Resources for Developmentally Appropriate Practice

Recommendations from the Profession

Gail Perry and Mary S. Duru, Editors

National Association for the Education of Young Children
Washington, D.C.

National Association for the Education of Young Children
1509 16th Street, NW
Washington, DC 20036-1426
202-232-8777 or 800-424-2460
Website: www.naeyc.org

Through its publications program the National Association for the Education of Young Children (NAEYC) provides a forum for discussion of major issues and ideas in the early childhood field, with the hope of provoking thought and promoting professional growth. The views expressed or implied are not necessarily those of the Association. NAEYC thanks the editors, who donated much time and effort to develop this book as a contribution to the profession.

Library of Congress Catalog Card Number: 99-067612
ISBN 0-935989-91-9
NAEYC #233

NAEYC Publications Editor: Carol Copple
Editing and production assistance: Debra Beland, Catherine Cauman, Millie Riley, and Lacy Thompson
Design and production: Malini Dominey

Printed in the United States of America

About the Editors

Gail Perry, Ph.D., is currently on the early childhood faculty in the Graduate School of Education at George Mason University in Fairfax, Virginia. After 10 years as a teacher of 3- to 7-year-olds, Gail spent the next 30 years in teacher education, educational program design, and consultation with early childhood programs in diverse cultural settings. Among her many memorable experiences are working with the Virgin Islands Head Start program, directing a Trinity College master's program for Washington, D.C., public school teachers at the National Child Research Center, and serving as an education consultant to an Appalachian Head Start program in Garrett County, Maryland. Her most important lessons, Gail says, have come from the teachers and children and students in all these settings.

Mary S. Duru, Ph.D., is a professional development specialist with NAEYC's National Institute for Early Childhood Professional Development. She has worked in teacher education and various early childhood settings for more than 25 years, including coordination of early childhood programs in the District of Columbia public schools and an assistant professorship of early childhood education at the University of Maryland–Baltimore County. Past experiences that continue to inspire and energize her present work, Mary says, are the mentoring of beginning teachers, studying childrearing practices in Igbo culture of rural Nigeria, and mothering two sons, Obidiugwu Kenrik and Nwamaegwu Jeremi.

Contents

Foreword

When we revised NAEYC's *Developmentally Appropriate Practice in Early Childhood Programs* in 1997, we knew that not even a 181-page book could fully define *developmentally appropriate practice* or explain its underlying principles and provide enough basic guidelines and examples. And no book on what is appropriate care and education for young children (from birth through age 8) is the last word. Developmentally appropriate practice continuously evolves and converges.

As we completed that edition, we also knew that to move from understanding general guidelines and principles to actually planning and carrying out programs, practitioners want and need other resources for encouraging and bolstering developmentally appropriate practices. Teachers must make everyday decisions across the span of concerns—children's ages, developmental domains, curriculum areas, and a wide array of social, cultural, and individual differences.

NAEYC's Panel on Revisions to Developmentally Appropriate Practice, which finished its work with the publication of the 1997 edition, and the Developmentally Appropriate Practice, Curriculum, and Assessment Panel, which began its term in November 1997, both agreed that NAEYC's next step should be bringing together a collection of resources for developmentally appropriate practice in published form. But where to start? We saw preparing such a resource bibliography as an enormous task, involving difficult and subjective choices about what to include. A list providing even a modest sampling of the numbers of wide-ranging relevant resources would itself be an entire book. Two years later, we are publishing that book.

From the outset NAEYC staff and the Panel members saw that it was not feasible or even desirable for a few NAEYC staff members to determine what to include in such a resource compilation. Rather, we needed to turn to expert early childhood educators to find out which books, articles, videos, and other resources they found most useful in making decisions about developmentally appropriate practice. Members of our profession from diverse roles were asked to identify and categorize resources that would be helpful to individuals who seek to implement and improve developmentally appropriate practice.

As the suggestions poured in, staff compiled preliminary lists within each category, and these were sent back to Panel members and other experts for review. Efforts were made to identify a representative range of high-quality references in each category that emphasized practical application and were accessible to practitioners at all levels of expertise. Books that describe classroom activities without providing the framework and rationale that enable teachers to make meaningful use of them were not included. Generally, research citations were included only when the research investigated the effects of developmentally appropriate practices.

This bibliography is fortunate in having as editors two respected early childhood experts with a strong commitment to helping early childhood professionals find good resources. Gail Perry, a teacher educator, has worked for many years as a consultant to NAEYC's editorial staff, reading the best new publications in the field and writing useful, concise annotations for inclusion in *Young Children*. Gail brings to this task a long-term engagement with teachers and children in preschool and elementary school settings, in agencies, and on college campuses: the places where our professional literature comes to life.

Mary Duru, in her role as a professional development specialist in NAEYC's National Institute for Early Childhood Professional Development, works closely with the National Council for Accreditation of Teacher Education (NCATE). She is a former assistant professor of early childhood education and coordinator of early childhood programs in an urban school district. Through these experiences, Mary gained broad familiarity with resources used in the education of early childhood professionals.

These editors worked under the pressures of limited available time to produce this extensive bibliography. In that time they contributed immeasurably to its quality. Any failings the book may have do not fall to their responsibility. Far from being exhaustive, this bibliography's wide selection is necessarily bound to omit many resources. And new materials are published continuously. At the same time, we are confident that readers will find a wealth of valuable resources and a framework and reference guide to which they will add year after year. The process has relied on and been strengthened by the suggestions of many professionals, bringing their own areas of expertise and being supplemented by the work of the editors.

We want to make explicit several important points about the book:

• **One-time publication.** *Resources for Developmentally Appropriate Practice: Recommendations from the Profession* will not be updated or revised in print form. Such a potentially major enterprise is not possible for NAEYC to take on. This publication is viewed only as a starting point for individuals to use in expanding their understanding of developmentally appropriate practice.

• **Accuracy of bibliographic entries**. Even with the hundreds of hours spent checking the bibliographic information, some resources may have errors in the citations or may subsequently have been published as new editions. With the many recent mergers, publishers have changed and a few of the recommended resources have been difficult to locate to ensure complete accuracy. To publish a book such as this, we had to be willing, as the saying goes, to not "let the *perfect* be the enemy of the *good*." We believe that these resources recommended by the profession will be extremely useful.

• **Categories.** Assigning resources to categories, not surprisingly, was very difficult. Nearly every entry could have been listed under more than one category. Yet making such multiple listings would have tripled the book's length, at the least. In some cases, in which two categories were equally applicable, the editors opted to use double listings to help readers find resources.

Resources for Developmentally Appropriate Practice: Recommendations from the Profession represents the experience and expertise of more than one hundred early childhood professionals. We are especially grateful to practitioners and teacher educators who reviewed drafts of the specific sections of this book in which they have expertise. The compiling of the recommended resources has truly been a cooperative venture undertaken to assist the reader in identifying resources useful in interpreting and implementing developmentally appropriate practice in programs for young children.

—Sue Bredekamp, NAEYC Director
of Professional Development, 1989–98;
and Carol Copple, NAEYC Publications Editor

Preface

More than a hundred early childhood educators and countless authors, voices from the profession, have contributed to this compilation of resources. The process of moving from an idea to a printed volume has indeed been a collaborative venture. We celebrate the sharing of insight, expertise, and experience that is the underlying theme of this publication.

Serving as editors of this book has been challenging, exhausting, yet ultimately rewarding. *Challenging* (some called accomplishing such a mission impossible)—because we really wanted to find all the best publications that represent the creative ways practitioners are engaging in developmentally appropriate practice. *Exhausting*—because the book's unavoidable production delay dealt us the new task of updating what had been done thus far and adding as many as possible of the good new books that had been published subsequently. Continued practitioners' requests for resources, however, served as a needed new catalyst driving forward the efforts of identifying, categorizing, annotating, checking, and rechecking to secure accurate citations. *Rewarding*—as we revisited some favorites on our own bookshelves and read and wrote annotations for new resources. In all, this has been a continuing professional development experience, with opportunities to hear and reflect on the thinking of a wide range of early childhood educators. We value it.

Readers will find the book organized into the following three parts.

Part 1 includes resources that define the concept of developmentally appropriate practice. This approach/philosophy has been emerging in our field for the better part of this century and will be reshaped and elaborated in the next century as society and the needs of children, families, and educators change. But the core qualities that were set forth in the first part of this century remain central to our profession. Thus this section begins with the roots and continues with the multiple viewpoints, debates, critiques, findings, issues, conclusions, and questions that frame the conceptual conversation about practice that is developmentally appropriate.

Part 2 includes resources that describe the main beneficiaries of developmentally appropriate practice—children and their families. The numerous and wide range of resources in this category inform the reader about the diverse nature of families, their values, beliefs, and ideas about parenting, and their lifestyles. Many excellent resources offer practical suggestions for teachers in establishing collaborative partnerships with families to engage in mutual support of children's care and education. Beliefs about how children learn and develop and theories about how children become socially, emotionally, cognitively, physically, and linguistically competent comprise the last category in this section.

Part 3 includes resources to support appropriate practices by teachers and caregivers of children at all ages in varied settings. It begins with resources that address all the components of practice with children in preschool and primary grades, then moves to teaching infants and toddlers, creating quality family child care, and enhancing programs for school-age children. In widening our view, we have included materials in Spanish and other languages, videorecordings, and Websites on the Internet.

Resources throughout were placed in categories based on their primary focus or because they make a special contribution to the topic. Some of the annotations are considerably shorter than others. This in no way reflects on the caliber of the particular publication, but is a result of our receiving a number of the recommended resources without annotations or with very brief descriptions.

In a project of this scope, we could never acknowledge by name all of the contributors, but we thank them immensely. In addition, to the members of NAEYC's Developmentally Appropriate Practice, Curriculum, and Assessment Panel, we express a deep gratitude. Several other individuals deserve our special thanks: Barbara Bowman and Lilian Katz not only responded readily to our call for help, but over the years their wise and visionary articulation of developmentally appropriate practice has continued to serve as a motivating force. We send special thanks too to Miriam Silver, who inspired and made substantial contributions to the "Roots" category of this book.

NAEYC's editorial production staff teamed with us to get this book on press in time for NAEYC's 1999 Annual Conference. We thank them all. Long overdue tribute goes to Jack Zibulsky, our chief production manager, who seems to be able to do several tasks simultaneously, working on *Young Children* and steering two or three books in the making. Malini Dominey gave the book cover and layout its polish and wrestled with all our changes in sequence and format. Millie Riley put form and clarity and exactness of detail to the citations, with precision help from Lacy Thompson, Debra Beland, and Catherine Cauman.

Abbey Showalter, a graduate student at the University of Maryland, dedicated countless hours to locating resources and verifying bibliographic citations.

Finally, we each express our gratitude to our families for their encouragement and support throughout the two-year process of gathering and publishing. Gail, as a mother to four and grandmother to six, has learned much about developmental expectations from the mature and creative ways that Kim, Tamara, Cheri, and Nick have met life's challenges. Her hugs go to Austin, husband of 40 years, who developed his own style DAP (devotion, acceptance, and patience) while she completed this project. Mary's grown sons, emerging new professionals in the practice of medicine and law, let her reflect personally on the outcomes of the investment in children so many teachers make in the earliest years.

We believe that this collection can be a source for teacher education students, both beginning and experienced practitioners, administrators, and teacher educators. Our hope is that each of you will find in it help and support in your work with young children and their families.

—The Editors

Part 1

...about the concept

This section begins with the roots of developmentally appropriate practice and continues with the concepts that undergird it—the viewpoints, debates, critiques, findings, issues, conclusions, and questions that comprise the frame. A final group lists selections from the research base supporting developmentally appropriate practice.

Roots of developmentally appropriate practice

The roots of developmentally appropriate practice reach back to the first half of this century when many of the ideas central to the philosophy of *developmentally appropriate practice* emerged. These are some of the writings that document the ideas of these early education pioneers who more often than not stood as solitary voices against the tide of traditional practices.

Reading through these books one finds the basis for child-centered education; play as a medium for learning; planning curriculum that is meaningful and based on children's real-life experiences, interests, and developmental needs; the importance of the family and parent education; quality toddler education; teaching and learning as a dynamic and inherently social enterprise; experience- and literature-based reading; and assessment based on observation.

We pay tribute to this rich heritage as well as to the current shapers of developmentally appropriate practice who have refined and redefined the practice in light of new knowledge and social contexts, while respecting and preserving these core values of our early childhood profession.

Alschuler, R.H, & the Pre-Primary Faculty of the Winnetka Public Schools. 1933. *Two to six.* New York: William Morrow.

> The staff director of a public-school nursery and junior kindergarten depicts the preparation of a unified, continuous curriculum adapted to the growth levels of 2-, 3-, 4-, 5-, and 6-year-old children.

Ashton-Warner, S. 1963. *Teacher.* New York: Bantam.

> A New Zealand teacher's definitive work illustrating ideas of developmentally appropriate practice. It's now a classic.

Baruch, D.W. 1939. *Parents and children go to school.* New York: Scott, Foresman.

Prefaced with the statement "Within the last two decades...we have become aware that the early years of a child's life play a fundamental and pervasive role" (p. vii). Delightful photographs and text portray what a good program for 4- and 5-year-olds looks like and how parents and teachers collaborate to meet the child's needs. Includes specific strategies for topics such as conferencing and parent education and the physical, emotional, social, language, and cognitive needs of the child.

Biber, B. 1969. *Challenges ahead for early childhood education.* Washington, DC: NAEYC.

A brief monograph reporting on a vision of the future of early childhood education foreshadows issues still faced today.

Biber, B. 1984. *Early education and psychological development.* New Haven, CT: Yale University Press.

A selection of articles written in the preceding 40-year period, constituting a chronicle of the early childhood profession's interest in child development and the prominence of early education scholars.

Biber, B., E. Shapiro, & D. Wickens, with E. Gilkeson. 1971. *Promoting cognitive growth: A developmental-interaction point of view.* New York: Bank Street College of Education.

Contains anecdotes from the Bank Street Early Childhood Center and School for Children to illustrate how a "whole child" approach to teaching promotes cognition.

Bronfenbrenner, U. 1970. *Two worlds of childhood: U.S. and USSR.* New York: Russell Sage Foundation.

A cross-cultural study that called attention to the gravity of the problems of childrearing in the American society.

Cohen, D., & V. Stern. 1958. *Observing and recording the behavior of young children.* New York: Teachers College Press.

Still in print, this booklet has served as a catalyst for generations of teachers, with techniques of focusing on and recording significant aspects of children's behavior as they engage with materials, their peers, and adults.

Dewey, J. 1900. *The child and the curriculum.* Chicago: University of Chicago Press.

Dewey, J. 1902. *The school and society.* Chicago: University of Chicago Press.

In these two volumes the early threads of progressive education were woven into the fabric of teaching and schooling that centered on the child. Nursery school education was based on these principles and endures today as a basis for developmentally appropriate practice. Two concepts of Dewey's educational philosophy—learning from experience and the social individual—are central in our work. Today's popular idea of establishing a "community of learners" was captured by Dewey. He believed that "classrooms should be participatory democracies...not mere proximity that endows significance or meaning to a community, it is the sharing of activity, in participating toward a common end that communities are created and sustained."

Eliot, A. 1924. Two nursery schools: Nurseries working on health, education and family life. *Child Health Magazine* (March): 97–101.

Abigail Eliot, as founder of Ruggles Street Nursery School in Boston, writes about her belief that children are persons and nursery school education is not custodial care but genuine education where the programs should be balanced to support both security and independence. Eliot served as director of the Eliot-Pearson Department of Child Study at Tufts University from 1922 to 1952, was a founding member of NAEYC, and established the Pacific Oaks College in Pasadena, California, in 1952.

Erikson, E.H. 1963. *Childhood and society.* New York: W.W. Norton.

Focuses on the dialectical pattern of development from infancy onward, an enfolding of our emotional and social selves, and the critical crises that must be resolved to establish trust, independence, initiative, and other personal elements key to successful living and learning.

Fraiberg, S. 1966. *The magic years.* New York: Scribner.

In the early years the child's conception of the world is a magical one. A sensitive story of personality development in the first five years, addressing typical problems that emerge at each stage.

Getzels, J., & P. Jackson. 1962. *Creativity and intelligence: Explorations with gifted students.* New York: John Wiley.

Studied the relationship between creativity and intelligence and ushered in the need to examine other distinctions of children's behavior as they entered school.

Gordon, I.J. 1972. *Children's views of themselves.* Washington, DC: Association for Childhood Education International.

Urged early childhood teachers to remove ethnic blinders and look at children as they are and how they feel. The narrative details the many individual ways children develop a concept of the self and suggests strategies to help teachers gain insight into children's views of themselves to help them achieve self-respect and confidence.

Hartley, R., L. Frank, & R. Goldenson. 1952. *Understanding children's play.* New York: Columbia University Press.

A classic interpretation of children's play that prepared teachers to "read" the language of play as an entry into the minds and hearts of young children. It made a definitive contribution to the study of play and its meaning.

Hawkins, F.P.L. 1998. *Journey with children: The autobiography of a teacher.* Boulder: University Press of Colorado.

Takes the reader from her first teaching assignment in a San Francisco second-grade classroom in 1936 to starting a nursery school in Los Alamos during the Second World War to a "Farm School" for 4-year-olds and so on. The commentary on teaching and children's lives is enriched by societal/ historical contexts, humorous and poignant moments in and out of class- rooms, portrayal of past educational friends, and the implications of all for teachers today.

Hill, P.S. 1913. *Second report—The kindergarten: Reports of the Committee of Nineteen on the Theory and Practice of the Kindergarten.* New York: Houghton Mifflin.

Documents the reform movement that called on kindergarten educators to help children come to new understandings by drawing on their real-life experiences, emphasizing the importance of subject-matter learning. Chil- dren were encouraged to represent the social life of the community through play and concrete materials in the classroom, such as blocks.

Hostler, A., & G. Bicknell. 1932. Science experiences in the nursery school. *Childhood Education* 8 (7): 342–48

Describes science activities for 2- through 5-year-olds at Western Uni- versity day care center and nursery school, highlighting instructional ac- tivities and background and the needs of children. One author helped to write standards for early childhood teachers in her roles as director of New York's Work Progress Administration nurseries, dean of the Mills School for kindergarten teachers, and president of NAEYC (then called the National Association for Nursery Education).

Hunt, J.M. 1961. *Intelligence and experience.* New York: Ronald Press.

Argues that intelligence is a product of environmental factors and high- lights the importance of the quality of early experiences in the human de- velopment cycle.

Hymes, J.L. 1949. *Teacher listen, the children speak.* New York: Committee on Mental Health of the State Charities Aid Association.

A guide for helping teachers deal with problem behavior effectively.

Hymes, J.L., Jr. [1955] 1995. *A child development point of view: A teacher's guide to action.* West Greenwich, RI: Consortium.
Hymes, J.L., Jr. 1995. *Behavior and misbehavior: A teacher's guide to discipline, revised edition.* West Greenwich, RI: Consortium.

Describe the essence of good teaching and include thoughtful, commonsense talk about establishing discipline and making a child devel- opment point of view an internal characteristic of teaching. Topics such as child development are as viable today as 43 years ago, about which Hymes wrote, "Teach right down your children's alley."

Hymes, J.L. 1975. *Early childhood education: An introduction to the profession.* Washington, DC: NAEYC.

Presents a history and status of early childhood as the field moves into the second decade of Head Start and a growing awareness of the importance of child care centers. Hymes ran Works Progress Administration day care centers during World War II, directed the early childhood education program at the University of Maryland, and was a president of NAEYC.

Isaacs, S. 1933. *Social development in young children.* New York: Routledge & Kegan Paul.

Detailed observations of the child gathered in the author's school for young children form the basis for the portrait of social development in the early years. Hostility, aggression, friendliness, cooperation, and sexuality are discussed along with the implications for teachers

Isaacs, S. 1966. *Intellectual growth in young children.* New York: Schocken.

Offers substantial insights that include content and methods that are now standard educational techniques. Suggests methods designed to assist the teacher in gaining understanding of the intellectual life of the very young.

Johnson, H. 1945. *The art of block building.* New York: Bank Street Publications.

The author was the director of the Harriet Johnson Nursery School from its organization in 1914 until her death. Like others around her, she took children's play seriously. She traces children's use of blocks from ages 2 through 5 and how they use unit blocks to represent their experiences.

Johnson, M. 1996. *Organic education: Teaching without failure.* Montgomery, AL: Communication Graphics.

Published originally as two books in 1929 and 1938, this edition combines Johnson's writing on progressive education and organic education. The portrayal of learning and schooling and of the nature and needs of children and parents is as fresh and applicable to late twentieth-century classrooms as it was in the early part of this century.

Lane, M.B., with Q. Baker. 1998. *Our schools: Frontline for the 21st century. What our schools must become. Essays in education.* Salt Lake City, UT: Publishers' Press.

In these essays, an 87-year-old early childhood educator reflects on seminal ideas about education from the forties and fifties, and the interdisciplinary theories in which they are grounded. Her vision of the key concepts of education, such as the development of the self in living and learning and the individualizing of expectations for children, are as true today as they were then.

Mead, M. 1962. *A creative life for your children.* Washington, DC: Children's Bureau, U.S. Department of Labor.

Elaborates on the essence of creativity with rare insight and sensitivity.

Mendham, A.C. 1942. Washington trains volunteers for day care of children. *The Child* 6 (11). Washington, DC: Children's Bureau, U.S. Department of Labor.

Describes the training that emphasized understanding of child development principles and observation techniques at local nursery schools where teachers were helped to understand the unique nature of young children and their interests as a basis for curriculum. The author started a nursery school in 1934 based on the progressive policies of John Dewey. Green Acres School continues today and serves children pre-K through eighth grade in Bethesda, Maryland.

Mitchell, L.S. 1934. *Young geographers: How they explore the world and how they map the world.* New York: Bank Street College of Education.

Shows teachers of 3- to 6-year-olds how to incorporate geography (both the concepts and skills) into the curriculum through time-worn techniques of trips into the community and how to represent these discoveries back in the classroom through such activities as map making with blocks and using other natural materials.

Montessori, M. 1948. *The discovery of the child.* 3d ed. Madras, India: Kalakshetra.

Maria Montessori describes her explorations with children and the scientific constraints she developed to validate her work. She discusses the work of colleagues with whom she collaborated.

Montessori, M. 1949. *The absorbent mind.* Madras: Kalakshetra.

Describes a phenomenon observed by Maria Montessori in her early study of how young children learn. She documents her explorations and explains appropriate adult responses to children's behavior.

Morgan, H. 1999. *The imagination of early childhood education.* Westport, CT: Bergin & Garvey.

Reaches back to Greco-Roman and Judeo-Christian influences on the development of education and into the twentieth century to examine historical features that are important to early childhood scholars. Author dedicates the book to the early childhood pioneers like Abigail Eliot and Lucy Sprague Mitchell as he expands on roots of the philosophy, theory, and curriculum of early childhood education.

Moustakas, C. 1956. *The teacher and the child.* Cambridge, MA: Howard A. Doyle. (Republished in 1966 as *The authentic teacher: Sensitivity and awareness in the classroom.*)

From his base at the Merrill-Palmer Institute, where he taught a human relations seminar for teachers beginning in 1949, the author describes the key interpersonal process in the classroom. He suggests ways the teacher can bring his or her unique self into the classroom and evoke the kind of open interaction with children that helps them realize their potential.

Murphy, L.B. 1949. *Methods for the study of personality in young children.* Vol. 1. New York: Basic.

Murphy, L.B. 1956. *Personality in young children.* Vol. 2. New York: Basic.

In collaboration with the teachers at Sarah Lawrence College nursery school, these two volumes demonstrate in detailed studies of preschool children the series of play and activity techniques devised for assessing personality development and insight into the way a child strives to live in his world.

Murphy, L.B. 1962. *The widening world of childhood: Paths toward mastery.* New York: Basic.

Incorporates ideas from some of the leading thinkers about childhood— Margaret Mead, Peter Blos, Lawrence Frank, Anna Freud, and Erik Erikson— in this accounting of children's ways of meeting challenges.

Peltzman, B. 1998. *Pioneers of early childhood education: A bio-bibliographical guide.* Westport, CT: Greenwood.

Offers a unique perspective on 34 of the educators who built the field of early childhood education. After brief biographies, the author provides their most important writings in an impressive annotated list of original works as well as secondary sources of their ideas. Included are works of Abigail Eliot, founding member of NAEYC, and Mary Church Terrell and the contributions of the National Association of Colored Women.

Pratt, C., with a Record of Group Seven. 1924. *Experimental practice in the city and country school.* New York: Dutton.

Documentary of a year in a second-grade classroom in a school begun in 1913 as an alternative to the traditional elementary school. Its purpose was to demonstrate the role of play in education and the result of planning curriculum and physical space centered on children's developing needs and interests. A school vacation farm was maintained as a part of the educational process.

Pratt, C. 1948. *I learn from children: An adventure in progressive education.* New York: Simon & Schuster.

A gem of a story of how this gifted teacher explored the world of children and their ways of growing and learning.

Prescott, D. 1957. *The child in the educative process.* New York: McGraw-Hill.

Portrays the teacher's multitudinous daily decisions as the fundamental bases of the educative process. A framework for helping teachers understand and interpret children's behavior is illustrated through case studies and examples of teacher-child interactions that show the links to a child's life space and how experiences outside of school have an impact on the child's learning.

Read, K. 1950. *The nursery school: A human relationships laboratory.* Philadelphia, PA: W.B. Saunders.

The author sets the stage for developing sensitive teaching practice with 3- and 4-year-old children, giving wise advice for helping children build feelings of security, handle their own feelings of hostility and aggressiveness, and develops many other components of what we now call social competence.

Rotzel, G. 1971. *The school in Rose Valley: A parent venture in education.* Baltimore, MD: Johns Hopkins University Press.

Disillusioned by war and traditional teaching, a group of parents who had been studying child development and the ideas of John Dewey started a school in 1929 with the support of some nursery school teachers and the education department of Swarthmore College. Among many innovations, the curriculum emphasized firsthand experience, because parents noted the brain's need for stimulation early in life. The 3- and 4-year-olds worked with many materials from which they could choose; first-graders chose books from the library for reading; second- and third-graders were encouraged to talk about what they knew and did a lot of creative writing; and fourth-graders built a solar system.

Sheehy, E.D. 1954. *The fives and sixes go to school.* New York: Henry Holt.

Sets the stage for the progressive kindergarten and first grade and ways teachers can be resourceful in creating classrooms for child-centered, active learning in whatever settings they find themselves—often less-than-ideal physical spaces. Traditional topics of schedules and teaching writing and arithmetic are framed in ideas still practiced today, such as children having many opportunities throughout the day to read good books, the importance of social relationships, and movement and learning through dramatic play.

Silver Spring Nursery School. 1949. *Our cooperative nursery school.* Silver Spring, MD: Author.

Describes a parent cooperative nursery school where parents participate as assistants to the teacher. This manual describing the school helped the parents understand the child-centered program and their role in the classroom. The close parent-teacher relationhip and parent education were invaluable.

Taylor, K.W. 1967. *Parents and children learn together.* New York: Teachers College Press.

Documents the parent cooperative movement begun in the 1930s during which parents participated in their children's preschool program on a weekly basis, filling the roles of assistant teacher (under the teacher's guidance) and administrative board member. Unique and comprehensive perspectives on parent-teacher relationships and on developing a sound parent education program connected to preschools.

Terrell, M.C. 1902. What role is the educated Negro woman to play in the uplifting of her race? In *Twentieth century Negro literature or Relating to the American Negro by 100 of America's greatest Negroes.* Toronto, Canada: J.L. Nichols.

Considers the role women must play to improve the lives of African Americans and the efforts of women's clubs in helping children through improved living and educational conditions. As a teacher in Washington, D.C., and a professor at Wilberforce University, the author used her leadership to encourage the development of kindergartens and nursery schools for Black children throughout the United States.

Veatch, J. 1966. *Reading in the elementary school.* New York: Ronald Press.

Presents a way of teaching reading very similar to what is recommended in recent reports. Details every aspect of teaching reading in developmentally appropriate ways.

Winsor, C.B., ed. 1979. *On teachers and teaching: Writings by Bank Street College faculty.* New York: Bank Street College of Education.

Articles by Bank Street's founder Lucy Sprague Mitchell and other early pioneers cover many facets of the teaching role in pre-K through sixth-grade classrooms, characteristics of classroom life such as building a classroom climate for learning and how to make discussion the heart of the classroom, and the process of developing good judgment.

Key concepts and issues in developmentally appropriate practice

Publications in this section explore the premises and concepts put forth in the first edition (1987) and revised edition (1997) of *Developmentally Appropriate Practice in Early Childhood Programs.* The dialogue is a lively one and includes both critics and supporters. The discussion illuminates the many dimensions of developmentally appropriate practice and serves as a continuing forum for early childhood practitioners, researchers, and other professionals interested in the education of young children.

Bredekamp, S., ed. 1987. *Developmentally appropriate practice in early childhood programs serving children from birth through age 8.* Exp. ed. Washington, DC: NAEYC.

Represents the early childhood profession's consensus definition of developmentally appropriate practice in early childhood programs. Intended for use by teachers, administrators, parents, policymakers, and others involved with programs serving young children. Contains chapters on appropriate practices, successful transitions, and strategies to inform others about developmentally appropriate practice.

Bredekamp, S. 1991. Redeveloping early childhood education: A response to Kessler. *Early Childhood Research Quarterly* 6 (2): 199–209.

Responding to a critique of the developmental basis for developmentally appropriate practice, Bredekamp explains the rationale for this approach and clarifies assumptions made by Shirley A. Kessler (1991a). Areas of agreement between the social reconstructionist and child-centered viewpoints are cited.

Bredekamp, S. 1993a. Myths about developmentally appropriate practice: A response to Fowell and Lawton. *Early Childhood Research Quarterly* 8 (1): 117–19.

States that Nancy Fowell and Joseph Lawton (1992) misrepresent developmentally appropriate practice, in both content and intent of the philosophy. Bredekamp clarifies the assumption made by the two authors that developmentally appropriate practice prohibits teacher-directed activity. She describes the appropriateness of the early childhood program at the University of Wisconsin–Madison.

Bredekamp, S. 1993b. The relationship between early childhood education and early childhood special education: Healthy marriage or family feud? *Topics in Early Childhood Special Education* 13 (3): 258–73.

Describes and clarifies common misconceptions about developmentally appropriate practice, identifies areas where the two disciplines could converge, and explains current collaborative efforts between the Division for Early Childhood of the Council for Exceptional Children and NAEYC.

Bredekamp, S., & C. Copple, eds. 1997. *Developmentally appropriate practice in early childhood programs.* Rev. ed. Washington, DC: NAEYC.

Expanding from the core ideas of the 1987 edition, this volume spells out more fully the principles underlying developmentally appropriate practice and the guidelines for classroom decisionmaking. The revised edition is explicit about the teacher's role and the importance of the social and cultural context in considering the appropriateness of practice.

Brooks, J.G., & M.G. Brooks. 1993. *In search of understanding: The case for constructivist classrooms.* Alexandria, VA: Association for Supervision and Curriculum Development.

Highlights the importance of creating a classroom environment in which children search for meaning, children's ideas are valued, and assessment practices are used to improve teaching. Provides actual classroom examples as well as helpful tables outlining the constructivist approach to teaching as it compares it to more traditional approaches. Part 1 addresses the need for constructivism; Part 2 outlines five guiding principles of constructivism; and Part 3 gives recommendations for creating constructivist settings.

Carta, J.J., J.B. Atwater, I.S. Schwartz, & S.R. McConnell. 1993. Developmentally appropriate practices and early childhood special education: A reaction to Johnson and McChesney Johnson. *Topics in Early Childhood Special Education* 13 (3): 243–54.

After an earlier article by Carta and colleagues in 1991 warned early childhood special educators to think of developmentally appropriate practice as a necessary contribution to the field of early childhood special education but not as the only approach, Johnson and McChesney Johnson (1992; see "Research" section that follows) defended developmentally appropriate practice. This article redirects the debate and clarifies the authors' perspective, identifying areas where developmentally appropriate practices and early childhood special education practices overlap and complement each other.

Cesarone, B. 1998. Developmentally appropriate practice. 1998. *Childhood Education* 74 (5): 332–34.

A collection of abstracts from articles about developmentally appropriate practice and related issues. Addresses early childhood and elementary education.

Chafel, J.A., & S. Reifel, eds. 1996. *Advances in early education and day care: Theory and practice in early childhood education.* Vol. 8. Greenwich, CT: JAI.

Aims to explicate the value of early education theory and its usefulness to practice. Examining the areas of classroom practice, teacher preparation, research, and conceptualization, this book features academic and practitioner perspectives and provides a synthesis of theory and practice.

Charlesworth, R. 1998a. Developmentally appropriate practice is for everyone. *Childhood Education* 74 (5): 274–82.

In this Annual Theme issue, Charlesworth addresses developmentally appropriate practice and states that it is appropriate for all children from diverse ethnic and socioeconomic communities. He describes the basic elements of quality practice and cites research that demonstrates the benefits of appropriate practice.

Charlesworth, R. 1998b. Response to Sally Lubeck's "Is developmentally appropriate practice for everyone?" *Childhood Education* 74 (5): 293–98.

Response to Lubeck's article (1998a, below). Comments that developmentally appropriate practice is not for everyone. Discusses the basic ideas of Lubeck's argument and points out the sources of differences between their perspectives.

Lubeck, S. 1998a. Is developmentally appropriate practice for everyone? *Childhood Education* 74 (5): 283–92.

Suggests that developmentally appropriate practice is not appropriate for all children because it is based on general principles that may not be appropriate in every situation and for every child.

Lubeck, S. 1998b. Is DAP for everyone? A response. *Childhood Education* 74 (5): 299–301.

Response to Charlesworth (1998b) in which Lubeck defends her position that developmentally appropriate practice may not be for everyone and argues that dichotomizing early childhood as appropriate or inappropriate ignores the complexities of teaching a diverse population of young children.

Elkind, D. 1993. Resistance to developmentally appropriate practice: A case study of educational inertia. In *Images of the young child,* 55–65. Washington, DC: NAEYC.

Discusses how a philosophy that views education from a quantitative perspective creates a barrier for contemporary classroom innovation and curricular reform. Presents information about the learner and the learning process as well as the practical implications of a developmental philosophy.

Fleer, M., ed. 1995. *DAPcentrism: Challenging developmentally appropriate practice.* Watson, ACT: Australian Early Childhood Association.

Questions the completeness of developmentally appropriate practice for all children, and claims that developmentally appropriate practice underestimates the role of the teacher. Contrasts developmentally appropriate practice with socially constructed learning.

Fowell, N., & J. Lawton. 1992. An alternative view of developmentally appropriate practice in early childhood education. *Early Childhood Research Quarterly* 7 (1): 53–73.

Provides an alternative view of developmentally appropriate practice and suggests that early childhood programs could incorporate instructional theory as well as developmental theory. The authors compare and contrast the theory and practices of their perspective to the description of developmentally appropriate and inappropriate programs as presented by NAEYC.

Fowell, N., & J. Lawton. 1993. Beyond polar descriptions of developmentally appropriate practice: A reply to Bredekamp. *Early Childhood Research Quarterly* 8 (1): 121–24.

Addresses four concerns raised by Bredekamp (1993a) in her commentary on Fowell and Lawton (1992). Authors argue that Bredekamp misrepresented their position on alternative perspectives to developmentally appropriate practice. Suggests that the concepts of appropriate and inappropriate practice represent two ends of a continuum rather than two discrete compartments.

Gabbard, C. 1995. P.E. for preschoolers: The right way. *Principal* 74 (5): 21–22, 24.

Written to provide information to principals and administrators about developmentally appropriate practices; contrasts some appropriate and inappropriate practices for early childhood programs.

Galen, H. 1994. Developmentally appropriate practice: Myths and facts. *Principal* 73 (5): 20–22.

Argues that the philosophy of developmentally appropriate practice can benefit and meet the needs of children from all backgrounds.

Gestwicki, C. 1999. *Developmentally appropriate practice: Curriculum and development in early education.* 2d ed. Albany, NY: Delmar.

Describes which practices are and are not considered developmentally appropriate and offers clear descriptions of practices that provide nurturing physical, social, emotional, and cognitive environments for various ages.

Hart, C.H., D.C. Burts, & R. Charlesworth. 1997. Integrated developmentally appropriate curriculum: From theory and research to practice. In *Integrated curriculum and developmentally appropriate practice: Birth to age eight,* eds. C.H. Hart, D.C. Burts, & R. Charlesworth. Albany: State University of New York Press.

This chapter outlines basic ideas behind developmentally appropriate practice and reviews the debate surrounding the ability of developmentally appropriate practice to meet the needs of diverse populations. In response to this debate, the authors provide an overview of research that supports developmentally appropriate practice.

Hyun, E. 1996. New directions in early childhood teacher preparation: Developmentally and culturally appropriate practice (DCAP). *Journal of Early Childhood Teacher Education* 17 (3): 7–19.

Suggests that teacher preparation must readdress cross-cultural child development and learning style and reintroduce self-awareness and ways of valuing the study of culture and ethnicity.

Hyun, E. 1998. *Making sense of developmentally and culturally appropriate practice (DCAP) in early childhood education.* New York: Peter Lang.

Attempts to expand developmentally appropriate practice as developmentally *and* culturally appropriate practice (DCAP) to pay greater attention to the cultural influences that form young children's growth and learning. By infusing into the texts voices of prospective early childhood educators and developmentally and culturally appropriate teaching experiences, the book presents a way to prepare teachers to be more sensitive to multiple and multiethnic perspectives in young children's learning.

Jipson, J. 1991. Developmentally appropriate practice: Culture, curriculum, connections. *Early Education and Development* 2 (2): 120–36.

Using journals and personal narratives of 30 early childhood teachers, the author questions the ability of developmentally appropriate practice to address and respond to cultural diversity. Research supports the inclusion of practitioners' perspectives in the discussion about what constitutes developmentally appropriate practice.

Kessler, S.A. 1991a. Alternative perspectives on early childhood education. *Early Childhood Research Quarterly* 6 (2): 183–97.

Compares curriculum studies about developmentally appropriate versus inappropriate practices and identifies problems with the justification of basing child-centered practices on developmental theory. Suggests a model of early childhood education as schooling for democracy.

Kessler, S.A. 1991b. Early childhood education as development: Critique of the metaphor. *Early Education and Development* 2 (2): 137–52.

Proposes that early childhood educators consider two other metaphors for describing the content of early childhood curriculum rather than development: early childhood education as caring and early education as schooling for democracy. It is hoped that these metaphors can guide discussion about curriculum content in early childhood classrooms.

Kessler, S.A., & B.B. Swadener, eds. 1992. *Reconceptualizing the early childhood curriculum: Beginning the dialogue.* New York: Teachers College Press.

Asks broad questions about the construction of and goals for early childhood curriculum. Attempts to bring into the dialogue voices that have gone largely unnoticed. The book aims to help educators and professionals begin asking new questions, which can guide the field to ask still more questions.

Kostelnik, M.J., A.K. Soderman, & A.P. Whiren. 1999. *Developmentally appropriate curriculum: Best practices in early childhood education.* 2d ed. Upper Saddle River, NJ: Merrill/Prentice Hall.

Brings together the best information currently available for developing an integrated approach to curriculum and instruction in the early years. It is designed for current and future early childhood professionals working in formal group settings with young children ranging in age from 3 to 8.

Lubeck, S. 1991. Reconceptualizing early childhood education: A response. *Early Education and Development* 2 (2): 168–74.

Reviews the articles contained in the issue and summarizes authors' ideas as they relate to reconceptualizing—defined as questioning the way things are done and then dreaming of what could be.

Mallory, B.L. 1992. Is it always appropriate to be developmental? Convergent models for early intervention practice. *Topics in Early Childhood Special Education* 11 (4): 1–12.

Three theoretical models of early intervention practice are discussed to identify the common values that characterize each. Although the developmental, functional, and biological models were each developed by different sets of practitioners and for different purposes and populations of children, it is possible to infer convergent principles that can guide professional practice. Previous assumptions that these models are discrete are questioned.

Mallory, B.L., & R.S. New, eds. 1994. *Diversity and developmentally appropriate practices: Challenges for early childhood education.* New York: Teachers College Press.

Critiques of early childhood education and developmentally appropriate practices help expand the current definition of developmentally appropriate practice to include alternative theoretical and practical perspectives necessary for addressing the needs of young children with cultural and developmental differences.

McLean, M.E., & S.L. Odom. 1993. Practices for young children with and without disabilities: A comparison of DEC- and NAEYC-identified practices. *Topics in Early Childhood Special Education* 13 (3): 274–92.

Points out where the differences and similarities exist between the Division for Early Childhood of the Council for Exceptional Children and NAEYC accepted practices in the areas of inclusion, family involvement, assessment, program planning, curriculum and intervention strategies, services-delivery models, and transition.

O'Brien, L.M. 1997. Turning my world upside down: How I learned to question developmentally appropriate practice: Issues in Education. *Childhood Education* 73 (2): 100–02.

Argues that the assumption of the universal applicability of developmentally appropriate practice is problematic. Supports the search for a middle ground between developmental and academic approaches to early childhood education. Also recommends that educators take a closer look at issues of inclusion, cultural diversity, and minority expectations, and continue to question whose experiences are represented by examining who is served by developmentally appropriate practices.

Pellegrini, A.D., & J. Dresden. 1991. The concept of development in the early childhood curriculum. In *Yearbook in early childhood education, vol. 2: Issues in early childhood curriculum,* eds. B. Spodek & O.N. Saracho. New York: Teachers College Press.

Discusses how the principles of development can inform practice for early childhood educators and researchers. Applies developmental concepts to the areas of literacy and numeracy.

Penn, H. 1999. *How should we care for babies and toddlers? An analysis of practice in out-of-home care for children under three.* Childcare Resource and Research Unit. Toronto, Canada: Centre for Urban and Community Studies, University of Toronto.

Reviews research on the values and beliefs in caring for babies and toddlers and concludes that some of the North American guidelines and rating scales (including DAP) have serious limitations. Author compares the Anglo-American approach to the European approach in domains such as the nature of relationships between adults and children, education content, and styles of instruction and training to work with young children.

Reifel, S., ed. 1993. *Advances in early education and day care: Perspectives on developmentally appropriate practice.* Vol. 5. Greenwich, CT: JAI.

Chapters in the first section are written by a variety of researchers who have attempted to identify developmentally appropriate practices and examine how these practices relate to children's school performances and development. The second section examines developmentally appropriate practice from a variety of perspectives such as social construction, inservice education, the teacher as researcher, parent involvement, and culture and language.

Schweinhart, L., & D. Wiekart. 1999. Why curriculum matters in early childhood education. In *Annual editions: Early childhood education 1999/2000, 20th editions,* eds. K. Paciorek & J. Munro. Guilford, CT: Dushkin/McGraw-Hill.

Responds to the debate over which type of early childhood program is best for young children. The authors report on their own 30 years of studying preschool programs, especially the roles of curriculum and the teacher. They conclude that developmentally appropriate programs are far superior to direct instruction programs in many areas.

Seefeldt, C., & A. Galper. 1998. *Continuing issues in early childhood education.* Upper Saddle River, NJ: Merrill/Prentice-Hall.

This volume addresses infant and toddler care, quality in child care, developmentally appropriate teacher education, parent involvement, standards, play, inclusion, diversity, assessment, and the role of government and business.

Singer, E. 1996. Prisoners of the method: Breaking open the child-centered pedagogy in day care centres. *International Journal of Early Years Education* 4 (2): 28–40.

Argues that the concepts of developmentally appropriate curriculum and child-centered teaching hinder interaction between teachers and children. This author advocates for approaches that assist children in working together as peers and that give increased value to peer relationships and scaffolding.

Spodek, B. 1991. Reconceptualizing early childhood education: A commentary. *Early Education and Development* 2 (2): 161–67.

Begins with a description of the historical setting for today's discussions about appropriate early childhood approaches. Summarizes the current debates on issues surrounding this discussion.

Vander Wilt, J.L., & V. Monroe. 1998. Successfully moving toward developmentally appropriate practice: It takes time and effort! *Young Children* 53 (4): 17–24.

Discusses what developmentally appropriate practice is, based on NAEYC's revised edition of *Developmentally Appropriate Practice in Early Childhood Programs.* Describes the implementation of developmentally appropriate practice in kindergarten through second grade in a midwestern school district.

Wakefield, A.P. 1993. Developmentally appropriate practice: "Figuring things out." *The Educational Forum* 57: 134–43.

Author contrasts developmentally appropriate practice with traditional practice in the form of a DAP Self-Assessment Inventory. Each of the ten characteristics on the inventory are discussed: integrated, meaning-driven, incidental, heterogeneous, ready now, child-centered, autonomy, previous knowledge, requires thinking, and human-as-instrument.

Walsh, D.J. 1991. Extending the discourse on developmental appropriateness: A developmental perspective. *Early Education and Development* 2 (2):109–19.

Argues that to date the discussion about developmental appropriateness has been limited. Identifies four main problems with the discussion: an assumed consensus, a suspect assumption of universal stages, an individualist perspective, and a reliance on developmental match while ignoring alternative perspectives (mainly Vygotsky).

Wardle, F. 1999. In praise of developmentally appropriate practice. *Young Children* 54 (6): 4–11.

Reviewing his professional and personal experiences, the author reaffirms his strong support for the philosophy of developmentally appropriate practice and lists and elaborates on 12 beliefs undergirding his support.

Research relating to developmentally appropriate practice

Citations of research articles are included that examine the effects of developmentally appropriate practice. Because the titles of the research studies are quite descriptive and most of the research is accessible through the Internet, annotations have not been included.

Barnett, W.S., & S.S. Boocok, eds. 1998. *Early care and education for children in poverty: Promises, programs, and long-term results.* Albany: State University of New York Press.

Bryant, D.M., R.M. Clifford, & E.S. Peisner. 1991. Best practices for beginners: Developmental appropriateness in kindergarten. *American Educational Research Journal* 28 (4): 783–803.

Buchanan, T.K, D.C. Burts, J. Bidner, F.V. White, & R. Charlesworth. 1998. Predictors of the developmental appropriateness of the beliefs and practices of first, second, and third grade teachers. *Early Childhood Research Quarterly* 13 (3): 459–83.

Burts, D.C., R. Charlesworth, P.O. Fleege, J. Mosley, & R.H. Thomasson. 1992. Observed activities and stress behaviors of children in developmentally appropriate kindergarten classrooms. *Early Childhood Research Quarterly* 7 (2): 297–318.

Burts, D.C., C.H. Hart, R. Charlesworth, D.M. DeWolf, K. Manuel, & P.O. Fleege. 1993. Developmental appropriateness of kindergarten programs and academic outcomes in first grade. *Journal of Research in Childhood Education* 8 (1): 23–31.

Burts, D.C., C.H. Hart, R. Charlesworth, & L. Kirk. 1990. A comparison of frequencies of stress behaviors observed in kindergarten children in classrooms with developmentally appropriate versus inappropriate instructional practices. *Early Childhood Research Quarterly* 5 (3): 407–23.

Buzzelli, C.A. 1992. Research in review. Young children's moral understanding: Learning about right and wrong. *Young Children* 47 (6): 47–53.

Carta, J.J. 1995. Developmentally appropriate practice: A critical analysis as applied to young children with disabilities. *Focus on Exceptional Children* 27 (8): 1–14.

Charlesworth, R., D.C. Burts, & C.H. Hart. 1994. The effectiveness of developmentally appropriate compared with developmentally inappropriate practices: Implications for teacher preparation. *Journal of Early Childhood Teacher Education* 15 (1): 8–12.

Charlesworth, R., C. Hart, D. Burts, & M. DeWolf. 1993. The LSU studies: Building a research base for developmentally appropriate practice. In *Advances in early education and day care, volume 5: Perspectives on developmentally appropriate practice*, ed. S. Reifel, 3–28. Greenwich, CT: JAI.

Charlesworth, R., C. Hart, D. Burts, R. Thomasson, J. Mosley, & P. Fleege. 1993. Measuring the developmental appropriateness of kindergarten teachers' beliefs and practices. *Early Childhood Research Quarterly* 8 (3): 255–76.

Colorado Department of Education. 1993. Recent research supports developmentally appropriate practice in the primary grades. *Of Primary Interest* 1 (1): 1–2.

Dunn, L., & S. Kontos. 1997a. Developmentally appropriate practice: What does research tell us? *ERIC Digest.* ED 413106. Champaign, IL: ERIC Clearinghouse on Elementary and Early Childhood Education.

Dunn, L., & S. Kontos. 1997b. What have we really learned about developmentally appropriate practice? *Young Children* 52 (5): 4–13.

Farran, D.C., W. Son-Yarbough, B. Silveri, & A.M. Culp. 1993. Measuring the environment in public school preschools for disadvantaged children: What is developmentally appropriate? In *Advances in early education and day care, volume 5: Perspectives on developmentally appropriate practice*, ed. S. Reifel, 75–93. Greenwich, CT: JAI.

Fox, L., & M.F. Hanline. 1993. A preliminary evaluation of learning within developmentally appropriate early childhood settings. *Topics in Early Childhood Special Education* 13 (3): 308–27.

Frede, E., A. Austin, & S. Lindauer. 1993. The relationship of specific developmentally appropriate practices in preschool to children's skills in first grade. In *Advances in early education and day care, volume 5: Perspectives on developmentally appropriate practice*, ed. S. Reifel, 95–111. Greenwich, CT: JAI.

Frede, E., & W.S. Barett. 1992. Developmentally appropriate public school preschool: A study of implementation of the High/Scope curriculum and its effects on disadvantaged children's skills at first grade. *Early Childhood Research Quarterly* 7 (4): 483–99.

Gould, N.P. 1992. Why public primary schools can, and should, adopt developmentally appropriate practice. *Day Care and Early Education* 20: 46–47.

Haupt, J., J. Larsen, C. Robinson, & C. Hart. 1995. The impact of DAP inservice training on the beliefs and practices of kindergarten teachers. *Journal of Early Childhood Teacher Education* 16: 12–18.

Hirsh-Pasek, K., M. Hyson, & L. Rescorla. 1990. Academic environments in preschool: Do they pressure or challenge young children? *Early Education and Development* 1 (6): 401–23.

Hirsch-Pasek, K., M.C. Hyson, L. Rescorla. 1990. The classroom practices inventory: An observation instrument based on NAEYC's guidelines for developmentally appropriate practices for 4- and 5-year-old children. *Early Childhood Research Quarterly* 5 (4): 475–94.

Hoot, J.L., R.S. Parmar, E. Hujala-Huttunen, Q. Cao, & A.M. Chacon. 1996. Cross-national perspectives on developmentally appropriate practices for early childhood programs. *Journal of Research in Childhood Education* 10 (2): 160.

Isenberg, J.P. 1990. Reviews of research: Teachers' thinking and beliefs and classroom practice. *Childhood Education* 66 (5): 322, 324–27.

Johnson, J.E., & K. McChesney Johnson. 1992. Clarifying the development perspective in response to Carta, Schwartz, Atwater, and McConnell. *Topics in Early Childhood Special Education* 12: 439–57.

 Carta, J.J., J.B. Atwater, I.S. Schwartz, & S.R. McConnell. 1993. Developmentally appropriate practices in early childhood education: A reaction to Johnson and McChesney Johnson. *Topics in Early Childhood Special Education* 13: 243–54.

Kagan, S.L., & M.J. Neuman. 1996. The relationship between staff education and training and quality in child care programs. *Child Care Information Exchange* (107): 65–70.

Kemple, K.M. 1996. Teachers' beliefs and reported practices concerning sociodramatic play. *Journal of Early Childhood Teacher Education* 17 (2): 19–31.

Kontos, S., & L. Dunn. 1993. Caregiver practices and beliefs in child care varying in developmental appropriateness and quality. In *Advances in early education and day care, volume 5: Perspectives on developmentally appropriate practice*, ed. S. Reifel, 53–74. Greenwich, CT: JAI.

Kontos, S., & A. Wilcox-Herzog. 1997. Research in review. Teachers' interactions with children: Why are they so important? *Young Children* 52 (2): 4–12.

Mangione, P., & H. Maniates. 1993. Training teachers to implement developmentally appropriate practice. In *Advances in early education and day care, volume 5: Perspectives on developmentally appropriate practice*, ed. S. Reifel, 145–66. Greenwich, CT: JAI.

Marcon, R. 1992. Differential effects of three preschool models on inner-city 4-year-olds. *Early Childhood Research Quarterly* 7 (4): 517–30.

Marcon, R.A. 1993. Socioemotional versus academic emphasis: Impact on kindergartners' development and achievement. *Early Child Development and Care* 96: 81–91.

Marcon, R.A. 1994. Doing the right thing for children: Linking research and policy reform in the District of Columbia public schools. *Young Children* 50 (1): 8–20.

Maxwell, K.L, & S.K. Eller. 1994. Children's transition to kindergarten. *Young Children* 49 (6): 56–63.

Penn, H. 1999. *How should we care for babies and toddlers? An analysis of practice in out-of-home care for children under three.* Childcare Resource and Research Unit. Toronto, Canada: Centre for Urban and Community Studies, University of Toronto.

Peters, D. 1993. Trends in demographic and behavioral research on teaching in early childhood settings. In *Handbook of research on the education of young children*, ed. B. Spodek, 493–505. New York: Macmillan.

Reifel, S., ed. 1993. *Advances in early education and day care: Perspectives on developmentally appropriate practice, volume 5.* Greenwich, CT: JAI.

Schweinhart, L.J. 1997. Child-initiated learning activities for young children living in poverty. *ERIC Digest.* ED 413105. Champaign, IL. ERIC Clearinghouse on Elementary and Early Childhood Education.

Schweinhart, L.J., & D.P. Weikart. 1993. *Significant benefits: The High/Scope Perry Preschool Study through age 27.* Ypsilanti, MI: High/Scope Educational Research Foundation.

Schweinhart, L.J., & D.P. Weikart. 1997. The High/Scope Preschool Curriculum Comparison Study through Age 23. *Early Childhood Research Quarterly* 12 (2): 117–43.

Smith, K.E. 1997. Student teachers' beliefs about developmentally appropriate practice: Pattern, stability, and the influence of locus of control. *Early Childhood Research Quarterly* 12 (2): 221–43.

Snider, M.H., & V.R. Fu. 1990. The effects of specialized education and job experience on early childhood teachers' knowledge of developmentally appropriate practice. *Early Childhood Research Quarterly* 5 (1): 69–78.

Stipek, D.J. 1993. Is child-centered early childhood education really better? In *Advances in early education and day care, volume 5: Perspectives on developmentally appropriate practice*, ed. S. Reifel, 29–52. Greenwich, CT: JAI.

Stipek, D.J., & P. Byler. 1997. Early childhood education teachers: Do they practice what they preach? *Early Childhood Research Quarterly* 12 (3): 301–25.

Stipek, D., R. Feiler, D. Daniels, & S. Milburn. 1995. Effects of different instructional approaches on young children's achievement and motivation. *Child Development* 66 (1): 209–23.

Zepeda, M. 1993. An exploratory study of demographic characteristics, retention, and developmentally appropriate practice in kindergarten. *Child Study Journal* 23 (1): 57–78.

Part 2

...about children and families

Diversity is not something that is added on to a curriculum, a classroom, or teaching. It is central to all components of developmentally appropriate practice. It is central to *development*. It is central to the implications of *appropriate*. It is central to good *practice*. *Learning to live with diversity* means helping children recognize diversity's value and its presence in our lives.

Resources that address diversity appear in every category of this book. Included in this section are those resources that help readers better understand different cultural, linguistic, and special abilities of children and families, along with ideas for creating environments that are sensitive to those needs.

Understanding cultural differences

This category includes resources that define the nature of culture and ways of thinking about multicultural education; social equity and discrimination; and the issues, challenges, and implications for teachers. Those references that portray the views, values, and practices of different cultures are also in this section.

Banks, J. 1998. *An introduction to multicultural education.* Needham Heights, MA: Allyn & Bacon.

Introduces preservice and practicing educators to the major issues, concepts, paradigms, and teaching strategies in multicultural education. Readers receive a brief, comprehensive overview of multicultural education and a helpful understanding of what it means for educational practice. Characteristics of a multicultural school are identified and described as well as ways multicultural education can transform curriculum to promote the attitudes and skills children need to become effective citizens.

Berns, R. 1997. *Child, family, school, community.* 4th ed. New York: Harcourt Brace.

Uses Bronfenbrenner's ideas to describe how children come to know about and effectively participate (or not) in their family, school, and community. Appropriate for those who work with preschool and primary. The author discusses how families become empowered, ethnic diversity, and the relationships between school and child care and families.

Billingsly, A. 1994. *Climbing Jacob's ladder: The enduring legacy of African American families.* New York: Touchstone/Simon & Schuster.

Describes the transitions of the African American family through history, highlighting sources of tradition. Includes a discussion of current issues for African American families.

Bowman, B.T. 1994. The challenge of diversity. *Phi Delta Kappan* 76 (3): 218–24.

Helps educators understand the nature of the problems faced by children at risk of school failure and how to design educational solutions that take into account the importance of the social context in which learning takes place.

Brown, B. 1998. *Unlearning discrimination in the early years.* Staffordshire, England: Trentham.

Encourages students and adults working with young children to enable the children to talk constructively about issues of discrimination. The author explains relevant research and theory about how racism, sexism, and homophobia develop and how to help engage in antidiscriminatory practice with preschoolers.

Chang, H.N., A. Muckelroy, & D. Pulido-Tobiassen. 1996. *Looking in, looking out: Redefining child care and early education in a diverse society.* San Francisco: California Tomorrow.

Responds to the challenges of how well our children develop pride in their cultural heritage and learn to work with people of other cultures. Shares five principles that define quality care, focusing on responsive partnerships with families.

Comer, J.P. 1997. *Waiting for a miracle. Why schools can't solve our problems— And how we can.* New York: Penguin.

Focuses on causes of the nation's growing social and economic problems and viable approaches for solving them. Calls for the creation of a new cultural mind-set—that children can succeed—and the investment in children's development. Provides successful strategies for troubled schools that involve families and communities working together to make schools become instruments of change.

Comer, J.P., & A.F. Pouissaint. 1992. *Raising Black children: Two leading psychiatrists confront the educational, social, and emotional problems facing Black children.* New York: Penguin.

Two noted Black psychiatrists provide a comprehensive assessment of how best to raise Black children from infancy through adolescence. Identifies universal aspects of growth and development while highlighting culturally relevant strategies to help parents, teachers, and social practitioners address issues of concern for Black children and families. A powerful resource for preparing children to counteract the effects of pervasive racism in America.

Delpit, L.D. 1988. The silenced dialogue. Power of pedagogy in educating other people's children. *Harvard Educational Review* 58 (3): 280–97.

Explores the culture of power that exists in society in general and the ways in which educational institutions maintain the status quo. Identifies the ways in which current power dynamics negatively affect poor and Black children. Targets educational strategies to promote cross-cultural dialogue and a vision of equity in supporting the growth and development of all children.

Derman-Sparks, L., S. Cronin, S. Henry, C. Olatunji, & S. York. 1998. *Future vision, present work: Learning from the Culturally Relevant Anti-Bias Leadership Project.* St. Paul, MN: Redleaf.

Offers the latest information addressing antibias and cultural relevancy issues, based on three leadership groups that performed cross-cultural advocacy work in Seattle, Minneapolis, and New Orleans for a three-year period. Also available in Spanish.

Derman-Sparks, L., & C.B. Phillips. 1997. *Teaching/learning anti-racism.* New York: Teachers College Press.

Based on the authors' experience in teaching adults, the book offers a guide to the development of an antiracist identity, awareness, and behavior. Organized chronologically from the first day of class to the last class, this book for teachers and trainers integrates methodology and course content descriptions with student writings and analyses of students' growth.

Dyson, A.H., & C. Genishi, eds. 1994. *The need for story: Cultural diversity in classroom and community.* Urbana, IL: National Council of Teachers of English.

Nineteen contributors explore the nature of *story*—the basic functions it serves, its connections to the diverse sociocultural landscape of our society, and its power in the classroom. Emphasizing the complex relationships between story, ethnicity, and gender, the book includes stories both told and written, those authored by children and by teachers, ones professionally produced, and those created in the classroom.

Espinosa, L.M. 1995. Hispanic parent involvement in early childhood programs. *ERIC Digest.* ED 382412. Urbana-Champaign, IL: ERIC Clearinghouse on Elementary and Early Childhood Education.

Stresses the importance of early childhood programs demonstrating successful approaches to working with Hispanic families. By forging closer communication and bridging the cultural gap between home and school, early childhood educators establish a basis for future school success. Lists seven strategies that work in early childhood programs.

Feng, J. 1994. Asian American children—What teachers should know. *ERIC Digest.* ED 369577. Urbana-Champaign, IL: ERIC Clearinghouse on Elementary and Early Childhood Education.

Provides information to help teachers gain a better understanding of Asian American children, from East and Southeast Asian cultures in particular, and identify culturally appropriate educational practices to use.

Fenson, C., B. Dennis, & S. Palsha. 1998. *¡Hola means hello! Resources and ideas for promoting diversity in early childhood settings.* 2d ed. Chapel Hill, NC: Frank Porter Graham Child Development Center.

Designed to assist child care providers, teachers, and others who provide services to young children and their families in promoting diversity and fostering discussion of different beliefs, values, and traditions. Sections include resources/materials for enhancing cultural awareness, a self-assessment checklist, booklists, and instructional resources.

Flynn, N., E. Thorp, K. Evans, & C. Takemoto, eds. 1996. *Infusing cultural competence in early childhood programs.* Fairfax, VA: George Mason University, Multicultural Early Childhood Team Training/Center for Human Disabilities.

Includes a participant's notebook and trainer's manual, an inservice training model promoting parent/professional collaboration in early childhood settings. Designed to target programs that serve families who represent multiple cultural and linguistic communities.

Garcia, E. 1997. The education of Hispanics in early childhood: Of roots and wings. In *Annual editions: Early childhood education, 1999/2000, 20th edition,* eds. K. Panciorek & J. Munro. Guilford, CT: Duskin/McGraw Hill.

Through a personal account of one man's early years of life, readers learn about the Hispanic culture. Information includes a focus on his lifestyle as a young child as well as demographic information about Hispanic families.

Garcia, E.E., B. McLaughlin, B. Spodek, & O.N. Saracho, eds. 1995. *Meeting the challenge of linguistic and cultural diversity in early childhood education.* Yearbook in Early Childhood Education, vol. 6. New York: Teachers College Press.

Contributors analyze a preschool program, review testing of language capacities, compare socialization and individuality, discuss family structure, look at support for disabled and diverse children, and discuss teacher preparation.

Garcia, S.B., ed. 1994. *Addressing cultural and linguistic diversity in special education: Issues and trends.* Reston, VA: Council for Exceptional Children.

Includes articles that focus on issues related to education reform, evaluation of instruction, and assessment for African American students, Asian and Pacific Islander students, Mexican American students, and other culturally and linguistically diverse students.

Gonzalez-Mena, J. 1998. *The child in the family and the community.* Upper Saddle River, NJ: Merrill.

An examination of the socialization process of young children, with a focus on the development of attachment, autonomy, initiative, and self-esteem in the family and the child's community. The author discusses how society's goals, cultural patterns, and values affect childrearing environments (including group and family child care settings).

Greenberg, P. 1992. Ideas that work with young children. Teaching about Native Americans? Or teaching about people, including Native Americans? *Young Children* 47 (6): 27–30, 79–81.

Stresses the importance of integrating information about Native Americans, as well as other cultural groups, into the curriculum rather than focusing specific units on them. Emphasizes the importance of stressing that people are people first, then discussing the similarities and differences between various cultures.

Hale, J.E. 1986. *Black children: Their roots, culture, and learning styles.* Baltimore: Johns Hopkins University Press.

Explains the effect of African and American cultures on African American child development. Suggests curriculum reforms that can enhance children's achievement.

Hale, J. 1991. The transmission of cultural values to young African American children. *Young Children* 46 (6): 7–14.

Alerts early childhood educators to the importance of ethnic image in formulating self-image.

Hall, N.S., & V. Rhomberg. 1995. *The affective curriculum: Teaching the anti-bias approach to young children.* Albany, NY: Delmar.

Enables anyone involved with young children to begin exploring personal values and attitudes toward diversity. The theoretical component examines the meaning of the anti-bias approach—the barriers to and the process of becoming empowered to carry out this philosophical orientation.

Harry, B. 1992. *Cultural diversity, families, and the special education system: Communication and empowerment.* New York: Teachers College Press.

Although aimed at special needs children and their families, this book provides valuable insight for all teachers through a profile of 12 real families. The treatment of the "world views" of different cultures is especially insightful when applied to educational services; case studies make principles more applicable and pragmatic.

Hildebrand, V., L.A. Phenice, M. Gray, & R. Hines. 2000. *Knowing and serving diverse families.* 2d ed. Columbus, OH: Merrill/Prentice Hall.

Helps teachers and parent specialists gain insight into families of different ethnicities, language, age, and socioeconomic levels. Current family research supports discussion of African American, Hispanic American, Asian American, Arab American, and Native American families. Addresses implications for working comfortably with diverse families.

Hilliard, A.G. 1995. *The Maroon within us: Selected essays on African American community socialization*. Baltimore: Black Classic.

Describes strategies for the education and socialization of African American children based on African values. Illustrates the effects of Eurocentric socialization on children of color and provides alternative assessments to culturally biased IQ testing.

Hilliard, A.G. 1997. *SBA: Reawakening the African mind*. Gainesville, FL: Makare.

SBA (seba) is a Kemetic (Ancient Egyptian) term that refers to teaching, wisdom, and study. Hilliard states, "It was through SBA that the great African civilizations of antiquity were produced." He discusses the genocide that results from institutional and covert forms of racism and focuses on the power of SBA for the liberation of future generations.

Hollins, E.R., J.E. King, & W.C. Hayman, eds. 1994. *Teaching diverse populations: Formulating a knowledge base*. Albany: State University of New York Press.

Covers a variety of cultures, ranging from Appalachian to Puerto Rican and Native American. Emphasis is on African American children, including a chapter on characteristics of effective African American teachers.

Kaeser, G., P. Gillespie, & G. Valentine. 1997. *Of many colors: Portraits of multiracial families*. Amherst: University of Massachusetts Press.

Documents the feelings and experiences of individuals in multiracial families. Parents and children speak candidly about their lives, their relationships, and the ways in which they have dealt with the issue of race.

Lewis, C.C. 1995. *Educating hearts and minds: Reflections on Japanese preschool and elementary education*. New York: Cambridge University Press.

Voices of Japanese teachers and examples from Japanese classrooms reveal education that reflects developmentally appropriate ideas. Teachers focus on the development of the whole child, show an interest in helping children build caring and responsible attitudes, as well as promote children's cognitive competence.

Little Soldier, L. 1992. Working with Native American children. *Young Children* 47 (6): 15–21.

Details the cultural discontinuity between the typical classroom experiences and home lives of Native American children.

Lynch, E.W., & M.J. Hanson. 1998. *Developing cross-cultural competence—A guide for working with children and their families*. Baltimore, MD: Brookes.

This book provides strategies for effective cross-cultural interactions with families of infants, preschoolers, and young children who may have or be at risk for a disability or chronic illness. Cultural perspectives are included from various ethnic groups.

Mallory, B.L., & R.S. New, eds. 1994. *Diversity and developmentally appropriate practices: Challenges for early childhood education.* New York: Teachers College Press.

Critiques of early childhood education and developmentally appropriate practices help expand the current definition of developmentally appropriate practice to include alternative theoretical and practical perspectives necessary for addressing the needs of young children with cultural and developmental differences.

Multicultural Initiative Project. 1995. *An introduction to cultural competence principles and elements: An annotated bibliography.* Portland, OR: Portland State University.

Resources for addressing topics that include cultural self-assessment, dynamics of difference, valuing diversity, adaptation to diversity, and incorporation of cultural knowledge.

NAEYC. 1996. *Responding to linguistic and cultural diversity—Recommendations for effective early childhood education: An NAEYC position statement.* Washington, DC: Author.

This brochure offers NAEYC's position regarding linguistic and cultural diversity and provides suggestions for educators working with children whose first language is not English.

Ramsey, P. 1998. *Teaching and learning in a diverse world.* 2d ed. New York: Teachers College Press.

Offers a comprehensive discussion of children's identity development in several areas such as race, culture, gender, class, disabilities, and family structure. Also provides principles and strategies for creating quality environments that support children of all backgrounds.

Reese, D. 1996. Teaching young children about Native Americans. *ERIC Digest.* EDOPS963. Urbana-Champaign, IL: ERIC Clearinghouse on Elementary and Early Childhood Education.

With much remaining to be done to counter stereotypes of Native Americans learned by young children in U.S. culture and society, this digest focuses on teaching about Native Americans in early childhood classrooms and provides teaching suggestions and positive strategies.

Sepulveda, C. 1996. *Seven keys: Learning and Latinos.* Leominister, MA: Biblos Press.

Explores the crisis we confront as a nation vis-à-vis Latino children and the belief that it can best be understood and resolved through a clear understanding of the process of learning as a progression through seven essential states. Discusses why the children of Latinos do not progress through these states with the ease that other children do.

Shartrand, A. 1996. *Supporting Latino families: Lessons from exemplary programs.* Cambridge, MA: Harvard Research Project.

Provides insightful strategies from 11 programs that have pioneered quality services to Latino families. Volume I provides an analysis of the programs' strategies and distills lessons for practitioners. Volume II gives an in-depth profile of each program, including its history, key features, evaluations, funding sources, and contacts for further information.

Stremel, A.J. 1997. Diversity and the multicultural perspective. In *Integrated curriculum and developmentally appropriate practice birth to age 8,* eds. C.H. Hart, D.C. Burts, & R. Charlesworth, 363–87. Albany: State University of New York Press.

Emphasizes the interactive process that emerges in the context of teaching and learning, while fostering respect for individual and cultural diversity. Offers a developmental framework that draws on the constructivist perspectives of both Piaget and Vygotsky.

Tacum, B.D. 1997. *"Why are all the Black kids sitting together in the cafeteria?" And other conversations about race.* New York: Basic.

Examines the awkwardness that stymies interracial communication and provides a new way of thinking and talking about race through the lens of racial identity. Also details the stages of identity development in children and adults and offers strategies for supporting healthy self-concepts.

Terzian, A.M. 1993. *The kids' multicultural art book.* Charlotte, VT: Williamson.

Explores the rhythms, designs, and traditions found in the art and artifacts of different cultures. Provides an informative section on each culture included.

Wilson, A. 1992. *Awakening the natural genius of Black children.* New York: Afrikan World InfoSystems.

Challenges us to broaden narrowly biased concepts of education to stimulate all aspects of growth and development. Provides strategies based on the developmental psychology of Black children to target the often-untapped genius of Black children. Contrasts the limits of traditional education models and the successes of culturally relevant pedagogy and practice.

Engaging in practices that value diversity

All teachers and caregivers will find in the resources in this section, help and support in responding to the cultural diversity in their classroom, responding to linguistic diversity, and including children with special needs and abilities. The three parts that follow interrelate and include resources that are mutually supportive.

Responding to cultural diversity

The focus of these resources is on specific strategies and activities and approaches for developing antibias and culturally responsive classrooms and relationships with families. Suggested practices address total approaches, the teacher's role, curriculum activities, materials, ways of setting up the physical environment, and communication techniques.

Ballenger, C. 1999. *Teaching other people's children: Literacy and learning in a bilingual classroom.* New York: Teachers College Press.

> Account of how a preschool teacher adapted the way she managed classroom behavior and learned the different ways her Haitian children and families viewed literacy and schooling. Text addresses the resources she used to learn about the cultural views—a teacher research group, adults from the community, and transcribed records of children's conversations.

Beaty, J. 1997. *Building bridges with multicultural picture books.* Columbus, OH: Merrill/Prentice Hall.

> Offers strategies for acquainting teachers and children with multicultural book characters as a strategy for helping them relate to and accept the real multicultural people they meet. Offers suggestions for choosing books, leading children into book-extension activities featuring multicultural characters, and developing multicultural curricula.

Boutte, G., S. Hendley, & I. Van Scoy. 1996. Multicultural and nonsexist prop boxes. *Young Children* 52 (1): 34–39.

> Stresses the importance of a rationale for using prop boxes to facilitate dramatic play and expands on ways to integrate multicultural and nonsexist learning experiences in curricula and activities.

Bromer, J. 1999. Cultural variations in child care: Values and actions. *Young Children* 54 (6): 72–78.

Conflicts and misunderstandings often arise when caregivers and parents hold different, culturally based beliefs about a child's expected behavior or an adult's appropriate response. Two profiles of care providers offer a point for beginning discussion; a table contrasts child-centered learning vs. academic preparedness; and other helpful charts outline perspectives in childrearing values, communicating childrearing values, and steps to practicing responsive caregiving.

Children's Foundation. 1994. *Helping children love themselves and others: Resource guide to equity materials for young children.* Washington, DC: Author.

The guide contains a checklist of books, toys, and materials to assist in determining equity resources; annotated bibliographies of children's literature and resources for adults that include books, curricula, magazines, newsletters and pamphlets; a listing of companies with antibias and/or multicultural books and materials available; and a listing of national support organizations. (Distributed by The Children's Foundation, 725 Fifteenth Street, NW, Suite 505, Washington, DC 20005-2109.)

Crawford, S.H. 1996. *Beyond dolls and guns: One hundred and one ways to help children avoid gender bias.* Portsmouth, NH: Heinemann.

Includes information on stereotypes and antibias activities. Offers suggestions for recognizing and overcoming sexism and gender bias and for developing healthy, respectful relationships.

Creaser, B., & E. Dau. 1996. *The anti-bias approach in early childhood.* Sydney, Australia: Harper.

Written by Australian early childhood teachers and includes strategies for working with 2-year-olds, preschoolers, linguistically diverse children, and families from a variety of backgrounds, all within the Australian context.

Cunningham, G. 1996. The challenges of responding to individual and cultural differences and meeting the needs of all communities. In *NAEYC accreditation: A decade of learning and the years ahead,* eds. S. Bredekamp & B.A. Willer, 79–82. Washington, DC: NAEYC.

Poses questions for the field to face regarding the real cost of developmentally appropriate practice, quality and affordability, and the role accreditation plays in guiding program improvement. Suggests that accreditation can serve the needs of low- and middle-income families and practitioners.

De Gaetano, Y., L.R. Williams, & D. Volk 1998. *Kaleidoscope: A multicultural approach for the primary school classroom.* Upper Saddle River, NJ: Merrill/ Prentice Hall.

Developed through a three-year cross-cultural project in kindergarten and primary grades. Highlights specific techniques that enable the teacher to learn about the child's culture and refine his or her practice in a step-by-step implementation process. The authors provide a framework for bridging theory and practice (including bilingualism), teaching strategies/ activities and directions for classroom set-up and making materials, and conducting parent workshops and evaluating the program and children.

Delpit, L. 1995. *Other people's children: Cultural conflict in the classroom.* New York: New Press.

Confronts the possibility that progressive practices have the potential to disadvantage children from nondominant cultures. Suggests ways for working with children without denigrating their primary cultures and languages.

deMelendez, W.R., & V. Ostertag. 1997. *Teaching young children in multicultural classrooms—Issues, concepts, and strategies.* Albany, NY: Delmar.

Provides a plan for developing and teaching a multicultural curriculum with 3- through 8-year-olds. Describes the social foundations and theory of multicultural education, past and current issues and directions, and guidelines and ideas for classroom implementation.

Derman-Sparks, L. 1992. Reaching potentials through antibias, multicultural curriculum. In *Reaching potentials: Appropriate curriculum and assessment for young children, volume 1,* eds. S. Bredekamp & T. Rosegrant, 114–27. Washington DC: NAEYC.

Provides information about applying curriculum guidelines to current practices, planning developmentally and contextually appropriate antibias, multicultural curriculum, and integrating antibias, multicultural planning into the total curriculum.

Derman-Sparks, L., & the A.B.C. Task Force. 1989. *Anti-bias curriculum: Tools for empowering young children.* Washington, DC: NAEYC.

Suggestions for helping staff and children respect each other as individuals and for confronting, transcending, and eliminating barriers based on race, culture, gender, or ability. Chapters include: why an anti-bias curriculum; creating an anti-bias environment; learning about racial differences and similarities; learning about disabilities; learning about gender identity; learning about cultural differences and similarities; learning to resist stereotyping and discriminatory behavior; and working with parents.

Derman-Sparks, L., & E. Jones. 1992. Meeting the challenge of diversity. *Young Children* 47 (2): 12–18.

Discusses how meeting the challenge of diversity is an essential component of quality early childhood programs.

Diller, D. 1999. Opening the dialogue: Using culture as a tool in teaching young African American Children. *The Reading Teacher* (May): 820–28.

A first-grade teacher poignantly shares how she learned to teach and reach her African American students once she understood and respected their rich culture and language. An excellent, insightful article for learning how to successfully meet the needs of children of diverse cultures.

Dyson, A.H. 1993. *Social worlds of children learning to write in an urban primary school.* New York: Teachers College Press.

Explores the way children's social relationships impact on their oral and written composing and thus literacy success in school. Based on a two-year ethnographic study of six K–3 children, describes efforts to make literacy accessible to culturally diverse populations.

Dyson, A.H. 1997. *What difference does difference make? Teacher reflections on diversity, literacy, and the urban primary school.* Urbana, IL: National Council of Teachers of English.

With commentaries in the voice of Dyson, a group of California K–3 teachers explore what is meant by *difference* and how to help children live in a world of differences. Contains conversational excerpts that focus on relationships, building a classroom community, negotiating access to the curriculum, and the qualities of a school culture in which teachers can openly communicate.

Fenson, C., B. Dennis, & S. Palsha. 1998. *¡Hola means hello! Resources and ideas for promoting diversity in early childhood settings.* 2d ed. Chapel Hill, NC: Frank Porter Graham Child Development Center.

Designed to assist child care providers and teachers to promote diversity and discussion of different beliefs, values, and traditions. Sections include resources/materials for enhancing cultural awareness, a self-assessment checklist, booklists, and instructional resources.

Ford, C.W. 1994. *We can all get along: Fifty steps you can take to help end racism.* New York: Dell.

Designed for caregivers, this text presents dos and don'ts of using nonracist-language cross-cultural communication to reinforce positive images in children.

Gallas, K. 1998. *Sometimes I can be anything: Power, gender and identity.* New York: Teachers College Press.

Explores how 6- and 7-year-olds come to understand gender, race, and the power structure as they interact in the classroom and collectively construct their social world. Implications for the teacher are portrayed through teacher commentary and the voices and actions of the children.

Gomez, R.A. 1991. Teaching with a multicultural perspective. *ERIC Digest.* ED 339548. Urbana-Champaign, IL: ERIC Clearinghouse on Elementary and Early Childhood Education.

Teaching with a multicultural perspective encourages children's appreciation and understanding of other cultures as well as their own, promotes a child's sense of the uniqueness of his own culture as a positive characteristic, and enables the child to accept the uniqueness of the cultures of others.

Certificate of

The National Association for th

NA

is pleased to prese

_____

for having participated in NA
Chicago—N

Mark R. Ginsberg, Ph.D.
NAEYC Executive Director

Attendance

Education of Young Children

C

this Certificate to

_____

C's 2003 Annual Conference

ember 5–8

1509 16th Street, N.W.
Washington, DC 20036-1426

Gonzalez-Mena, J. 1998. *The child in the family and the community.* Upper Saddle River, NJ: Merrill.

An examination of the socialization process of young children, with a focus on the development of attachment, autonomy, initiative, and self-esteem in the family and the child's community. Discusses how society's goals, cultural patterns, and values affect child care settings and family child care settings.

Hale, J.E. 1994. *Unbank the fire: Visions for the education of African American children.* Baltimore, MD: Johns Hopkins University Press.

Emphasizes the need for educating young children within the context of their culture. Proposes reforms in educational practice, offers a detailed description of an early childhood demonstration program, and explains how all schools can develop new, culturally appropriate ways of teaching.

Hall, N.S. 1999. *Creative resources for the anti-bias classroom.* Toronto: Canadian Mothercraft Society.

Integrates information about developmental-based planning and child development that reflects diversity. Experiences have been designed to promote the positive self-esteem of each individual child, support the value of others' uniquenesses.

Kendall, F.E. 1996. *Diversity in the classroom: New approaches to the education of young children.* 2d ed. New York: Teachers College Press.

Addresses many aspects of antibias education—from the stages of child development to strategies for educating parents—focusing particularly on the teacher's role as an agent of change. The author promotes teachers' self-awareness and provides guidelines for setting up multicultural environments and curricula for 3- through 5-year-olds.

Neugebauer, B., ed. 1992. *Alike and different: Exploring our humanity with young children.* Rev. ed. Washington, DC: NAEYC.

Provides teachers with suggestions and rationales for exploring with young children the unique qualities that make each person an individual. Considers gender, age, physical differences, ethnic background, intellectual abilities, and economic status.

Opitz, M.F., ed. 1998. *Literacy instruction for culturally and linguistically diverse students.* Newark, DE: International Reading Association.

Shows how cultural background affects reading and writing and offers ideas for elementary school classroom practice and a list of recent multicultural children's books. The teaching strategies include opportunities for students to reveal who they are as learners and how they connect their own cultural/linguistic experiences with a given text to ensure comprehension.

Schmidt, P.R. 1995. Working and playing with others: Cultural conflict in a kindergarten literacy program. *The Reading Teacher* 48 (5): 404–12.

Uses specific examples to show ways that literacy learning by children of ethnic minority backgrounds may be hampered by informal social interactions that take place in the classroom. Gives suggestions for improving the classroom culture for ethnic minorities.

Strickland, D.S. 1991. Multicultural education. In *Creating the learning environment: A guide in early childhood education,* ed. D. Strickland, 24–29. Orlando, FL: Harcourt Brace Jovanovich.

Presents a brief introduction to multicultural education and the reasons behind its importance in the early childhood classroom. Includes a number of themes, multicultural activities, and ideas for including multicultural elements into all areas of the curriculum.

Strickland, D.S. 1994. Educating African American learners at risk: Finding a better way. *Language Arts* 71: 328–36.

Discusses the features of good language arts instruction for all children and stresses education for meaning and constructivist teaching strategies.

Teaching Tolerance Project. 1991. *Starting small: Teaching tolerance in preschool and early grades.* Montgomery, AL: Southern Poverty Law Center.

Combines video and text to profile innovative classrooms. Offers research-based commentary on essential themes such as racial awareness, ability differences, and friendship. These reflections provide a conceptual framework for both close-up problem solving and long-range curriculum planning.

Terzian, A. 1993. *The kid's multicultural art book.* Charlotte, VT: Williamson.

Introduces artifacts from Native American, Hispanic, African, and Asian cultures. Each set of cultural artifacts is preceded by an explanation of the cultural traditions and evolution of the artifact, such as the Native American's close relationship to the natural world—the sea, fish, trees, birds, and other wildlife—that played a critical role in their lives and is seen in their crafts. Teacher suggestions for constructing the artifacts includes materials needed and step-by-step directions.

Thompson, B.J. 1993. *Words can hurt you: Beginning a program of anti-bias education.* Menlo Park, CA: Addison-Wesley.

Presents activities, resources, materials, and rationale for creating a supportive antibias environment and curriculum for 3- through 8-year-olds and their families. Main topic areas include same and different, cultural respect, disability awareness, and prejudice in the classroom and throughout the school.

Vold, E.B., ed. 1992. *Multicultural education in early childhood classrooms.* Washington, DC: National Education Association.

A source of practical ideas, sample lessons, and teaching strategies for infusing every aspect of your curriculum with a multicultural component. Gives specific techniques for increasing diversity training in school and broadening the multicultural scope of every teacher and child.

Whitney, T. 1999. *Kids like us: Using Persona dolls in the classroom.* St. Paul, MN: Redleaf.

Guides teachers of 2- to 8-year-old children through the process of storytelling with persona dolls to help the children confront bias by expanding their comfort with differences and ability to talk about their feelings. The author outlines five steps for using the dolls, incorporating ideas for creating characters, inventing stories, and working with children in a group.

Responding to linguistic diversity

The resources here are designed for teachers who have children in their early childhood classrooms who speak little or no English. The content encompasses the linguistic development of second-language learners and children who are bilingual and the implications of learning through a second language. Practical recommendations for working with linguistically diverse children cover curricular and assessment issues and setting up relationships with parents whose home language is other than English.

Barrera, R.M., C. Alvarado, A. Lopez, R. Booze, C. Greer, & L. Derman-Sparks. 1995. Bilingual education. *Child Care Information Exchange* (107): 43–62.

This article offers frank words on the needs of bilingual children or children whose home language is not English. The authors provide suggestions for establishing relationships with bilingual parents as well as suggestions for culturally consistent and inclusive programs.

Cary, S. 1997. *Second language learners.* York, ME: Stenhouse.

Outlines the basic ideas of how language is best acquired and provides a range of techniques for bringing second-language learners into the curriculum. Charts, visuals, and students' samples support the text to illustrate how engaging instruction and support for children's primary language means that children acquire more content and more language.

Cummins, J. 1996. *Negotiating identities: Education for empowerment in a diverse society.* Ontario, CA: California Association for Bilingual Education.

Provides an in-depth theoretical discussion of and strategies for working with linguistically diverse children in kindergarten through sixth grade.

Edwards, V. 1998. *The power of Babel.* Stoke on Trent, Great Britain: Trentham.

Examines a range of initiatives for promoting linguistic and cultural diversity in the primary classroom, bringing together practical teaching suggestions, case studies, and information on resources. Emphasizes the importance of a sound foundation in the first language for development in the second language. The author also recognizes that all members of the class—including monolingual English speakers—can benefit from the expertise of bilingual children. (Distributed in the United States by Stylus Publishing; 800-232-0223.)

Escamilla, K., A.M. Andrade, A.G.M. Basurto, O.A. Ruiz, & M. Clay. 1995. *Instrumento de observacion de los logros de la lecto-escritura inicial: Spanish reconstruction of an observational survey, A bilingual text.* Portsmouth, NH: Heinemann.

Draws on the theoretical framework of Marie Clay's *An Observation Survey* not as a literal translation, but a conceptual re-creation. Provides teachers with a tool to consider how children who come into contact with two languages use those languages to make sense of their world and monitor their progress. Based on extensive research in bilingual education, this book expands the knowledge base of K–3 bilingual teachers in a way that enables them to be better observers of children's literacy behaviors and improve their teaching.

> *Arena: Del cuento "Sand" por Marie Clay.* 1995. Portsmouth, NH: Heinemann.
>
> These are "Concepts About Print" tests (by M. Clay) that can be used with a new entrant or to enable the child to point to certain features as the examiner reads the book (the foregoing reference *Instrumento observacion),* which presents the theoretical background, administration details, and scoring interpretation of the tests.

Freeman, Y.S., & D.E. Freeman. 1998. *ESL/EFL Teaching: Principles for success.* Portsmouth, NH: Heinemann.

Provides a readable explanation of second-language teaching methodology, supported by numerous primary classroom examples. Includes detailed discussions and examples of EFL (English as a Foreign Language) teaching as well as many scenarios from ESL (English as a Second Language) classes. The emphasis is on teaching language through meaningful content.

Genesee, F., & E. Nicoladis. 1995. Language development in bilingual preschool children. In *Meeting the challenge of linguistic and cultural diversity in early childhood education.* Yearbook in Early Childhood Education, vol. 6, eds. E. Garcia & B. McLaughlin with B. Spodek & O.N. Saracho. New York: Teachers College Press.

An accounting of the linguistic development of children who are raised bilingually during the preschool years. Highlights developmental milestones, the understanding of bilingual language performance, the language socialization of bilingual children, and classroom implications.

Genishi, C., & M.B. Brainard. 1995. Assessment of bilingual children: A dilemma seeking solutions. In *Meeting the challenge of linguistic and cultural diversity in early childhood* education. Yearbook in Early Childhood Education, vol.6, eds. E. Garcia & B. McLaughlin with B. Spodek & O.N. Saracho. New York: Teachers College Press.

An overview of the issues that need to be understood as early childhood educators make decisions about the assessment of English-language learners.

Gibbons, P. 1993. *Learning to learn in a second language.* Portsmouth, NH: Heinemann.

An approach based on the assumption that the classroom program is a major resource for language development and that a responsive program takes into account the fact that children are not only learning a new language but learning *in* that language as well. Exemplifies current theories of second-language development through a wide range of strategies and practical suggestions for the classroom teacher.

Grant, R. 1995. Meeting the needs of young second language learners. In *Meeting the challenge of linguistic and cultural diversity in early childhood* education. Yearbook in Early Childhood Education, vol. 6, eds. E. Garcia & B. McLaughlin with B. Spodek & O.N. Saracho, 1–17. New York: Teachers College Press.

Addresses important dimensions of second-language proficiency, the way in which cultural beliefs and values provide a classroom context for learning a new language, and the kinds of instructional approaches, materials, strategies, and tasks that support language-minority learners.

Kuball, Y.E. 1995. Goodbye dittoes: A journey from skill-based teaching to developmentally appropriate language education in a bilingual kindergarten. *Young Children* 50 (2): 6–14.

Written by a kindergarten teacher, this article uses descriptions and photographs to demonstrate an approach to emergent literacy that works in a bilingual setting with English-language learners.

Mirmontes, O.B., A. Nadeau, & N.L. Commins. 1997. *Restructuring for linguistic diversity: Linking decisionmaking to effective programs.* New York: Teachers College Press.

Provides pre-K–12 teachers with basic premises about second-language learning and a framework within which to restructure their classrooms and teaching interactions. Specific classroom activities described include suggestions for scaffolding the teacher-student dialogue.

Opitz, M.F., ed. 1998. *Literacy instruction for culturally and linguistically diverse students.* Newark, DE: International Reading Association.

Shows how cultural background affects reading and writing and offers ideas for elementary school classroom practice and a list of recent multicultural children's books. The teaching strategies include opportunities for students to reveal who they are as learners and how they connect their own cultural/linguistic experiences with a given text to ensure comprehension.

Ovando, C.J., & V.P. Collier. 1998. *Bilingual and ESL classrooms: Teaching in multicultural contexts.* New York: McGraw-Hill.

A classic review of research, policy, and effective practices for all teachers, not just specialists, who work with primary-school language-minority children. Focuses on teaching strategies; first- and second-language acquisition; intercultural awareness; math, science, and social studies; and assessment.

Rennie, J. 1993. ESL and bilingual program models. *ERIC Digest.* ED 362072. Washington, DC: ERIC Clearinghouse on Languages and Linguistics.

Summarizes successful program models for promoting the academic achievement of language-minority students and the importance of local decisionmaking.

Rosegrant, T. 1992. Reaching potentials in a multilingual classroom: Opportunities and challenges. In *Reaching potentials: Appropriate curriculum and assessment for young children, volume 1,* eds. S. Bredekamp & T. Rosegrant, 145–47. Washington, DC: NAEYC.

Discusses the challenges one teacher faced in her efforts to create a multilingual classroom environment.

Soto, L.D. 1991. Understanding bilingual/bicultural young children. *Young Children* 46 (2): 30–36.

Examines demographic and educational trends of bilingual/bicultural children, misconceptions about young children learning a second language, successful educational approaches in early childhood bilingual education, and practical applications of existing research.

Soto, L.D. 1997. *Language, culture and power.* Albany: State University of New York Press.

In this case study of the Puerto Rican community in an industrial city, the author details the experiences of bilingual parents in their struggle to preserve the bilingual education programs in their schools.

Spodek, B., & O.N. Saracho, eds. 1993. *Language and literacy in early childhood education: Yearbook in early childhood education, vol. 4.* New York: Teachers College Press.

Addresses language-learning skills that relate to literacy, including becoming bilingual and biliterate, the whole-language philosophy, research implications for classrooms, the role of the parent in supporting language and literacy, and appropriate children's literature and assessment.

Stefanakis, E. 1998. *Whose judgment counts? Assessing bilingual children K–3.* Portsmouth, NH: Heinemann.

Written to provide teachers with the skills they need to make informed assessments of bilingual children in their class and make sense of their learning and language capacity. Author explains the issues involved for bilingual students and gives examples of informal techniques that can be used to assess children on a daily basis.

Tabors, P.O. 1997. *One child, two languages: A guide for preschool educators of children learning English as a second language.* Baltimore, MD: Brookes.

Details the second-language acquisition process for young children in classroom settings. Also includes information about providing children with a supportive environment, working with parents, and assessing children's progress—all in the context of a developmentally appropriate setting.

Valdez, G. 1996. *Con respecto: Bridging the distance between culturally diverse families and schools.* New York: Teachers College Press.

Describes the issues, challenges, and emotions families and children face as they enter schools when their home language is other than English. In their own words, parents explain what they want for their children.

Wolfe, L. 1992. Reaching potentials through bilingual education. *Reaching potentials: Appropriate curriculum and assessment for young children, volume 1,* eds. S. Bredekamp & T. Rosegrant, 139–44. Washington DC: NAEYC.

Discusses the history of bilingual education, the effects of primary-language instruction in preschool, multilingual classrooms, collaboration with parents and community, and assessment.

Including children with special needs and abilities

In this category, the materials presented give background information, varying viewpoints concerning the meaning of inclusion, and discussion on including children with disabilities in regular classrooms. The resources focus on developing inclusive programs, give descriptions of various disabling conditions, and offer guidelines for designing environments, curriculums, and assessments that accommodate the special needs of children and techniques for addressing the attitudes and feelings of teachers, children, and families.

Abraham, M.R., L.M. Morris, & P.J. Wald. 1993. *Inclusive early childhood education.* Tucson, AZ: Communications Skill Builders.

Shows how to use thematic planning to accomplish Individualized Education Plan (IEP) objectives.

Allen, K.E., & I.S. Schwartz. 1992. *The exceptional child: Inclusion in early childhood education.* 3d ed. Albany, NY: Delmar.

Provides current information on developing inclusive programs for all children, 0- through 6-year-olds, including those with special needs. The authors consider twelve disabilities in four categories—developmental, sensory, physical, and behavioral.

Bailey, D.B., & M. Wolery. 1992. *Teaching infants and preschoolers with disabilities.* 2d ed. New York: Merrill/Prentice Hall.

Provides a comprehensive overview of the framework and concepts associated with early intervention/early childhood special education. Also provides specific intervention strategies service providers can use in teaching young children with disabilities and in working with their families.

Bailey, P., D. Cryer, T. Harms, S. Osborn, & B. Kniest. 1996. *Active learning for children with disabilities: A manual for use with the active learning series.* New York: Addison Wesley/Longman.

Targeted to care providers and family members. Provides suggestions and resources for helping young children with disabilities learn through play. Learning situations found throughout the book can be adapted into training activities.

Blenk, K., & D.L. Fine. 1995. *Making school inclusion work: A guide to everyday practices.* Cambridge, MA: Brookline Books.

Describes how to conduct an inclusive school program that educates a diverse student body as a whole. Stresses that true inclusion demands involvement, imagination, and dedication to ensure its goals.

Bowe, F. 2000. *Birth to five: Early childhood special education.* 2d ed. Albany, NY: Delmar.

Presents major disabilities and developmental delays seen in young children and the laws that authorize and fund early intervention and preschool special education. Concrete examples illustrate techniques for fostering child development in inclusive settings including information on using technology to enhance the special education environment.

Bunnett, R., N.L. Davis, V. Youcha, K. Wood, K. Haugen, A.P. Meyer, L. Adams, W. Hayslip, & T. Norman-Murch. 1997. Environments for special needs. *Child Care Information Exchange* (114): 41–63.

Contains articles on the subjects of designing, enhancing, and evaluating inclusive environments. Also contains information about creating an inclusive outdoor setting and enriching center activities in order to include all children.

Catlett, C., & P. Winton, eds. 1999. *Resource guide: Selected early childhood/ early intervention training materials.* 8th ed. Chapel Hill: Frank Porter Graham Child Development Center, University of North Carolina.

An annotated bibliography listing for more than 400 entries divided into 18 sections that correspond with key early childhood/early intervention and instructional content and process areas. Includes resources on cultural diversity and evaluation and assessment. Also lists primary and supplemental print resources and videos.

Chandler, P.A. 1994. *A place for me: Including children with special needs in early care and education settings.* Washington DC: NAEYC.

Provides practical answers to real concerns, including dealing with one's negative feelings about inclusion, preparing the environment, assisting other children, and working with parents.

Cook, R., F. Tessier, & M. Klein. 2000. *Adapting early childhood curricula for children in inclusive settings.* New York: Merrill/Macmillan.

Reflects the most recent developments in the recommended strategies for adapting curriculum for infants, young children, and their families. Features parent-professional collaboration through avenues such as developing Individualized Family Service Plans (IFSPs) and safety tips for home visitors.

Davis, M.D., J.L. Kilgo, & M. Gamel-McCormick. 1998. *Young children with special needs: A developmentally appropriate approach.* Boston: Allyn & Bacon.

Provides readers with the skills and knowledge to make curriculum decisions to foster the development of young children with special needs in regular early childhood settings.

Dennis, B.C., S.T. Tyndall, & P. Wesley. 1997. *Quicknotes: Inclusion resources for early childhood professionals.* Chapel Hill: University of North Carolina.

A 10-module set of bilingual, English and Spanish, information sheets in a portable crate. Modules include these titles: Developmental Disabilities, Setting Up the Early Childhood Environment, Early Childhood Curriculum, What Is Early Childhood Inclusion, Including Children with Special Needs, Health & Safety, Promoting Appropriate Behavior, Families, and Early Intervention Lending Library Catalog.

Derman-Sparks, L., & the A.B.C. Task Force. 1989. Learning about disabilities. In *Anti-bias curriculum: Tools for empowering young children,* 39–48. Washington, DC: NAEYC.

Provides information on how to create an inclusive educational environment in which all children can succeed. Presents developmental tasks and guidelines as well as activities for teachers to use in their classrooms.

Division for Early Childhood Task Force on Recommended Practices. 1993. *DEC recommended practices: Indicators of quality in programs for infants and young children with special needs and their families.* Reston, VA: Council for Exceptional Children.

Includes validated practices in the areas of assessment, family participation, IFSPs and IEPs, intervention strategies, transition, personnel competence, evaluation, and specific skills interventions.

Dolinar, K., C. Boser, & E. Holm. 1994. *Learning through play: Curriculum and activities for the inclusive classroom.* Albany, NY: Delmar.

Discusses field-tested strategies for developing language-based curriculum for preschool children with special emphasis on adaptations for children with disabilities in inclusive classrooms.

Dugger-Wadsworth, D.E. 1997. The integrated curriculum and students with disabilities. In *Integrated curriculum and developmentally appropriate practice birth to age 8,* eds. C.H. Hart, D.C. Burts, & R. Charlesworth, 335–61. Albany: State University of New York Press.

Explores question about whether or not the two fields of early childhood education and early childhood special education can coexist in the same classroom, serving the needs of all children. Argues that the conceptual bases that guides recommendations for best practice are much the same. Addresses assessment issues, and provides suggestions for modification and integration of the approaches.

Dunn, N.S., D.R. Hoge, & H.P. Parette. 1995. Low-cost communication devices for children with disabilities and their family members. *Young Children* 50 (6): 75–81.

Describes many low-cost auxiliary aids and gives information on technical assistance services.

Froschl, M., L. Colon, E. Rubin, & B. Sprung. 1984. *Including all of us: An early childhood curriculum about disability.* New York: Educational Equity Concepts.

A guide for creating an early childhood curriculum that is inclusive, nonsexist, multicultural, and incorporates role models of children and adults with disabilities. The material fosters children's cognitive, social, and emotional growth by expanding their world view to include people with disabilities and by teaching appreciation of and respect for human differences. For example, activities are described that model experiences for hearing, visual, and mobility impairment.

Gargiulo, R., J.L. Kilgo, & S. Graves. 1999. *Young children with special needs: An introduction to early childhood special education.* Albany, NY: Delmar.

Explains early childhood special education and intervention methods in great detail, yet remains easy to understand. The authors focus on children from birth to age 5 who are at risk due to congenital disorders, developmental problems, or such environmental factors as poverty and abuse.

Gould, P., & J. Sullivan. 1999. *The inclusive early childhood classroom: Easy ways to adapt learning centers for all children.* Beltsville, MD: Gryphon House.

Suggests ways of approaching activities and daily routines to support children with special needs. Each chapter focuses on a learning center or daily routine, with particular attention to the needs of children who have developmental delays, orthopedic impairments, attention deficit hyperactivity disorder (ADHD) or behavioral issues, motor-skill problems, or visual impairments.

Greenspan, S.I. 1998. *The child with special needs: Encouraging intellectual and emotional growth.* 1998. Reading, MA: Addison-Wesley.

A key work that lays out a complete step-by-step approach for parents, educators, and others who work with children with development challenges, including autism, pervasive developmental disorders (PDD), language and speech problems, Down syndrome, cerebral palsy, ADHD, and other related disorders.

Hoskins, B. 1995. *Developing inclusive schools: A guide.* Reston, VA: Council for Exceptional Children.

Designed to help administrators, teachers, and special education staff work in a coordinated way to redesign services. Informs about roles in inclusive schools, resistance, motivation, curriculum, systems of support, collaborative consultation, school-based teams, leadership, and developing an inclusive culture.

Johnson, J.L., R.J. Gallagher, M.J. LaMontagne, J.B. Jordan, J.J. Gallagher, P.L. Hutinger, & M.B. Karnes, eds. 1994. *Meeting early intervention challenges: Issues from birth to three.* Reston, VA: Council for Exceptional Children.

Details critical new approaches to services delivery and provides concrete strategies for staff development and policy application. Shows how states have successfully resolved today's questions concerning administration, collaboration, competency issues, eligibility, evaluation, programmatic practices, parental involvement, and public policy.

Kitano, M. 1989. The K–3 teacher's role in recognizing and supporting young gifted children. *Young Children* 44 (3): 57–63.

Looks at ways kindergarten and primary teachers can meet the needs of children with special abilities.

Klein, S.M., & S. Kontos. 1993. *Best practices in integration inservice training model.* Bloomington, IN: BPI Outreach Project, Indiana University.

Intended as an inservice training model for those providing services for infants, toddlers, and preschool children with special needs.

Linder, T.W. 1993. *Transdisciplinary play-based intervention: Guidelines for developing a meaningful curriculum for young children.* Baltimore, MD: Brookes.

Discusses play and play materials in relation to developmental levels and categorizes them according to cognitive, social-emotional, communication, and sensory-motor disabilities. Provides detailed information on how to integrate children with special needs into regular classrooms.

Mahoney, G., A. Wheeden, &. D. Janas. 1996. *INDAP: Individualized developmentally appropriate practices for young children with special needs.* Tallmadge, OH: Family Child Learning Center.

Provides a series of guidelines and suggestions to help teachers adapt the classroom environment, instructional activities, and daily routines to the individual needs of each child. A good resource for all preschool teachers who are attempting to address the individual needs of children with disabilities in the context of constructivist/play-oriented curricula.

Mallory, B.L. 1998. Educating young children with developmental differences: Principles of inclusive practice. In *Continuing issues in early childhood education,* 2d ed., eds. C. Seefeldt & A. Galper, 213–37. Upper Saddle River, NJ: Merrill/Prentice Hall.

Helpful for practitioners seeking to implement the practical, ethical, and legal dimensions of inclusive early childhood education. Discusses the field of early childhood special education and principles for establishing an inclusive classroom.

Mallory, B.L., & R.S. New, eds. 1994. *Diversity and developmentally appropriate practices: Challenges for early childhood education.* New York: Teachers College Press.

Chapters 2, 4, and 10 provide a forum on the challenges to the concepts and indicators of developmentally appropriate practice. Issues surrounding diversity and inclusion in early childhood education practices are discussed.

Maryland Child Care Resource Network. 1992. *ENABLE: The day care resource project for children with special needs.* Baltimore: Maryland Committee for Children.

Tool for trainers in preparing child care providers to accept children with special needs. Topics include adapting the program, working with families, and using the arts in inclusive programs. Provides an outline for each training session and a resource kit.

McWilliam, P.J., & D.B. Bailey. 1993 *Working together with children and families: Case studies in early intervention.* Baltimore, MD: Brookes.

Provides vivid case studies of early intervention professionals working with families of children with disabilities, birth through 5 years of age.

Miller, R. 1996. *The developmentally appropriate inclusive classroom in early education.* Albany, NY: Delmar.

Melds the practices of early childhood education and early childhood special education into a practice that promotes and supports of inclusion. Provides many suggestions for using or adapting typical preschool equipment to suit special requirements of children with disabilities.

Moore, R.C., S.M. Goltsman, & D.S. Iacofano. 1992. *Play for all guidelines: Planning, design and management of outdoor play settings for all children.* 2d ed. Berkeley, CA: MIG Communications.

Details ideal playground design and offers suggestions for modifying equipment to conform to the Americans with Disabilities Act.

Neugebauer, B., ed. 1992. *Alike and different: Exploring our humanity with young children.* Washington, DC: NAEYC.

Provides a resource for exploring with children the unique qualities that make people individuals, including differences in physical and intellectual ability, economic situation, cultural heritage, gender, and age. Several chapters focus on inclusion of children with special needs.

Odom, S., & M. McLean. 1996. *Early intervention/early childhood special education: Recommended practices.* Austin, TX: Pro-Ed.

Discusses issues of standards and recommended practice in early intervention and early childhood special education. Topics include development and implementation of IFSPs (Individualized Family Services Plans) and IEPs (Individualized Education Plans), indicators of quality in communication intervention, preservice and inservice practices for early education personnel, and intervention strategies to promote social, emotional, and motor skills development. Includes DEC/CEC (Division for Early Childhood of the Council for Exceptional Children) recommended practices.

Rab, V., & K. Wood. 1995. *Child care and the ADA: A handbook for inclusive programs.* Baltimore, MD: Brookes

Supports teacher efforts to serve all children well as more and more atypical children are integrated into classrooms.

Russell-Fox, J. 1997. Together is better: Specific tips on how to include children with various types of disabilities. *Young Children* 52 (4): 81–83.

Contains guidelines for working with parents, physicians, and special education teachers in an inclusive preschool setting. Explains ways of using commonsense ideas and available materials to adapt the environment to meet the needs of children.

Solit, G., M. Taylor, & A. Bednarczyck. 1992. *Access for all: Integrating deaf, hard of hearing, and hearing preschoolers.* Washington, DC: Gallaudet University.

Developed for those interested in establishing integrated early childhood programs that include young children who are deaf, hard of hearing, as well as typically hearing. Provides information about deafness, inclusion, and adaption.

Spodek, B., & O.N. Saracho. 1994. *Dealing with individual differences in the early childhood classroom.* New York: Longman.

Covers aspects of working with children who have special needs. Includes a chapter on fostering creative expression that covers movement education, music, and art for children.

Tertell, E.A., S.M. Klein, & J.L. Jewett, eds. 1998. *When teachers reflect: Journeys toward effective, inclusive practice.* Washington, DC: NAEYC.

Comprised of teachers' reflections, this book includes firsthand accounts of creating classrooms and learning environments that are inclusive of all children. Covers the topics of individualizing, guidance, play, collaboration, working with families, inclusion, and emergent curriculum.

Villa, R.A., & J.T. Thousand, eds. 1995. *Creating an inclusive school.* Alexandria, VA: Association for Supervision and Curriculum Development.

Shows how instructive strategies such as cooperative learning, teaming, and multiage grouping contribute to planning an inclusive curriculum for children of primary-school age.

Walker, B., N.L. Hafenstein, & L. Crow-Enslow. 1999. Meeting the needs of gifted learners in the early childhood classroom. *Young Children* 54 (1): 32–36.

An integrated-thematic curriculum incorporates disciplines and skills appropriate for all preschoolers. This adaptable curriculum, which emphasizes exploration, manipulation, and play, allows teachers to individualize activities to meet the abilities of gifted learners. An overarching theme and monthly study units provide the intellectual framework for different levels of learning guided by inquiry questions.

Whitney, T. 1999. *Kids like us: Using Persona dolls in the classroom.* St. Paul, MN: Redleaf.

Guides teachers of 2- to 8-year-old children through the process of storytelling with persona dolls to help the children confront bias by expanding their comfort with differences and ability to talk about their feelings. The author outlines five steps for using the dolls, incorporating ideas for creating characters, inventing stories, and working with children in a group.

Wolery, M., P.S. Strain, & D.B. Bailey, Jr. 1995. Reaching potentials of children with special needs. In *Reaching potentials: Appropriate curriculum and assessment for young children, volume 1,* eds. S. Bredekamp & T. Rosegrant, 92–111. Washington, DC: NAEYC.

Discusses children with special needs and goals for their early education, current best practices, and the relevance of NAEYC and NAECS/SDE (National Association of Early Childhood Specialists in State Departments of Education) guidelines in relation to students with special needs.

Wolery, M., & J. Wilbers, eds. 1994. *Including children with special needs in early childhood programs*. Washington, DC: NAEYC.

Noted authorities relay the implications of research for practice with respect to including children with special needs in early childhood programs, working with families, collaborating with other professionals, designing inclusive environments, planning instruction and assessment, and implementing transitions to other programs.

Wolfle, J. 1989. The gifted preschooler: Developmentally different, but still 3 or 4 years old. *Young Children*. 44 (3): 41–48.

Suggests ways preschool teachers can meet the needs of gifted children. Also offers clues for looking for giftedness in young children.

Partnerships with Families

The focus of these resources is on ways that teachers and families can collaborate and establish relationships, engage in reciprocal ongoing communication and interaction, foster parent involvement in the curriculum and assessment, and share techniques for home visiting. Parent perspectives are represented in this category, along with discussions of current conceptions of "family" and ways in which family well-being is affected by social changes. The resources also demonstrate ways that teachers can increase their knowledge of children's lives outside the classroom.

Barbour, C., & N. Barbour. 1997. *Families, schools, and communities: Building partnerships for educating the child*. Columbus, OH: Merrill/Prentice Hall.

Seeks to combine the knowledge and experiences that emerge from the three social settings of a child's life—home, community, and school—into educational strategies that result in nurturing learning environments. Incorporates a wealth of activities and questions into real-life situations in schools and families in pre-K through third-grade settings.

Beisel, R. 1997. *HomeLink: Home activities for the emergent reader*. Carlsbad, CA: Dominie.

Designed to encourage parent participation in children's literacy development through enjoyable literacy activities. The program addresses Early Literacy Learning, Learning the Alphabet, Learning Words and How They Work, Supporting Reading at Home, and Supporting Writing at Home. Includes simply written parent letters, suggestions for reading and writing activities accompanied by uncomplicated directions, enjoyable games, and puzzles.

Berger, E.H. 2000. *Parents as partners in education: Families and schools working together*. 5th ed. Upper Saddle River, NJ: Merrill/Prentice Hall.

Provides in-depth discussions of ways to generate positive teacher-parent partnerships and specific suggestions for both school-based and home-based programs for children birth through 8. Author addresses recent developments such as Goals 2000, family resource centers, and involving parents in the beginning of the educational process.

Berns, R. 1997. *Child, family, school, community*. 4th ed. New York: Harcourt Brace.

Uses Bronfenbrenner's ideas to describe how children come to know about and effectively participate (or not) in their family, school, and community. Appropriate for those who work with preschool and primary. The author discusses how families become empowered, ethnic diversity, and the relationships between school and child care and families.

Bickart, T., D.T. Dodge, & J. Jablon. 1997. *What every parent needs to know about 1st, 2nd, and 3rd grades: An essential guide to your child's education*. Naperville, IL: Sourcebooks and Washington, DC: Teaching Strategies.

Takes parents inside classrooms where children are challenged to become thinkers, problem solvers, and enthusiastic learners. The authors detail how children learn reading, writing, science, math, and social skills. Parents also learn how best to work with their child's teachers, survive homework, and more.

Blank, H., & N.O. Poersche. 1996. *Working together for children: Head Start and child care partnerships*. Washington, DC: Children's Defense Fund.

Examines the efforts of several visionary partnerships that have pioneered in bringing Head Start and child care services together for the children in their programs. While the partnerships vary in scope and design, all of the initiatives discussed provide comprehensive services to children and families, including: full-day care and education, social services, health services, parent involvement, and a commitment to quality.

Boone, E., & K. Barclay. 1995. *Building a three-way partnership: The leader's role in linking school, family, and community*. New York: Scholastic.

Examines parent involvement by focusing upon written communication through school handbooks and newsletters, group meetings during open houses and parent programs, and one-on-one meetings during conferences and home visits.

Bowman, B. 1997. Preschool as family support. In *Advances in early education and day care, vol. 9: Family policy and practice in early child care,* eds. C. Dunst & M. Wolery, 157–70. Greenwich, CT: JAI.

Looks at the contribution preschool has made to families within a historic context. Highlights various roles preschool has played and how they have changed over the century in response to changing family needs and theories. Even with the wide range of preschool programs in the United

States, day care to Head Start, there remains the commitment to educating both the child and the family.

Bundy, B.F. 1991. Fostering communication between parents and preschools. *Young Children* 46 (2): 12–17.

Effective communications between home and school are a vital ingredient in quality early childhood education. By employing a variety of communication techniques, early childhood educators can reach out to parents.

Clay, W.J. 1990. Working with lesbian and gay parents and their children. *Young Children* 45 (3): 31–35.

Focuses on how early childhood programs can work with lesbian and gay parents and their children.

Cochran, M. 1993. *Extending families: The social network of parents and their children.* New York: Cambridge University Press.

Discusses the personal networks that parents and their preschool children develop and how they affect parent and child development. The authors also consider the ways that those networks change over time and the impact that a community-based family support program has on parents' networks.

Corbett, S. 1993. A complicated bias. *Young Children* 48 (3): 29–31.

Discusses how early childhood educators must confront prejudice related to homosexuality so that no child feels ashamed of his or her family and as a way to promote children's acceptance of differences.

Developmental Studies Center. 1995. *Homeside activities: Conversations and activities that bring parents into children's schoolside learning (Grades K–3).* Oakland, CA: Author.

The volumes (kindergarten and grades one, two, and three) provide a simple way for teachers to initiate parent involvement in their children's learning. The activities, which honor cultural diversity, structure conversations or simple games between child and parent that encourage an exchange of ideas, develop the child's critical thinking and communication skills, and provide an open-ended framework for adult and child to explore significant social and ethical issues. Each activity is printed in English and Spanish.

Developmental Studies Center. 2000. *Homeside math.* Oakland, CA: Developmental Studies Center.

Supports parent involvement in mathematics through a series of activities introduced in kindergarten and first-grade classrooms and sent home for children and a home partner to do together. Activities are designed to foster discussion and exploration between children and their families in the areas of number, geometry, and measurement and will culminate in a class discussion or project.

Diffily, D., & K. Morrison, eds. 1996. *Family-friendly communication for early childhood programs*. Washington, DC: NAEYC.

Directed at teachers and directors, this work contains 93 sample messages dealing with everything from biting to the role of play, each designed either to be used as-is in newsletters or as handouts or tailored to meet specific needs.

Dodge, D.T., A.L. Dombro, & L.J. Colker. 1998. *A parent's guide to infant/toddler programs*. Washington, DC: Teaching Strategies.

Shows parents how warm and responsive care helps shape the future development of infants and toddlers and their ability to learn. It outlines what children learn and how during these crucial years and suggests ways that caregivers/teachers and parents can work together.

Dombro, A., & P. Bryan. 1991. *Sharing the caring: How to find the right child care and make it work for you and your child*. New York: Simon & Schuster.

Addresses both parents and providers on ways to build partnerships that will help children feel safe and secure in child care.

Donegan, M., D.B. Fink, S.A. Fowler, & M.W. Wischnowski. 1994. *Entering a new preschool: How service providers and families can ease the transitions of children turning three who have special needs*. Urbana: University of Illinois.

Discusses some of the issues children and families may experience when children enter group settings at age three. Authors detail strategies related to planning for transition, preparing children for the change, and working with families and staff.

Downing-Leffler, N., & T.M. Kokoski. 1995. Boosting your science and math programs in early childhood education: Making the home-school connection. *Young Children* 50 (5): 35–39.

Home-school connections can be extended through science and math learning activities. This article explains the importance of this connection and ways it can be strengthened.

Duffy, R., G. Zeller, K. Albrecht, L.G. Miller, J. Gonzalez-Mena, & L. Lee. 1997. Parent conferences. *Child Care Information Exchange* (116): 41–56.

Provides parents' perspectives on conferencing. The authors also offer suggestions for various types of conferences: three-way, cross-cultural, and involving non-English-speaking families.

Dunn, L., N. Kling, & J. Oakley. 1996. Homeless families in early childhood programs: What to do and what to expect. *Dimensions of Early Childhood* 24 (1): 3–8.

The authors explain how some homeless families live and provide strategies and expectations that may need to be adjusted in early childhood classrooms for children without homes.

Education Department of Western Australia. 1995. *Parents as partners: Helping your child's literacy and language development.* Portsmouth, NH: Heinemann.

Describes activities and strategies for parents to support their children's learning. The concise explanations of developmental stages, practical strategies, and the many resource pages/parent handouts on how parents can help their children with reading, writing, speaking, and listening make this a valuable resource.

Edwards, P.A., with H.M. Pleasants & S.H. Franklin. 1999. *A path to follow: Learning to listen to parents.* Portsmouth, NH: Heinemann.

Describes the approach to parent involvement that helps teachers meet the needs of their children by capitalizing on parents' literacy stories, narratives gained from open-ended conversations about home literacy activities. The author describes all the steps involved in creating a parent story program that gives parents a chance to participate in personally meaningful ways.

Fuller, M.L. 1998. *Home-school relations: Working successfully with parents and families.* Boston: Allyn & Bacon.

Documenting the changing role of the teacher and parent in the school, this volume covers a wide range of often neglected topics. Examples include family life—past and present, information on family violence, the legal and policy aspects of home-school relations, the home-schooling movement, and working with parents of children with special needs.

Gestwicki, C. 2000. *Home, school, and community relations: A guide to working with families.* 4th ed. Albany, NY: Delmar/Thomson Learning.

Presents creative suggestions for establishing reciprocal relationships that are satisfying and beneficial to both teachers and families. Current family issues and techniques for informal communication, home visiting, conferencing, and involving parents in the classroom are some of the topics discussed.

Goldberg, S. 1997. *Parent involvement begins at birth: Collaboration between parents and teachers of children in the early years.* Boston: Allyn & Bacon.

Presents a dynamic model for parent involvement, an overview of child development from birth to age 5, and a summary of key competencies needed for school readiness. Information is based upon research conducted in public-school-based parent education seminars and home-based infant/toddler play-and-learn activities.

Gonzalez-Mena, J. 1998. *The child in the family and the community.* Upper Saddle River, NJ: Merrill.

An examination of the socialization process of young children, with a focus on the development of attachment, autonomy, initiative, and self-esteem in the family and the child's community. The author discusses how society's goals, cultural patterns, and values affect childrearing environments (including group and family child care settings).

Hannigan, I. 1998. *Off to school: A parent's-eye view of the kindergarten year.* Washington DC: NAEYC.

When the author's son headed off to school for the first time, she used her journal to capture not only his reactions through that first year but also her own observations and concerns. Also included are the teacher's messages sent home to keep families well informed about their children's school lives.

Heath, H.E. 1994. Dealing with difficult behaviors—Teachers plan with parents. *Young Children* 49 (5): 20–24.

Presents a hypothetical situation in which a teacher meets with parents to discuss the difficult behavior their daughter is exhibiting in class. Uses this model to explore the various concerns and solutions parents and teachers bring to a difficult situation.

Hildebrand, V., L.A. Phenice, M. Gray, & R. Hines. 2000. *Knowing and serving diverse families.* 2d ed. Columbus, OH: Merrill/Prentice Hall.

Helps teachers and parent specialists gain insight into families of different ethnicities, language, age, and socioeconomic levels. Current family research supports discussion of African American, Hispanic American, Asian American, Arab American, and Native American families. Addresses implications for working comfortably with diverse families.

Klass, C.S. 1996. *Home visiting: Promoting healthy parent and child development.* Baltimore, MD: Brookes.

Addresses the complex role of the teacher as home visitor, including the dilemmas that typically occur; makes recommendations for professional development and supervision. Information is given on key developmental topics from birth through age 5 and ways the home visitor can help parents develop understandings and skills.

Koch, P.K, & M. McDonough. 1999. Improving parent-teacher conferences through collaborative conversations. *Young Children* 54 (2): 11–15.

Describes how to use conversations between school staff, families, and others to help bring about successful resolution of problems in childhood programs, such as disruptive behavior, and to create supportive relationships.

Lakey, J. 1997. Teachers and parents define diversity in an Oregon preschool cooperative—Democracy at work. *Young Children* 52 (4): 20–28.

Describes how the introduction of an antibias curriculum on an expanded scale divides a school and ultimately brings about lasting change. The article discusses how assembling a Curriculum Advisory Committee allowed parents to voice thoughts and concerns.

Larner, M. 1995. *Linking family support and early childhood programs: Issues, experiences, opportunities.* Chicago: Family Resource Coalition.

Outlines family support principles along with descriptions of programs that demonstrate such support. Principles include partnership relationships, empowerment, cultural competence, and inclusion. Model programs across the United States are included.

Larsen, J.M,. & J.H. Haupt. 1997. Integrating home and school: Building a partnership. In *Integrated curriculum and developmentally appropriate practice birth to age 8,* eds. C.H. Hart, D.C. Burts, & R. Charlesworth, 389–415. Albany: State University of New York Press.

Discusses ways in which a partnership between home and school can be initiated and developed through an integrated curriculum.

Lee, F.Y. 1995. Asian parents as partners. *Young Children* 50 (3): 4–9.

Based on interviews with Asian parents, the author discusses their attitudes toward education, methods for communication, using them as volunteers, and how to reach out to this segment of the parent population.

Levin, D.E. 1997. *Remote control childhood? Combating the hazards of media culture.* Washington, DC: NAEYC.

A handbook for reducing media culture's negative impact on children's lives—the heavy doses of violence, stereotypes, and commercialism, the hours spent watching instead of doing. Provides effective guidance and strategies for teachers and parents to minimize harmful media effects and reshape the media environment in which children grow up.

Levin, D.E., & N. Carlsson-Paige. 1994. Developmentally appropriate television: Putting children first. *Young Children* 49 (5): 38–44.

Discusses the ways in which caregivers can develop a framework for assessing television programs.

Levine, J., D. Murphy, & S. Wilson. 1993. *Getting men involved: Strategies for early childhood programs.* New York: Scholastic.

Outlines specific strategies for getting men involved in children's lives and highlights programs that have been successful in involving men.

Levine, J., & W. Pitt. 1995. *New expectations: Community strategies for responsible fatherhood.* New York: Families and Work Institute.

Goes beyond the current rhetoric about responsible fatherhood to examine promising strategies being used by community-based agencies—to engage and reengage men in the lives of their children. It is a must for practitioners, policymakers, and funders in the private and public sector who are planning, developing, and delivering services to families.

Mathias, B., & M.A. French. 1996. *Forty ways to raise a nonracist child.* New York: Harper Perennial.

Meant to help caregivers and families talk with children about racism and teach respect and appreciation for cultural differences. Authors include practical suggestions for teaching children to be nonracist.

Mathias, M., & B. Gulley, eds. 1995. *Celebrating family literacy through intergenerational programming.* Wheaton, MD: Association for Childhood Education International.

Provides practical examples of ways to include families in literacy activities.

McBride, S.L. 1999. Research in Review. Family-centered practices. *Young Children* 54 (3): 62–68.

Suggests overarching principles that drive family-centered priorities: establishing the family as the focus of services; supporting and respecting family decisionmaking; and providing flexible, responsive, and comprehensive services designed to strengthen child and family functioning.

McWilliam, R.S., B.J. McMillen, K.M. Sloper, & J.S. McMillan. 1997. Early education and child care program philosophy about families. In *Advances in early education and day care,* vol. 9, eds. C. Dunst & M. Wolery, 61–104. Family Policy and Practice in Early Child Care, series ed. S. Reifel. Greenwich, CT: JAI.

Discusses prevailing philosophies for working with parents, using examples of programs that reflect a range of issues. A rating scale is included for assessing which philosophy predominates within an early childhood program.

Moles, O., ed. 1996. *Reaching all families: Creating family-friendly schools.* Washington, DC: U.S. Department of Education.

Designed to stimulate thinking and discussion about how schools can better involve families in their children's education regardless of family circumstances or student performance

NAEYC. 1995. When parents and professionals disagree: Using NAEYC's code of ethics. *Young Children* 50 (3): 64–65.

This ethical dilemma revolves around conflict between a parent, a teacher, and after-school program staff over a 7-year-old's homework.

National PTA. 1997. *National standards for parent/family involvement programs.* Chicago: Author.

Presents standards to guide parent-involvement programs and evaluates their quality and effectiveness. The purpose of the standards is to promote meaningful parent and family participation, raise awareness of components of effective programs, and provide guidelines for programs that serve children and families who wish to improve their programs.

Neugebauer, B. 1997. Perspectives on discipline. *Child Care Information Exchange* (113) (Beginnings Workshop suppl.): 50–62.

The author focuses on parent/staff partnerships and uses interviews by Cam Do Wong, Karen Kelly, Robin Gadsden-Dupree, and Cecelia Alvarado to provide different perspectives on discipline.

Powell, D.R. 1989. *Families and early childhood programs.* Washington, DC: NAEYC.

In-depth and critical review of the literature on rationales for working with parents, relations between families and programs, and strategies for addressing home-school relations.

Power, B. 1999. *Parent power: Energizing home-school communication.* Portsmouth, NH: Heinemann.

Enhances connections with parents through a collection of 30 letters to parents and a teacher's guide with ideas such as personalizing the communication, designing newsletters, best books for promoting learning at home, and making involvement easier for parents. The letters address curriculum and school concerns and general parenting issues such as coping with sibling conflict. All letters are translated into Spanish as well and one chapter addresses strategies for relating to non-English-speaking parents.

Regional Educational Laboratories Early Childhood Collaboration Network. 1995. *Continuity in early childhood: A framework for home, school, and community linkages.* Oak Brook, IL: North Central Regional Educational Laboratory.

Starting with the belief that school and community ease children's transition from early interventions to school, this document provides a comprehensive framework for creating and sustaining home-school-community partnerships. The framework consists of eight elements of continuity: families as partners, shared leadership, comprehensive and responsive services, culture and home language, communication, knowledge and skill development, appropriate care and education, and evaluation of partnership success.

Rockwell, R.E, L.C. Andre, & M.K. Hawley. 1996. *Parents and teachers as partners: Issues and challenges.* Ft. Worth, TX: Harcourt Brace/College.

Features a family-centered approach to parent involvement and discusses ways to communicate with parents and work with parents of children with special needs and families from diverse backgrounds. Strategies for developing support systems are provided.

Sawyers, J., & C.S. Rogers. 1988. *Helping young children develop through play: A practical guide for parents, caregivers, and teachers.* Washington, DC: NAEYC.

Reminds parents and teachers of the importance of play for young children. It offers practical suggestions for adults as they support the play of babies, toddlers, preschoolers, and primary-age children.

Scheinfeld, D.R., & L.B. Wallach. 1997. *Strengthening refugee families: Designing programs for refugee and other families in need.* Chicago: Lyceum.

Describes a program designed to help families prepare young children for entering public school and nurture school learning in the early years.

The program has four components: parent/child preschool sessions, after-school homework classes, family services, and language instruction for parents.

Simpson, R.L. 1996. *Working with parents and families of exceptional children and youth: Techniques for successful conferencing and collaboration.* Austin, TX: Pro-Ed.

Deals with school-age children and their families as they deal with special needs. The role of the teacher as collaborator is emphasized.

Springate, K., & D. Stegelin. 1999. *Building school and community partnerships through parent involvement.* Columbus, OH: Merrill/Prentice Hall.

Examines the interrelationships between children, school, and families in the school system and features an in-depth look at the complexities of parenting and diversity of families that shape the approaches teachers should use to work effectively with parents in school settings. Suggested strategies include use of the portfolio approach and ways of supporting parents as decisionmakers.

Stevens, J.H. 1991. Strategies for family involvement. In *Creating the learning environment: A guide in early childhood education,* ed. D. Strickland, 61–65. Orlando, FL: Harcourt Brace Jovanovich.

Discusses ways in which teachers can involve families in the education of their children. Suggestions are given on how educators can create family-friendly environments such as toy libraries and family reception areas and establish mentor relationships.

Stipek, D., L. Rosenblatt, & L. DiRocco. 1994. Making parents your allies. *Young Children* 49 (3): 4–9.

Offers advice on enlisting parent support for and interest in a developmentally appropriate, child-sensitive classroom.

Stone, J. 1987. *Teacher-parent relationships.* Washington, DC: NAEYC.

Discusses the importance of warm and respectful relationships between parents and teachers during the early childhood years. Full of practical guidance on this essential aspect of teaching.

Stonehouse, A. 1995. *How does it feel? Child care from a parent's perspective.* Redmond, WA: Exchange Press.

Helps center directors and teachers understand child care from a parent's perspective. The author gives readers a resource for developing with parents sensitive, mutually rewarding relationships that benefit children.

Sturm, C. 1997. Creating parent-teacher dialogue: Intercultural communication in child care. *Young Children* 52 (5): 34–38.

Teachers in a culturally diverse area realize that some of their assumptions clash with the cultural background of the children in their care, so they begin a parent-teacher dialogue project.

Swap, S.A. 1993. *Developing home-school partnerships.* New York: Teachers College Press.

Describes practices that support two-way communication and mutual support between parents and the elementary school. The author discusses benefits, barriers, and specific steps to establishing effective home-school partnerships.

Swick, K. 1993. *Strengthening parents and families during the early childhood years.* Champaign, IL: Stipes.

Provides early childhood educators with perspectives and tools that will enable them to strengthen parents and families during the child's earliest years of development. Examines the process of relating to the special needs of families from a supportive, yet realistic, framework and describes a proactive approach to developing positive and equitable relations with families experiencing special needs.

Vopat, J. 1994. *The parent project: A workshop approach to parent involvement.* York, ME: Stenhouse.

Provides a framework for increasing parent involvement. Materials are provided for conducting workshops with parents in areas of writing, reading, self-esteem, and community building. Workshop formats in Spanish are included.

Washington, V., V. Johnson, & J.B. McCracken. 1995. *Grassroots success! Preparing schools and families for each other.* Washington, DC: NAEYC.

Twenty grassroots initiatives, funded by W.K. Kellogg Foundation, show that success for children, families, schools, and communities can be a reality. Discusses how school and communities can work together in providing high-quality experiences that are known to enhance readiness.

Wickens, E. 1993. Penny's question: "I will have a child in my class with two moms—What do you know about this?" *Young Children* 48 (3): 25–28.

Discusses examining and modifying curriculum, selecting stories and songs that present parents of both sexes in protective and nurturing roles, and creating a climate in which children can talk about their family structure regardless of how conventional or unconventional it is.

Winton, P.J. 1991. *Working with families in early intervention: An interdisciplinary preservice curriculum.* Chapel Hill: University of North Carolina.

Designed as a preservice curriculum for graduate students, this resource consists of 11 three-hour modules or semester-long courses. Includes modules on developing a rationale for an interdisciplinary approach to early intervention, family theories, family adaption, application of principles to practices, communication strategies for assessment and goal setting, and service coordination.

Developmental and Theoretical Bases of Practice

The collection of books and readings from professional journals in this category present current perspectives about the nature and development of children. The dominant theories and philosophies that influence our field are discussed with an emphasis on readings that make clear links to teaching practice. The resources represent all the developmental domains and a range of complexity, and their portraits of children are drawn from a variety of professional literature—child development texts, teaching books with a strong developmental knowledge base, and readings that foster our understanding of children's development through their interactions, their drawings, their language, and their social contexts.

Allen, K.E., & L.R. Marotz. 1994. *Developmental profiles: Prebirth to 8.* Albany, NY: Delmar.

A concise yet comprehensive guide to the development of young children. Includes extensive listings of developmental changes that are useful for planning developmentally appropriate learning experiences. The manual can also be used in the observation and early identification of developmental problems and delays.

American Association for the Advancement of Science. 1999. *Dialogue on early childhood science, mathematics, and technology education.* Washington, DC: Author.

Takes a broad look at the state of preschool and kindergarten programs in America and beliefs about how children learn and develop concepts in the early years. Papers address issues of equity, professional development, family/teacher/community partnerships, and the teaching of math, science, and technology.

Azar, B. Defining the trait that makes us human. 1999. In *Annual editions: Human development, 1999/2000, 27th edition,* ed. K. Freiberg. Guilford, CT: Dushkin/McGraw-Hill.

A short article that traces the development of empathy in early childhood. Described as both a cognitive and emotional achievement, the ability to empathize with others is critical to our survival as a species. Psychologists discuss the functions empathy serves and how it can be nurtured in the early years.

Berk, L.E. 1997. *Child development.* Boston: Allyn & Bacon.

Provides heightened attention to the relationship between theory, research, and applications. Includes discussion of biological influences, cross-cultural findings, and social issues. This text has an accompanying video-cassette, *Child Development in Action Observation Video Program,* as well as a corresponding observation guide.

Berk, L.E., & A. Winsler. 1995. *Scaffolding children's learning: Vygotsky and early childhood education.* Washington, DC: NAEYC.

Describes an integrated approach to learning and assessment based on concepts of Vygotsky who stresses the influence of social interaction on children's learning. Vygotsky views effective teaching and assessment as dependent upon careful observation of children, followed, as appropriate, by modeling and discourse (scaffolding) to help them achieve new levels of understanding.

Berns, R. 1997. *Child, family, school, community.* 4th ed. New York: Harcourt Brace.

Uses Bronfenbrenner's ideas to describe how children come to know about and effectively participate (or not) in their family, school, and community. Appropriate for those who work with preschool and primary. The author discusses how families become empowered, ethnic diversity, and the relationships between school and child care and families.

Bjorkland, D., & B. Bjorkland. 1992. *Looking at children: An introduction to child development.* Pacific Grove, CA: Brooks/Cole.

Organized by developmental topics such as cognitive, social, and physical development. Sections at the end of each chapter highlight contemporary issues related to the topic under discussion.

Black, S. 1994. Different kinds of smart. *The Executive Educator* 16 (1): 24–27.

Provides a concise summary of Howard Gardner's theory of multiple intelligences. The author describes in this National School Boards Association publication an elementary school program in which teachers offer children opportunities to explore their multiple intelligences and encourage them to use their strongest domains, while helping them develop their less dominant abilities.

Bodrova, E., & D.J. Leong. 1976. *Tools of the mind: The Vygotskian approach to early childhood education.* New York: Merrill/McGraw-Hill.

Introduces the major principles of Vygotsky's theory of development and how his concepts, such as the *zone of proximal development, independent and assisted performance,* and *mediators,* can be applied to teaching and learning activities with infants/toddlers through second-graders.

Brazelton, T.B. 1992. *Touchpoints: The essential reference—Your child's emotional and behavioral development.* Reading, MA: Addison-Wesley.

A child care resource by a distinguished pediatrician offers a comprehensive explanation of all aspects of child development from physical and emotional to cognitive and behavioral.

Brewer, J. 1998. *Introduction to early childhood education: Preschool through primary grades.* 3d ed. Boston: Allyn & Bacon.

Provides a brief overview of the best known developmental theories before moving into a discussion of the essential components for building a curriculum, such as (1) an environment for learning, (2) a plan for learning, (3) guided behavior, (4) a way of planning and assessing learning activities, (5) language, (6) literacy development, (7) mathematics, (8) science, (9) the arts, (10) social studies, and (11) motor development and health and safety.

Brownlee, S. 1999. Baby talk. Reprinted from *U.S. News and World Report* in *Annual editions: Early childhood education, 1999/2000, 20th edition*, eds. K. Panciorek & J. Munro. Guilford, CT: Dushkin/McGraw-Hill.

Reports current research on the development of oral language. The author gives particular attention to the role of the environment and its effects on how language is learned.

A bundle of emotions. 1997. Reprint from *Newsweek* Special Issue, Spring/Summer in *Annual editions: Early Childhood education, 1999/00, 20th edition*, eds. K. Paciorek & J. Munro. Guilford, CT: Dushkin/McGraw Hill.

Describes the ways in which infants are able to communicate their needs from birth. Stages of emotional development in the first 36 months of life are detailed in this essay.

Charlesworth, R. 1996. *Understanding child development: For adults who work with young children.* 4th ed. Albany, NY: Delmar.

Designed for teachers in training and teachers in service whose major interest is in the development of the prekindergartner, kindergartner, and primary-school child. Includes information on prenatal and infancy periods, physical and motor growth, and children's cognitive growth and development from preschool to primary school age.

Child Care Services Branch, Kentucky Cabinet for Human Resources. 1992. *Developmentally appropriate practices: An orientation training curriculum for child care providers.* Lexington, KY: Author.

Designed to give child care providers three hours of orientation to child development and developmentally appropriate practices. Contains a list of suggested activities, materials for handouts, videos, overheads, and flip charts.

Corsaro, W.A. 1997. *The sociology of childhood.* Thousand Oaks, CA: Pine Forge.

Shows how young children contribute to both social stability and social change as they collectively participate in and ultimately produce "peer cultures" throughout early childhood. Examples are taken from the author's analysis of children's friendship and conflict in three preschools located in different cultural settings.

Cox, M. 1997. *Drawings of people by the under-5s.* Bristol, PA: Falmer.

Follows children's development from toddler through the preschool years by careful study of hundreds of children's drawings of a human figure, a cross-sectional examination of many children from different cultures rather than a following of each child longitudinally. The implications for understanding a child's intelligence, personality or emotional stability, physical disability, and learning difficulties are examined.

Craig, G. 1999. *Human development.* 8th ed. Upper Saddle River, NJ: Prentice Hall.

A major portion of this text documents birth-to-age-8 development in easy-to-read language. Snapshots throughout highlight developmental implications for early childhood practice, such as early infant care and cultural variations in the meaning of play.

Cuffaro, H. 1995. *Experimenting with the world: John Dewey and the early childhood classroom.* New York: Teachers College Press.

Offers a detailed account of how the educational philosophy of John Dewey may be translated into the everyday life of the classroom. Particular attention is given to learning from experience and to the complexities involved in experiential learning.

David, J., & L. Dombro. 1992. Child development. In *Explorations with young children: A curriculum guide from the Bank Street College of Education,* eds. A. Mitchell & J. David, 23–46. Beltsville, MD: Gryphon.

Profiles typical behavior of infants and toddlers, 3- to 5-year-olds, and 6- to 8-year-olds in easy-to-understand language and vivid examples from group settings. Developmental theory is integrated into the profiles.

de Villiers, P.A., & J.G. de Villiers. 1979. *Early language.* Cambridge, MA: Harvard University Press.

Documents how the toddler learns language, with a focus on infants, toddlers, and preschoolers. Vivid examples illustrate the course of learning to talk and communicate, with attention to how the adult learns what a child knows about language.

DeVries, R., & L. Kohlberg. 1987. *Constructivist early childhood education: Overview and comparison with other programs.* Washington, DC: NAEYC.

Provides a classic overview of constructivist early childhood education, comparing it with other models such as Montessori and Bank Street.

Essa, E. 1999. *Introduction to early childhood education.* Albany, NY: Delmar.

A planning and program development focus that includes instructions on working with parents and discussions of all other areas of child development and education that a person learning to work with young children needs to know.

Gallahue, D.L. 1995. *Understanding motor development: Infants, children, adolescents, adults.* Dubuque, IA: Brown & Benchmark.

Covering the entire life span, this text focuses on phases of motor development and provides a solid introduction to the biological, affective, cognitive, and behavioral aspects within each developmental stage.

Gardner, H. 1993a. *Frames of mind: The theory of multiple intelligences.* 10th anniversary ed. New York: Basic.

Provides adults with a knowledge base that will facilitate the cultivation of each child's talents. Chapter 13 allows parents to critically reflect on how their children are being educated—crucial for educators as Gardner forces us to make choices about each individual child's learning environment.

Gardner, H. 1993b. *The unschooled mind: How children think and how schools should teach.* New York: Basic.

Merges cognitive science with the educational agenda, beginning with a fascinating look at the young child's mind and concluding with a sweeping program for educational reform.

Goleman, D. 1995. *Emotional intelligence.* New York: Bantam.

Discusses the meaning and development of emotional intelligence. The author states that the ability to manage the social and emotional aspects of one's life in a complex world is an important yet different way of being smart. Implications for the teacher are presented.

Golinkoff, R.M., & K. Hirsch-Pasek. 1999. *How babies talk.* New York: Dutton/ Penguin.

A chronology of oral language development in easy-to-read language highlights the linguistic accomplishments in the first three years and the most current understanding of what it takes to make language happen. The authors report on new methods of studying language and how caregivers can use the latest knowledge to enhance everyday interactions.

Gonzalez-Mena, J. 1998. *The child in the family and the community.* Upper Saddle River, NJ: Merrill.

An examination of the socialization process of young children, with a focus on the development of attachment, autonomy, initiative, and self-esteem in the family and the child's community. Author discusses how society's goals, cultural patterns, and values affect childrearing environments (including group and family child care settings).

Gordon, A.M., & K. Williams-Browne. 2000. *Beginnings and beyond.* 5th ed. New York: Delmar.

A comprehensive text begins with an examination of what distinguishes early childhood education from other levels of education and continues through development, curriculum, and all other areas of our field. Guest editorials by well-known early childhood educators focus on current issues.

Greenspan, S.I, & N.Thorndike Greenspan. 1989. *First feelings: Milestones in the emotional development of your baby and child.* New York: Penguin.

Shows how to recognize critical stages of a child's emotional growth from birth until age 4 and how to promote a child's psychological development. Covers vital topics such as building trust and relationships and encouraging curiosity and independence.

Healy, J.M. 1994. *Your child's growing mind: A guide to learning and brain development from birth to adolescence.* (New edition, completely revised and updated). New York: Doubleday.

Uses the latest advances in brain research to back competent advice for parents and educators, including how to promote (not push) readiness at home, how to raise children's levels of motivation, and how to help children become problem solvers.

Hendrick, J.B. 1995. *The whole child: Developmental education for the early years.* Upper Saddle River, NJ: Prentice Hall.

Offers teachers of children ages 2 to 5 a complete, developmental approach to early childhood education, providing them the specific skills they need to function effectively with the children in their care. Focuses on the whole child and what he or she needs from the learning environment in order to thrive. Recommends methods and materials for enhancing growth in emotional, social, physical, creative, and cognitive areas of child development. Available in French and Chinese.

Hopson, J. 1999. Fetal Psychology. In *Annual editions: Early childhood education, 1999/2000, 20th edition,* eds. K. Panciorek & J. Munro. Guilford, CT: Dushkin/McGraw Hill.

Presents new research about the extraordinary development that takes place in the womb. The author describes the capabilities of the fetus in sensory areas—hearing, tasting, smelling, seeing, and learning.

Hymes, J.L., Jr. 1994. *The child under six.* 2d ed. West Greenwich, RI: Consortium.

An updated classic about the nature of the 2- to 6-year-old. In down-to-earth language, Hymes's perceptive views highlight each stage of development, including traditional topics of interest to teachers and parents, such as separation, temper tantrums, or group living for young children.

Hyson, M.C. 1994. *The emotional development of young children: Building an emotion-centered curriculum.* New York: Teachers College Press.

Provides a comprehensive review of recent research on emotional development. In addition the second part of the book gives advice on honoring and supporting the role of emotions in the classroom.

Isenberg, J.P., & M.R. Jalongo. 1997. *Major trends and issues in early childhood education: Challenges, controversies, and insights.* New York: Teachers College Press.

Provides essential social, historical, and philosophical perspectives in the early childhood field. Well-known contributors examine a variety of the most significant and challenging subjects, including child development research, play, program models, assessment, diversity, inclusion, public policy, and advocacy.

Katz, L.G. 1997. *Child development knowledge and teachers of young children.* Urbana-Champaign, IL: ERIC Clearinghouse on Elementary and Early Childhood Education.

Discusses the meaning of a developmental approach to early childhood education and explores different methods of judging the appropriateness of early childhood curricula and pedagogy and defining the developmental approach. The author describes several principles to be considered in developing appropriate curricula for young children.

McClane, J.B., & G.D. McNamee. 1990. *Early literacy.* Cambridge, MA: Harvard University Press.

Explores the ways young children begin to learn about written language—the skills, behaviors, attitudes, and relationships with adults and peers that are involved in becoming literate. Addresses early literacy development at home and in the neighborhood, in preschool and kindergarten.

McDonough, S.C., & A. Sameroff. 1994. Educational implications of developmental transitions: Revisiting the 5- to 7-year shift. *Phi Delta Kappan* 76 (3): 188–93.

Helps teachers to understand the nature of the shift from being 5 to 7 years old, a major prerequisite if educators are to help children make a successful transition into elementary school.

Myers, B.K. 1997. *Young children and spirituality.* New York: Routledge.

Designed for teachers, teacher educators, and researchers who seek a theoretical and practical language to talk about spiritual development and its nurturance in the early years of life. This book is not about a specific religion, nor does it teach comparative religion. Spirituality is a feeling, an attitude, a way of life.

Nicolson, S., & S.G. Shipstead. 1999. *Through the looking glass: Observations in the early childhood classroom.* Columbus, OH: Merrill/Prentice Hall.

Describes highlights of development during the preschool and primary-grade years. This text maintains there is a close relationship between observing, understanding what one observes, and improving the educational program and environment.

Pruett, K.D. 1999. *Me, myself and I: How children build their sense of self, 18 to 36 months.* New York: Goddard.

Conveys key aspects of toddlerhood. Chapters feature topics such as brain development and how everyday patterns of sensation, perception, and cognition transform behavior into personality; emerging temperament and style; language explosions and behavior that speak when words fail; anxieties of toddlerhood; and good ways to help children establish inner controls.

Ramey, S.L., & C.T. Ramey. 1994. The transition to school: Why the first few years matter for a lifetime. *Phi Delta Kappan* 76 (3): 194–98.

Emphasizes the critical importance of children's positive transitions to school as representing the real world. Calls for rethinking the concept of school readiness in terms of how educators can work with home and community to tailor education to the developmental and cultural needs of children and thus promote their success.

Read, K., P. Gardner, & B. Mahler. 1993. *Early childhood programs: Human relationships and learning.* 9th ed. New York: Harcourt Brace Jovanovich.

Offers a unique approach with emphasis on understanding human behavior—the child's, the teacher's, and the parent's. Written for preparing teachers who need to understand the significance of behavior and the needs of individuals so as to guide children wisely and help them learn. Focuses on learning through exploring and discovery in early childhood programs.

Schickedanz, J., D.I. Schickedanz, P.D. Forsyth, & G.A. Forsyth. 1997. *Understanding children and adolescents.* Needham Heights, MA: Allyn & Bacon.

Includes sections that deal with educational issues, assessment, and health, safety, and recreational concerns. Focus boxes add depth to these issues as well as to special education and other current topics in areas of research and public policy.

Shore, R. 1997. *Rethinking the brain: New insights into early development.* New York: Families and Work Institute.

Provides readers with a basic reference guide that documents new research supporting the importance of the early years in relation to the development of mental capacity.

Singer, D.G., & T.A. Revenson. 1997. *A Piaget primer: How a child thinks.* Rev. ed. Madison, CT: International Universities Press.

Gives clear focus on and practical application to Piaget's work, clarifying his view of a child's thought processes through illustrations drawn from *Alice in Wonderland, Winnie the Pooh, Peanuts,* and other classic and popular literature.

Spodek, B., & O. Saracho. 1994. *Right from the start: Teaching children from 3 to 8.* Boston: Allyn & Bacon.

A comprehensive textbook for early childhood teachers with a thorough overview of developmental theories as well as curriculum development, working with parents, and program evaluation.

Trawick-Smith, J. 2000. *Early childhood development: A multicultural perspective.* Columbus, OH: Merrill/Prentice Hall.

Portrays development from birth through the primary years with a focus on multicultural applications of early childhood educators by providing multiethnic cases and examples at each level. Special features include second-language learning, the unique play styles of children from other cultures, and families in diverse cultures.

Wadsworth, B.J. 1997. *Piaget's theory of cognitive and affective development.* 5th ed. White Plains, NY: Longman.

Summarizes Piaget's four stages of intellectual development—sensorimotor development, preoperational thought, concrete operations, and formal operations—and applies theory to math, reading, and writing.

White, C.S., & M. Coleman. 2000. *Early childhood education: Building a philosophy for teaching.* Columbus, OH: Merrill/Prentice Hall.

Designed to help beginning teachers and student teachers develop a sense of professional identity by understanding the development and diversity of childhood life experiences and social contexts that influence the care and education of children birth through age 8. Content includes historical precedents and current trends of early childhood education, extensive examination of family development and involvement in schools, organizing classrooms and integrating curriculum.

Wortham, S.C. 1998. *Early childhood curriculum: Developmental bases for learning and teaching.* 2d ed. Upper Saddle River, NJ: Merrill/Prentice Hall.

Addresses the need for present and future teachers to understand the benefits of developmentally appropriate curricula and the role of the child's development in the curriculum. Combines theory with practice by providing concrete examples of how to plan meaningful activity for children from infancy through age 8 in child care, preschool, and primary-school settings.

Zero to Three. 1992. *Heart start: The emotional foundations of school readiness.* Arlington, VA: ZERO TO THREE.

Looks at the characteristics that children develop in their first three years of life that enable them to be prepared for school and propelled to learn and work well with others. Those characteristics discussed include confidence, curiosity, intentionality, self-control, relatedness, capacity to communicate, and cooperation.

Part 3

...about the practice

In this broad category, the resources address many aspects of the process of teaching and implementing curriculum. References that focus primarily on a particular content area are located in the appropriate curriculum area in the sections that follow this general category.

A wide range of topics are addressed in this category, such as the multiple roles and responsibilities of the teacher; descriptions of early childhood education models and approaches; curriculum planning and daily schedules, including emergent curriculum; teaching based on the Child Development Associate competencies; multiage practices; communication skills for early childhood staff; implications of the standards movement; and applying theory in the early childhood setting.

Abramson, S., K. Ankenman, & R. Robinson. 1995. Project work with diverse students: Adapting curriculum based on the Reggio Emilia approach. *Childhood Education* 71 (4): 197–202.

Describes applications of a project approach in settings serving young children from diverse backgrounds. Explains the Reggio Emilia approach and gives examples of successful adaptions.

Beaty, J. 2000. *Skills for preschool teachers.* 6th ed. Columbus, OH: Merrill/ Prentice Hall.

Builds content around the 13 functional areas of the Child Development Associate credential, including such topics as webbing, emergent curriculum, and implications of brain research on the development of communication skills. The author reviews 25 computer programs and includes numerous checklists to assess areas such as children's curiosity and child involvement.

Bickart, T.S., J.R. Jablon, & D.T. Dodge. 1999. *Building the primary classroom: A complete guide to teaching and learning.* Washington, DC: Teaching Strategies.

This updated version describes six strategies that form a framework for making decisions and implementing a curriculum responsive to each child. Also shows how concepts and skills are taught using the framework in subject areas—language and literacy, mathematical thinking, social studies, scientific thinking, technology, and the arts.

Birchak, B., C. Connor, K.M. Crawford, L.H. Kahn, S. Kaser, S. Turner, & K.G. Short. 1998. *Teacher study groups: Building community through dialogue and reflection.* Urbana, IL: National Council of Teachers of English.

Describes how collaborative inquiry in a teacher study group gave teachers time to discuss professional changes they were asked to make in their classroom and became an essential aspect of their teaching. Guidelines are given on how to organize and maintain a study group, including topics such as dealing with group dynamics or incorporating teacher research into the study-group process.

Booth, C. 1997. The fiber project: One teacher's adventure toward emergent curriculum. *Young Children* 52 (5): 79–85.

Explains the step-by-step process one teacher used for developing an integrated unit. The author also points out that even experienced teachers continue to grow and learn as they work to provide appropriate experiences for young children.

Bredekamp, S., & T. Rosegrant, eds. 1992. *Reaching potentials: Appropriate curriculum and assessment for young children, volume 1.* Washington, DC: NAEYC.

Details the guidelines developed jointly in 1991 by NAEYC and NAESC/SDE (National Association of Early Childhood Specialists in State Departments of Education).

Bredekamp, S., & T. Rosegrant, eds. 1995. *Reaching potentials: Transforming early childhood curriculum and assessment, volume 2.* Washington, DC: NAEYC.

Builds on volume 1 of *Reaching Potentials* by elaborating on developmentally appropriate guidelines and describing content that is most acceptable by administrators and has the greatest intellectual integrity.

Burchfield, D. 1996. Teaching all children: Four developmentally appropriate curricular and instructional strategies in primary-grade classrooms. *Young Children* 52 (1): 4–10.

A principal and a former first-grade teacher provide developmentally appropriate instruction for 5- through 8-year-olds. Strategies include basing instruction on children's multiple intelligences and different ways of knowing, using the project approach, employing the writer's workshop method, and developing a balance of reading approaches and cuing systems.

Cadwell, L.B. 1997. *Bringing Reggio Emilia home.* New York: Teachers College Press.

An American teacher describes her year-long internship in the Reggio preschools as she worked along with the staff and children, noting especially the language and other symbols the children used as they related to each other and the natural environment. The second part addresses the way she adapted these ideas to a school in the United States.

Carter, M., & D. Curtis. 1996. *Spreading the news: Sharing the stories of early childhood education*. St. Paul, MN: Redleaf.

Offers suggestions for informing parents and center visitors of the value and components of high-quality early childhood care. Adapted from the work done at Reggio Emilia, this resource provides suggestions for making a dynamic display panel, using everyday tools.

Chard, S.C. 1994a. *The project approach: Developing the basic framework. Practical guide 1*. New York: Scholastic.

The first section provides an account of children's learning and examines what classroom techniques best support project work, what a rich learning climate looks like, and what is and is not a project. The second section identifies the phases of a project, describes children at work on projects, and discusses the evaluation of children's development and the roles of teachers, learners, and parents.

Chard, S.C. 1994b. *Project approach: Developing curriculum with children. Practical guide 2*. New York: Scholastic.

The first three sections discuss activities related to the three phases of a project: getting started, developing the project work, and concluding the project. Section four examines what classroom environment best supports project work.

Charney, R.S. 1992. *Teaching children to care: Management in the responsive classroom*. Greenfield, MA: Northeast Foundation for Children.

Provides a theoretical framework for elementary-school teaching, with guidelines and techniques to put that theory into practice. Discusses how to organize classrooms, develop appropriate curricula, and develop social competence.

Child Care Services Branch, Kentucky Cabinet for Human Resources. 1992. *Developmentally appropriate practices: An orientation training curriculum for child care providers*. Lexington, KY: Author.

Designed to give child care providers three hours of orientation to child development and developmentally appropriate practices. Contains a list of suggested activities, materials for handouts, videos, overheads, and flip charts.

Coughlin, P.A., K.A. Hansen, D. Heller, R.K. Kaufmann, J.R. Stolberg, & K. Walsh. 1997. *Creating child-centered classrooms: 3–5 year olds*. Washington, DC: Children's Resources International.

Defines child-centered thinking and how it translates into practice. This comprehensive guide addresses family participation, building community, and all the components of implementing an integrated curriculum, including a section on outdoor play and sand and water.

Cummings, C. 1995. *Creating good schools for young children: Right from the start. A study of eleven developmentally appropriate primary school programs.* Alexandria, VA: National Association of State Boards of Education.

Features 11 exemplary public school programs for children ages 4 through 8 and discusses how the programs were developed and the outcomes. Describes the learning environment, curriculum, assessment, classroom configuration, and parent involvement in each program.

Curtis, D., & M. Carter. 1996. *Reflecting children's lives: A handbook for planning child-centered curriculum.* St. Paul, MN: Redleaf.

Primarily designed for preschool teachers (one chapter is for infant/toddler teachers), this guide to curriculum development includes topics such as self-assessment, with checklists for teachers to examine their own skills and dispositions, developing curriculum themes that emerge from the children, and revitalizing the classroom. Includes detailed suggestions for scheduling, planning, and routines.

Devault, L. 1999. *Getting ready to teach kindergarten.* Torrance, CA: Frank Schaffer.

Especially helpful for beginning teachers or early childhood students. This practical handbook contains an overview of the curriculum and an explanation of each subject area illustrated by creative activities. Useful advice is given on topics such as setting up the classroom, creating a caring environment, relationships with school staff, and record keeping and assessment.

Dodge, D.T., & L.J. Colker. 1992. *The creative curriculum for early childhood.* 3d ed. Washington, DC: Teaching Strategies.

Explains how to work with children at different developmental levels, how to adapt the environment to make it increasingly challenging, and how to actively involve parents in the program. The book also includes a child development and learning checklist to help teachers learn about each child in their class and individualize the curriculum. Available in standard Spanish, appropriate for the majority of Spanish speakers.

Dodge, D.T., D.G. Koralek, & P.J. Pizzolongo. 1996. *Caring for preschool children.* 2d ed. Washington, DC: Teaching Strategies.

Presents a competency-based training program for teachers working with children in center-based settings. The set contains modules covering the 13 functional areas of the competency standards established by the Child Development Associate (CDA) credential. A trainer's guide is also available.

Driscoll, A. 1995. *Cases in early childhood education: Stories of programs and practices.* Needham Heights, MA: Allyn & Bacon.

Provides real classroom examples of developmentally appropriate practice and reflective teaching that instructors need for modeling the concepts, strategies, and issues they teach about.

Eddowes, E.A., & K.S. Ralph. 1998. *Interactions for development and learning: Birth through eight years.* Upper Saddle River, NJ: Merrill/Prentice Hall.

Stresses the importance of thoughtful interactions between adults and young children. Especially helpful to new teachers; practical applications throughout include a matrix correlating the Child Development Associate (CDA) competencies with different chapters.

Edwards, C., L. Gandini, & G. Forman, eds. 1993. *The hundred languages of children: The Reggio Emilia approach to early childhood education.* Norwood, NJ: Ablex.

Describes an innovative approach to early childhood education that is practiced in the public schools for infants through 6-year-old children in Reggio Emilia, Italy. Children's intellectual development is fostered in a focus on exploring and representing through words, movement, and exceptionally creative art media. The philosophy, curricula, use of space and physical environments, and role of teachers are portrayed both in Italy and as applied in North American schools.

Edwards, C., L. Gandini, & G. Forman, eds. 1998. *The hundred languages of children: The Reggio Emilia approach—Advanced reflections.* 2d ed. Greenwich, CT: Ablex.

Provides the history, ideas, and basic philosophy of the Reggio Emilio approach to early childhood education, as well as a description of the extension of the Reggio Emilio approach into American classrooms.

Feeney, S., D. Christensen, & E. Moravcik. 1996. *Who am I in the lives of children: An introduction to teaching young children.* 5th ed. Englewood Cliffs, NJ: Merrill/Prentice Hall.

Focuses on the link between personal development of teachers and their ability to work effectively with young children. Supports the affective as well as cognitive development of teachers and encourages teachers to develop self-knowledge and an individual style of teaching.

Feinburg, S., & M. Mindess. 1994. *Eliciting children's full potential: Designing and evaluating developmentally based programs for young children.* Pacific Grove, CA: Brooks/Cole.

Explains how to implement a developmentally based cross-cultural, inclusion program for 3- through 8-year-olds, with particular focus on providing an intellectual challenge, stimulate creativity, and strengthen social understanding. Observation and assessment are also addressed.

Fisher, B. 1995. *Thinking and learning together: Curriculum and community in a primary classroom.* Portsmouth, NH: Heinemann.

Describes a classroom in which trust is fostered and children practice and share what they learn. Illustrations of children pursuing their own areas of interest and inquiry are included.

Fisher, B. 1998. *Joyful learning in kindergarten.* Portsmouth, NH: Heinemann.

Describes what an observant knowledgeable kindergarten teacher does in her classroom on a typical day and why she does it. Each chapter highlights a specific aspect of the classroom and includes many ideas, themes, routines, and record keeping suggestions. Chapters on assessment, dramatic play, and questions teachers ask are especially strong.

Fisher, J. 1996. *Starting from the child? Teaching learning from 4 to 8.* Bristol, PA: Open University Press.

Discusses a range of theories about young children as learners and the implications of these theories for classroom practice. The author addresses the key issues of planning and assessment, explores the place of talk and play in the classroom, and examines the teacher's role in keeping a balance between the demands of the curriculum and the learning needs of the child.

Fleer, M., ed. 1996. *Conversations about teaching and learning in early childhood settings.* Watson, ACT: Australian Early Childhood Association.

Begins with the vision of early childhood education from the perspectives of teachers of 4- to 8-year-olds in Australia. These conversations then move to rethinking classroom organization and parent relationships in primary schools, working in partnership with Aboriginal children, educating for peace, reconsidering play, and addressing gender construction.

Forman, G.E., & D.S. Kuschner. 1983. *The child's construction of knowledge: Piaget for teaching children.* Washington, DC: NAEYC.

Explains why and how to apply Piaget in the classroom. Emphasizes that for young children to acquire the necessary basis for understanding language, mathematics, and social relationships, they must be presented with practical activities and spontaneous play.

Forsten, C., J. Grant, & I. Richardson. 1999a. *The looping evaluation book.* Peterborough, NH: Crystal Springs.

Helps teachers and administrators identify and consider all the factors that will lead to a thriving looping classroom. Part 1 explains looping and the kinds of instructional practices associated with it. Part 2 details the steps necessary to implement looping. Part 3 identifies which elements need to be evaluated, including checklists, and how results should be used. Part 4 has resources, sample surveys, letters, forms, and charts.

Forsten, C., J. Grant, & I. Richardson. 1999b. *The multiage evaluation book.* Peterborough, NH: Crystal Springs.

Contains detailed checklists for understanding the concept of multiage and the reason for implementing it. Provides suggestions on how to design, prepare for, implement and assess, and begin a multiage classroom. For those educators already engaged in multiage practice, this book will help in evaluating which components are working well and which need revising. Support pages include sample parent questionnaires in English and Spanish.

Fromberg, D.P. 1995. *The full-day kindergarten: Planning and practicing a dynamic themes curriculum.* 2d ed. New York: Teachers College Press.

Primary focus is on organizing the curriculum and classroom space for independence, responsibility, caring, and meaningful choice. Demonstrates how different children doing different things at different times can have equivalent experiences. Each of the content areas includes activity projects and materials lists.

Funqa, J.D., & T.T. Harris. 1996. To build a house: Designing curriculum for primary-grade children. *Young Children* 52 (1): 77–84.

Describes a project designed to meet the needs of children from diverse backgrounds. Provides an excellent example of developing a project based on children's interests and experiences.

Gestwicki, C. 1999. *Developmentally appropriate practice: Curriculum and development in early education.* 2d ed. Albany, NY: Delmar.

Describes which practices are and are not considered developmentally appropriate and offers clear descriptions of practices that provide nurturing physical, social, emotional, and cognitive environments for various ages.

Glover, M. 1992. *Two years: A teacher's memoir.* Portsmouth, NH: Heinemann.

Records a two-year segment of life in a classroom with the author teaching history to first- and second-grade children. Provides insight into how classrooms can be organized so that learning and the sense of well-being become central. The book is testimony to the value of children having consecutive years with the same teacher.

Goffin, S.G., & D.G. Murphy. 1992. *Project construct: A curriculum guide to understanding the possibilities.* Columbia: University of Missouri.

Provides a process-oriented curriculum and assessment framework for working with primary-school-age children. Also included are a theoretical base and suggestions for implementing constructivist education.

Gordon, A.M., & K. Williams-Browne. 2000. *Beginnings and beyond.* 5th ed. New York: Delmar.

A comprehensive text begins with an examination of what distinguishes early childhood education from other levels of education and continues through development, curriculum, and all other areas of our field. Guest editorials by well-known early childhood educators focus on current issues.

Grant, J., I. Richardson, & A. Fredenburg, eds. 1996. *Multiage handbook: A comprehensive resource for multiage practices.* Peterborough, NH: Crystal Springs.

Draws from a variety of schools in urban, suburban, and rural settings to present practical suggestions for multiage teaching and learning. The articles cover issues such as managing the change to multiage classrooms, curricular planning, assessment, implementing parent relationships, grouping, and acceptance by teachers and communities.

Graves, M. 1996. *The teacher's idea book 2: Planning around children's interests.* Ypsilanti, MI: High/Scope.

The second book in a High/Scope series for teachers, it offers teaching strategies, classroom examples of teacher-child interactions, and ideas for drawing on children's interests in curriculum planning.

Gronlund, G. 1995. Bringing the DAP message to kindergarten and primary teachers. *Young Children* 50 (5): 4–13.

Explains the three key elements of developmentally appropriate practice that the author has found help build the foundation for introducing developmentally appropriate practice to kindergarten and primary teachers.

Gullo, D.F. 1992. *Developmentally appropriate teaching in early childhood.* Washington, DC: National Education Association.

Explores matching early childhood education practices to how children learn, creating a classroom environment that facilitates learning and development, recognizing and planning for the continuity of child development, and promoting parent involvement.

Hale, J. 1992. An African American early childhood education. In *Reconceptualizing the early childhood curriculum,* eds. S. Kessler & B.B. Swadener, 205–24. New York: Teachers College Press.

Discusses the need for ethnic identity and describes Visions for Children, a preschool program that emphasizes the special characteristics of African-American children. Details of teaching methods, curriculum, organization, and research evaluating the program effectiveness are presented.

Hansen, K.A., R.K. Kaufmann, & S. Saifer. 1997. *Education and the culture of democracy: Early childhood practice.* Washington, DC: Children's Resources International.

Contends that there are subtle yet effective techniques that encourage choice, creativity, equality, and appreciation of individual needs while keeping group needs in focus. This book describes an educational initiative that introduced developmentally appropriate teaching and the connections to democracy to well-established early childhood programs in Eastern and Central Europe.

Helm, J.H., ed. 1996. *The project approach catalog.* Urbana-Champaign, IL: ERIC Clearinghouse on Elementary and Early Childhood Education.

In addition to the Project Approach Study Group summaries that include teachers' comments and photographs, this publication contains articles on implementing the project approach, documenting projects, frequently asked questions about the project approach, incorporating projects into a traditional curriculum, and notes for brainstorming sessions on project work.

Hendrick, J., ed. 1997. *First step toward teaching the Reggio way.* Columbus, OH: Merrill/Prentice Hall.

Explores the essential features and principles that underlie the philosophy of the Reggio Emilia schools and gives examples of preschool and public school settings where aspects of the Reggio Emilia approach are being incorporated into the classroom. Teachers, teacher educators, and an art educator discuss the application of features such as documentation, collaboration, projects, and facilitating good conversations, and how they made changes in their work with children.

Hendrick, J.B. 1998. *Total learning: Developmental curriculum for the young child.* 5th ed. Upper Saddle River, NJ: Merrill/Prentice Hall.

Emphasizes the developmental needs of 2-, 3-, and 4-year-old children, thus curriculum and teaching suggestions are organized by developmental goals, for example, achieving emotional competence, developing verbal competence, and so on. Covers all components of a learning environment, including relationships with families and building for future academic competence.

Hohmann, M., & D.P. Weikart. 1995. *Educating young children: Active learning practices for preschool and child care* programs. Ypsilanti, MI: High/Scope.

Presents essential strategies adults can use to make active learning a reality in their programs. Describes key components of the adult role: planning the physical setting and establishing a consistent daily routine, creating a positive social climate, and using "key experiences" to understand and support young children. Other topics include family involvement, daily team planning, creating interest areas, choosing appropriate materials, the plan-do-review process, and small- and large-group times. A study guide is also available.

Hughes, P., & G. Macnaughton. 1999. *Communication in early childhood services: A practical guide.* Melbourne, Australia: RMIT.

Presents current thinking in the area of communications to help staff in early childhood settings and early childhood students develop professional communication skills (verbal, written, and electronic) in interviews and meetings, advocacy and public speaking, reports and media relations, or on the Internet. Topics include the nature of good communication, working with colleagues to establish community, team leadership, and communicating with families and communities.

Humphryes, J. 1998. The developmental appropriateness of high-quality Montessori programs. *Young Children* 53 (5): 4–16.

Presents the Montessori philosophy of education in relation to developmentally appropriate practice. Discusses elements of the Montessori classroom, such as the importance of observation, use of learning materials, role of the teacher, and emphasis on reality.

Jackman, H. 1997. *Early education curriculum: A child's connection to the world.* New York: Delmar.

Focuses on child-directed experiences, process-oriented curriculum, and creating an environment that encourages creativity. Chapters include examples of room arrangements, how to encourage children's explorations, and lesson plans.

Jalongo, M.R., & J.P. Isenberg. 2000. *Exploring your role: A practitioner's introduction to early childhood education.* Columbus, OH: Merrill/Prentice Hall.

Organizes the text around the professional roles that early childhood teachers play, such as child development specialist, environment designer, and curriculum developer. Each chapter describes the role and illustrates how the role is realized in classrooms of current teachers in infant/toddler, preschool, and primary settings. The many examples include materials used, webs or charts developed, or actual discussions such as the question-and-answer session with parents on portfolios in the chapter on becoming a family resource person.

Jensen, E. 1998. *Teaching with the brain in mind.* Alexandria, VA: Association for Supervision and Curriculum Development.

Provides the latest research on learning and the brain. Balances the research and theory on the brain with successful recommendations and techniques for using the information in primary classrooms.

Jones, E., & J. Nimmo. 1994. *Emergent curriculum.* Washington, DC: NAEYC.

Listens to the ongoing discussion among teachers in one center as they and the children move through the year, weaving the curriculum. A stimulating resource for getting teachers or aspiring teachers thinking about developing meaningful curriculum.

Jones, E., & E. Prescott. 1984. *Dimensions of teaching-learning environments: A handbook for teachers in elementary schools and day care centers.* Pasadena, CA: Pacific Oaks College.

Translates research concepts into ideas that can be used by teachers to informally analyze their own classroom learning environments. Physical setting and teacher behavior are measured against the following values: open/closed, soft/hard, simple/complex, intrusive/seclusive, and high/low mobility.

Katz, L.G. 1993. Dispositions as educational goals. *ERIC Digest.* ED363454. Urbana-Champaign, IL: ERIC Clearinghouse on Elementary and Early Childhood Education.

Concludes that the acquisition of both knowledge and skills is taken for granted as an educational goal and most educators agree that many feelings are also worthy of inclusion among learning goals. Examines the meaning of the term *disposition* and suggests the implications for practice.

Katz, L.G. 1994. The project approach. *ERIC Digest.* ED368509. Urbana-Champaign, IL: ERIC Clearinghouse on Elementary and Early Childhood Education.

Describes what a project is and details how the three phases of a project proceed. The author notes that project work is complementary to other aspects of a curriculum and explains how projects differ from themes and units. Available in Spanish.

Katz, L. 1995. *Talks with teachers of young children: A collection.* Norwood, NJ: Ablex.

Focuses on the real situations of classroom life as well as the broader context of the profession of early childhood education. Collected writings by Lilian Katz that represent her perspectives on meaningful development of self-esteem, her exploration into the differences between being a teacher and a mother, her drawing of the line between excitement and education, and her stages of teaching.

Katz, L.G., & S.C. Chard. 1989. *Engaging children's minds: The project approach.* Norwood, NJ: Ablex.

An approach to teaching and curriculum planning that promotes children's intellectual development through in-depth study of topics of interest to children. All steps in putting projects into action are illustrated with samples of projects, curriculum web and the teacher's interaction.

Katz, L.G., D. Evangelou, & J.A. Hartman. 1990. *The case for mixed-age grouping in early education.* Washington, DC: NAEYC.

Offers suggestions for making mixed-age settings work and answers key questions teachers may have about the benefits of a mixed-age classroom. Includes research supporting the theory that social development can be enhanced by experiences available in mixed-age groupings.

Kohn, A. 1998. *What to look for in a classroom and other essays.* San Francisco, CA: Jossey-Bass.

Invites readers to reconsider some of the most basic practices and premises about educational traditions. This collection of 19 of the author's most popular essays (the majority of which were written since 1995) covers subjects such as classroom (mis)management, grading, unsettling questions about the ADHD label, television and children, and the false premises of school-choice plans. The last three essays lay out some educational practices that underscore children having a voice and the creation of caring classroom communities in which children's curiosity is nourished.

Koralek, D.G., L.J. Colker, & D.T. Dodge. 1995. *The what, why, and how of high-quality early childhood education: A guide for on-site supervision.* Rev. ed. Washington, DC: NAEYC.

Deals with environment, equipment and materials, schedules, activities, interactions, and resources for caregivers, teachers, and directors in early childhood programs. The book is useful in helping caregivers and teachers take a thoughtful look at their own practices.

Kuball, Y.E. 1999. A case for developmental continuity in a bilingual K–2 setting. *Young Children* 54 (3): 74–79.

Focuses on using multiage groupings to allow for developmental continuity at the primary level. The author describes designing a K–2 continuous-progress program and discusses challenges faced.

Lambert, B. *Beating burnout.* 1994. AECA Resource Book/series 1 , no. 2. Watson, ACT: Australian Early Childhood Association.

Describes the multidimensional nature of burnout in an early childhood center: a process that occurs over time and involves all aspects of a center's functioning. Recommends ongoing strategies to prevent burnout, strategies that should be enshrined and incorporated into a center's philosophy and administrative procedures.

Lillard, P.P. 1972. *Montessori: A modern approach.* New York: Schoken.

Explains the purpose of Montessori education from both teachers' and parents' perspectives. Includes descriptions of Montessori materials for these areas: practical life, the sensory, language, cultural extension, and mathematics.

Mardell, B. 1999. *From basketball to the Beatles: In search of compelling early childhood curriculum.* Portsmouth, NH: Heinemann.

Tells how a child care teacher of 3- and 4-year-old children constructed an innovative curriculum by engaging the children in serious study of their world through an interplay of reality and fantasy and by bringing his own passions into the classroom. His South African curriculum examines the life and work of Mandela, who then becomes a hero in their dramatic play, a hero whose standards for equality and justice become a moral compass for them. In the study of astronomy the loft is an observatory to search for new planets.

Marfey, A. 1998. *The miracle of learning: How to inspire children. A multicultural approach to early childhood development.* Albany, NY: Windflower.

Presents a model of teaching that the author developed in a multicultural child care setting that uses association, imagination, and stimulation to help the 3- to 5-year-olds learn to accept and learn about themselves and each other. All aspects of this program are covered, such as setting up beautifully designed environments to using stories of the children and adults.

Miller, B. 1994. *Keeping children at the center: Implementing the multiage classroom.* Portland, OR: Northwest Regional Education Laboratory.

Explores the experience of creating multiage groupings (two or more grade levels intentionally placed together to improve learning) at four Northwest elementary schools and shares the firsthand insights of teachers and administrators who have made such changes. The author presents guidelines for smoothing the transition to multiage and bolstering program success.

Mitchell, A., & J. David. 1992. *Explorations with young children: A curriculum guide from the Bank Street College of Education.* Beltsville, MD: Gryphon.

Provides an integrated approach to the preschool curriculum, giving teachers a framework to address the individual needs and interests of their children. Suggests ways of developing an integrated curriculum from infant/toddler through third graders, with many curricular ideas.

Morelock, M.K., & K. Morrison. 1996. *Gifted children have talents too!: Multidimensional programmes for the gifted in early childhood.* Victoria, Australia: Hawker Brownlow Education.

A guidebook for identifying and developing talents in young gifted children in preschool and primary classrooms. Presents the psychological and educational theoretical frameworks and practical strategies for providing stimulating and developmentally appropriate curricula for children manifesting gifted development.

NAESP (National Association of Elementary School Principals). 1997. Special issue on early childhood education. *Principal* 76 (5).

Includes an article addressing several areas related to developmentally programs in kindergarten and primary grades. Additional articles address multiculturalism, documentation using a Reggio Emilia model, and play.

NAESP (National Association of Elementary School Principals). 1998. *Early childhood education and the elementary school principal: Standards for quality programs for young children.* Alexandria, VA: Author.

Details the move to extend public elementary schooling to younger children and create an early childhood unit in an elementary school. It provides elementary-school principals a means of assessing progress and broadening the impact of such programs.

NAEYC. 1998. *Code of ethical conduct and statement of commitment: Guidelines for responsible behavior in early childhood education.* Washington, DC: Author.

Prepared by the NAEYC's Panel on Professional Ethics in Early Childhood Education, this pamphlet details the nationally recognized guidelines for ethical conduct. The four sections include: ethical responsibilities to children; to families; to community and society; and to co-workers.

New, R.S. 1993. Reggio Emilia: Some lessons for U.S. educators. *ERIC Digest.* ED354988. Urbana-Champaign, IL: ERIC Clearinghouse on Elementary and Early Childhood Education.

Provides a summary of the features of a municipal early childhood program in Reggio Emilia, Italy—an internationally acclaimed program that supports and challenges the American notions of appropriate early education.

Northeast Foundation for Children. 1991. *A notebook for teachers.* Greenfield, MA: Author.

Designed to help elementary teachers create classrooms that are responsive to the needs of children, this book gives background on developmental theory as well as many practical ideas for creating a developmentally appropriate classroom environment and curriculum.

Northeast Foundation for Children (NEFC). 1997. *Off to a good start: Launching the school year.* The Responsive Classroom Series, no.1. Greenfield, MA: Author.

Contains popular excerpts from past NEFC newsletters, including descriptions of the first six weeks of school: establishing rules, building a sense of group, introducing and displaying materials in the classroom, and reaching out to parents.

Olien, R. 1998. *Walk this way: Classroom hikes to learning.* Portsmouth, NH: Heinemann.

Tells how to plan an outdoor education program for K–3 children to enrich projects on ecological concepts and an aesthetic appreciation of the environment and to complement the math and science learning in the classroom. Strategies for conducting minihikes in the community surrounding the school (both urban and rural) encompass topics such as questioning techniques and keeping nature notebooks.

Pelander, J. 1997. My transition from conventional to more developmentally appropriate practices in the primary grades. *Young Children* 52 (7): 19–25.

The author explains some of the key points of developmentally appropriate practice as he traces his movement from a traditional teaching approach to one that adheres to developmentally appropriate principles.

Phipps, P. 1997. *Multiple intelligences in the early childhood classroom.* Santa Rosa, CA: McGraw Hill/SRA.

A perspective that teachers can use to assess and apply the theory of multiple intelligences. Suggestions are offered for using the idea of multiple intelligences in planning and implementing a curriculum for diverse learners in preschool and the early years of schooling.

Puckett, M.B., & D. Diffily. 1999. *Teaching young children: An introduction to the profession.* Philadelphia, PA: Harcourt Brace .

Defines high-quality programs for the birth-through-age-8 group and the historical roots of early childhood education. Chapters address all the components of teaching such as understanding development, assessment, parent involvement, creating curricula, and setting up the physical environment.

Rooparine, J. 2000. *Approaches to early childhood education.* 3d ed. Columbus, OH: Merrill/Prentice Hall.

A comprehensive look at the range of approaches to early childhood education such as the family center model, Montessori, the project approach, and the perspective of the Erikson Institute and Reggio Emilia on early childhood education. Specific programs are also described, such as the Portage model (home visitor model), Bank Street, High/Scope, and the Ausebelian preschool classroom.

Seefeldt, C., & N. Barbour. 1998. *Early childhood education: An introduction.* Columbus, OH: Merrill.

Provides a comprehensive guide to the education of young children based on developmentally appropriate practices. Themes include parent education, curriculum for inclusion, and child development theory and practice.

Siraj-Blatchford, I., ed. 1998. *A curriculum development handbook for early childhood educators.* Staffordshire, England: Trentham.

Introduces criteria for determining quality in early learning—a framework for planning a curriculum for 3- to 6-year-old children, focusing on core learning experiences in all the subject areas. These include movement, dance, and gymnastics; use of computers; and the humanities, experiences that introduce children to time and place.

Smutney, J., S. Walker, & E. Meckstroth. 1997. *Teaching young gifted children in the regular classroom: Identifying, nurturing and challenging ages 4–9.* Minneapolis, MN: Free Spirit.

Describes the process of identifying and engaging gifted children in pre-K and primary classrooms before they become bored or lose hope that school is worthwhile. The authors present creative ways to introduce challenging activities that help children solidify their ideas and inspire new ones and that prompt children's deeper inquiry.

Splitter, L., & T. Sprod. 1999. *Places for thinking.* Melbourne, Victoria: Australian Council for Educational Research.

Resource manual based on the idea that children in the first years of school are inspired to think through wonder. The authors invite children to explore a collection of philosophical ideas embedded in four illustrated picture books. Provides discussion plans to help teachers identify and explore possible ways to develop an idea, activities to enhance children's reasoning skill by considering a number of different situations, and the active exploration of ideas through writing, drawing, physical exploration, and role playing.

Stephens, K., E. Jones, J. Nimmo, D. Levin, & L. Torgerson. 1996. Circle time. *Child Care Information Exchange* (109): 43–62.

Discusses means of making circle time developmentally appropriate and using circle times to build a sense of classroom community.

Taylor, B. 1999. *A child goes forth: A curriculum guide for preschool children.* Columbus, OH: Merrill/Prentice Hall.

Highlights how the developmental characteristics of preschool children should shape instructional planning, curriculum, and the teacher's expectations. Curriculum subject matter includes use of recent technology, social studies and field trips, and a section on violent play, its causes and effects, and recommendations for curbing violence.

Trepanier-Street, J. 1993. What's so new about the project approach? *Childhood Education* 70 (1): 25–28.

Discusses the emergent curriculum approach. It contains practical, concrete examples of ways children can assume responsibility for their own learning as teachers scaffold their experiences.

Vander Wilt, J.L., & V. Monroe. 1998. Successfully moving toward developmentally appropriate practice: It takes time and effort! *Young Children* 53 (4): 17–24.

Discusses what developmentally appropriate practice is, based on NAEYC's revised edition of *Developmentally Appropriate Practice in Early Childhood Programs.* Describes the implementation of developmentally appropriate practice in kindergarten through second grade in a midwestern school district.

Waite-Stupiansky, S. 1997. *Building understanding together: A constructivist approach to early childhood education.* Albany, NY: Delmar.

Relates Piaget's constructivist theory to classroom practice and describes activity ideas related to curriculum areas such as math and science. Vignettes, visuals, and photographs illustrate the outlined processes.

Walsh, K. 1997. *Step by Step: A program for children and families. Creating child-centered classrooms (for 6- to 7-year-olds).* Washington, DC: Children's Resources International.

Presents a comprehensive guide for teaching first- and second- graders based on democratic principles. Curricular activities and assessment strategies are unified by four themes: communication is the key concept for literacy, visual arts, and math; caring is the impetus for science and character education; community helps children see the links between history, geography, and civics, and between teachers and families; connections help children bridge new concepts and develop an empathetic world view.

Weber, L. 1997. *Looking back and thinking forward: Reexaminations of teaching and schooling.* Edited by B. Alberty. New York: Teachers College Press.

A collection of writings by a noted educator Lilian Weber, whose ideas revolutionized public elementary schools in New York City. She reflects on issues confronting early childhood educators, such as the place in the curriculum of equity for minority students, the meaning of education in a democracy, and educational implications of moral development.

Wien, C.A. 1995. *Developmentally appropriate practice in "real life": Stories of teacher practical knowledge.* New York: Teachers College Press.

A documented study using observations, interviews, and review of videotapes with teachers shows how some teachers can have simultaneously an allegiance to two contradictory frameworks for action: developmentally appropriate practice and teacher dominion.

Williams, K.C. 1997. What do you want? Involving children in curriculum planning. *Young Children* 52 (6): 78–81.

Explains one teacher's method of including 3- through 8-year-olds when developing units of study. The author includes a step-by-step process for including children in all aspects of planning and implementing curriculum.

Wishon, P., & K. Crabtree. 1998. *Curriculum for the primary years: An integrative approach.* Columbus, OH: Merrill/Prentice Hall.

Promotes the idea of teachers as reflective practitioners and covers the development, implementation, and assessment of an integrated curriculum. Addresses subject matter content, parent relationships, and the classroom environment.

Developing competence in curriculum areas

These resources are designed as guides for teachers. They illustrate practical activities, materials, and teaching strategies and give classroom examples of how to implement curriculum in a particular domain. Increasing the content knowledge of teachers is represented by thorough explanations of disciplinary concepts. Authors also detail the way in which children's learning proceeds in a given subject area.

Art, music, drama, and dance

Andress, B. 1991. Research in Review. From research to practice: Preschool children and their movement responses to music. *Young Children* 47 (1): 22–27.

Discusses implications found for the manner in which we provide movement experiences that can more effectively help children express the music they hear.

Andress, B. 1995. Transforming curriculum in music. In *Reaching potentials: Transforming early childhood curriculum and assessment, volume 2,* eds. S. Bredekamp & T. Rosegrant, 99–108. Washington, DC: NAEYC.

Includes music curriculum guidelines. Presents information about a child-centered curriculum, music learning environments in early childhood, young children's musical behaviors, appropriate music curriculum for children in a variety of age groups, and assessing the music experiences of young children.

Andress, B., & L. Walker. 1992. *Readings in early childhood music education.* Reston, VA: Music Educators National Conference.

Offers a compilation of reports and articles on the role of music in the education and development of young children. Includes articles on assessment, multicultural music, and children with special needs.

Barlin, A.L. 1979. *Teaching your wings to fly: The nonspecialists guide to movement activities for young children.* Santa Monica, CA: Goodyear.

Presents a program of dance movement activities for teachers of 3- to 12-year-olds, including a large selection of potential music and instruments. Specific techniques communicate how to introduce the activities and support children's natural instincts and imagination.

Benzie, T. 1987. *A moving experience: Dance for lovers of children and the child within.* Tucson, AZ: Zephyr.

Details creative movements to help 4- through 8-year-olds discover their bodies, rhythm, and space. Children learn to feel good about themselves through creative movement.

Blackburn, L. 1998. *Whole music: A whole language approach to teaching music.* Portsmouth, NH: Heinemann.

Introduces a point of view about music—many parallels exist between the way a child internalizes the language and the music of a culture. Written primarily for elementary teachers with and without musical experience, this book takes the child-centered holistic ways used to nurture language and applies them to movement, singing, listening, and creating music. Teaching strategies and classroom activities can be carried out separately or woven into the curriculum.

Brokering, L. 1989. *Resources for dramatic play.* St. Paul, MN: Redleaf.

Includes 26 play themes, props, suggestions for furniture and costumes, and play possibilities suitable for 3- through 5-year-olds, plus suggestions for teachers and ideas for extending the themes into other areas of the classroom or home. Unit ideas are suggested that fit with the dramatic-play settings.

Chenfeld, M. 1995. *Creative experiences for young children.* 2d ed. Orlando, FL: Harcourt Brace.

Helps teachers provide the conditions that allow children to display their creative and reasoning abilities in ways unique to their temperaments and experiences.

Christie, J.F. 1990. Dramatic play: A context for meaningful engagement. *The Reading Teacher* 43 (8): 542–45.

Shows the ways that dramatic play gets 3- to 8-year-olds engaged in the curriculum.

Church, E. 1991. How many ways can you move? *Pre-K Today* 5 (5): 26–35.

Focuses on ways to enhance movement in the classroom and provides examples of activities.

Colbert, C. 1997. Visual arts in the developmentally appropriate integrated curriculum. In *Integrated curriculum and developmentally appropriate practice: Birth to age eight*, eds. C.H. Hart, D.C. Burts, & R. Charlesworth, 201–23. Albany: State University of New York Press.

Discusses two views of the teacher's role: nonintervention by teacher or instruction of children and discussion of the child's work with her or him. The author presents an overview of how children's artistic abilities develop and how to provide meaningful art experiences that are not trivial.

Cornett, C. 1999. *The arts as meaning makers: Integrating literature and the arts throughout the curriculum.* Upper Saddle River, NJ: Merrill.

Shows elementary school teachers how to integrate literature, art, drama, dance, and music throughout the curriculum. The author summarizes appropriate concepts and skills in the five art forms to teach children. Recommends activities that emphasize active and meaning-oriented learning.

Dighe, J., Z. Calomiris, & C. Van Zutphen. 1998. Nurturing the language of art in children. *Young Children* 53 (1): 4–9.

Teachers share experiences of translating the Reggio Emilia approach to art into a vision for their classrooms. Discusses the importance of observing children, child-centered planning, teacher-child interactions and the classroom environment.

Edwards, C. 1997. *The creative arts: A process approach for teachers and children.* Columbus, OH: Merrill/Prentice Hall.

Frames curriculum development using the National Standards for Arts and Education and developmentally appropriate practice. The author explains the nature of the creative process and Howard Gardner's multiple intelligences theory and shows teachers how to tap into their own creativity to foster children's creative growth. Beginning with a chapter that explores feelings and images, the book is full of creative experiences in the arts for K–6 children.

Engel, B.S. 1995. *Considering children's art: Why and how to value their works.* Washington, DC: NAEYC.

A thoughtful, in-depth approach to children's artwork shows how much we are missing and how to begin having rich, mutually informative interactions with children about their works. For art to take its proper place in children's education, this author believes teachers need to learn how to look at children's art.

Ernst, K. 1994. *Picturing learning: Artists and writers in the classroom.* Portsmouth, NH: Heinemann.

Describes an entire framework for incorporating the arts into the literacy conversation. In showing how the visual can be a vital component of literacy, it demonstrates how close observation and teacher research can bring important changes to classrooms and schools.

Ewart, F. 1998. *Let the shadows speak: Developing children's language through shadow puppetry.* Staffordshire, England: Trentham.

Intended for preschool and primary teachers who are looking for effective ways to help children express themselves—be it a bilingual child, a child with learning difficulties, a bored or shy child—or as a means of discussing sensitive social problems or furthering curriculum projects. A Scottish primary school teacher introduces techniques for making imaginative and magical puppets and screens, writing plays, and using shadow puppetry in a variety of ways in the classroom. (Distributed by Stylus Publishing, Herndon, Virginia.)

Feinburg, S.G., C. Genishi, & L. Malaguzzi. 1993. Learning through art. *Early Childhood Today* 8 (2): 58–73.

Addresses how art connects to all the developmental areas and develops in young children. Colorful photographs illustrate suggestions for setting up an art area and implementing a creative program, including how to use art to document children's growth.

Gallas, K. 1994. *The language of learning: How children talk, write, dance, draw, and sing their understanding of the world.* New York: Teachers College Press.

Describes how all forms of expression can be used in a classroom community to reveal and refine children's thinking about the world.

Haines, J. 2000. *Leading young children to music.* 6th ed. Columbus, OH: Merrill/ Prentice Hall.

Weaves the growth and development of young children into a rich and diverse tapestry of musical experiences. Covers all aspects of music— rhythm, song, movement, playing instruments, and listening to music. Introduction techniques and facilitation guides for musical experiences for children, preschool through third grade, are presented.

Herberholz B., & L. Hanson. 1995. *Early childhood art.* 5th ed. Madison, WI: Brown & Benchmark.

Provides an illustrated introduction to the characteristics of children's artistic development. Also includes practical suggestions for varied and engaging learning experiences for 3- through 8-year-olds in collage, drawing and painting, clay and construction, and discussion of works of art.

Howell, J., & L. Corbey-Scullen. 1997. Out of the housekeeping corner and onto the stage: Extending dramatic play. *Young Children* 52 (6): 82–88.

Presents concrete ways to extend drama for young children and to create child-centered plays. In addition, the authors outline step-by-step processes for teachers working with 3- through 5-year-olds.

Isenberg, J.P., & M. Jalongo. 1997. *Creative expression and play in early childhood.* Upper Saddle River, NJ: Merrill.

Suggests strategies and activities to facilitate creative expression in 2- through 8-year-olds in art, music and movement, creative drama and play. Sections address how to set up the classroom and to conference with parents on ways to support creativity. A discussion on the nature of creativity helps teachers develop their own creative ideas.

Jalongo, M.R., & L.N. Stamp. 1997. *The arts in children's lives.* Needham Heights, MA: Allyn & Bacon.

Aims at unifying the arts into a holistic concept of aesthetic education for young children. Shows teachers that arts are an essential part of the daily curriculum.

Johnson, P. 1997. *Pictures and words together: Children illustrating and writing their own books.* Portsmouth, NH: Heinemann.

Illustrates, both literally and figuratively, how preschool and primary children can create books that infuse their drawing and writing in ways that help children enrich their meaning. The author gives practical advice such as helping preschoolers deal with drawing difficulties, which they sometimes have initially when using two-dimensional space, by collecting lots of tiny drawings from outside (playground, supermarket, etc.) to put into a sketchbook for later use when illustrating their stories.

Kelner, L.B. 1993. *The creative classroom: A guide for using creative drama in the classroom.* Portsmouth, NH: Heinemann.

Filled with creative drama strategies for use in the classroom on a daily basis and across the curriculum. For teachers who may not have prior knowledge or experience with creative drama, the book presents activities for 3- through 13-year-olds that are uncomplicated and versatile with a step-by-step procedural guide to help in implementing the activities successfully.

Kenney, S.H. 1997. Music in the developmentally appropriate integrated curriculum. In *Integrated curriculum and developmentally appropriate practice birth to age 8,* eds. C.H. Hart, D.C. Burts, & R. Charlesworth, 103–44. Albany: State University of New York Press.

Explores ways of creating music curriculum based on how children learn. Includes a position statement by the Music Educators National Conference concerning the musical learning of young children.

Khol, M. 1996. *Discovering great artists: Hands-on-art for children in the style of the great masters.*Bellingham, WA: Bright Ring.

Lets 4- through 12-year-old children experience and enjoy painting, sculpture, drawing, and building works of art in the styles of the great masters such as Van Gogh, Michelangelo, and Rembrandt. Some 150 art ideas divide into five chapters that focus on different artistic movements.

Lasky, L., & R. Mukerji-Bergeson. 1990. *Art: Basic for young children.* Washington, DC: NAEYC.

Reflects the view that a child's growing/learning is central to early childhood education and that art is an important pathway to development. Includes research about child development and creativity and how they relate to art.

McDonald, D. 1979. *Music in our lives: The early years.* Washington, DC: NAEYC.

Contains titles of recommended songbooks and guidelines for presentations of music. Also recommends classical music selections that appeal to children.

Micklethwait, L. 1993. *A child's book of art.* New York: Dorling Kindersley.

Couples colorful images from the art of many cultures with simple words and invites 3- through 8-year-olds to look carefully to find subtle clues in complex pictures. Images are grouped by themes.

Myhre, S. 1993. Enhancing your dramatic-play area through the use of prop boxes. *Young Children* 48 (5): 6–11.

This article discusses the use of prop boxes. Children come to know their world as they role-play and interact with props. As they play out their ideas they make sense of their experiences.

Perlmutter, J. 1990. Fostering children's fantasy play. *Dimensions* 18 (3): 23–24.

Presents ideas for designing a creative environment and teaching interactions that support fantasy and pretend play in preschool settings.

Perry, G. 1991. Sociodramatic play. In *Creating the learning environment: A guide in early childhood education,* ed. D.S. Strickland, 46–53. Orlando, FL: Harcourt Brace Jovanovich.

Discusses the benefits of sociodramatic play, such as cognitive development, development of communication skills, social development, and creative expression. Also provides information on how to construct two complete sociodramatic play environments, a hospital and a pizza parlor.

Pica, R. 2000. *Experiences in movement with music, activities, and theory.* 2d ed. Albany, NY: Delmar.

Provides knowledge for all that would like to understand and use movement curriculum in early childhood education.

Pleydell, S., & V. Brown. 1999. *The dramatic difference: Drama in the preschool and kindergarten classroom.* Portsmouth, NH: Heinemann.

Portrays use of drama as teaching tool that accommodates curricular demands while nurturing the need for play and active learning. Drama work is not performance art. It is experiential, an exploration of ideas and situations through drama-like story dramatizations and the processing of emotions through drama. Strategies for planning and guiding curriculum-based drama sessions include the use of props and adapting to special needs.

Rodger, L. 1996. Adding movement throughout the day. *Young Children* 51 (3): 4–6.

Explains how movement can be added to the classroom throughout the day and how it enhances learning.

San José, C. 1989. Classroom drama: Learning from the inside out. In *Learning from the inside out,* eds. S. Hoffman & L. Lamme, 69–76. Wheaton, MD: Association for Childhood Education International.

Explores ways that teachers can make the curriculum come alive for children: by using the power of drama for learning in the content area rather than viewing it as an adjunct to regular learning and rediscovering the learning connections that are possible when cognitive and affective experiences come together through the expressive arts.

Schiller, M. 1995. An emergent art curriculum that fosters understanding. *Young Children* 50 (3): 33–38.

Explains "discipline-based art education" with suggestions as to how this approach can be applied in preschool classrooms. Presents experiences of children being exposed to works of famous artists.

Schirrmacher, R. 1998. *Art and creative development for young children.* 3d ed. Albany, NY: Delmar.

This revised edition includes topics such as inclusion, multicultural activities, music and movement, and assessment.

Seefeldt, C. 1995. Art—A serious work. *Young Children* 50 (3): 39–45.

Stresses the importance of teachers' understanding cognitive theories of art, motivating children, and carefully selecting teaching strategies.

Sims, W. 1995. *Strategies for teaching prekindergarten music.* Reston, VA: Music Educators National Conference.

Designed for teachers of four-year-olds with various levels of music background, teaching strategies help children respond to and understand music, sing, play instruments, and create music. Spontaneous, small, and whole group activities are included.

Smith, N.R., C. Fucigna, M.T. Kennedy, & L. Lord. 1997. *Experience and art: Teaching children to paint.* New York: Teachers College Press.

Offers teachers guidance in helping children develop the mental and physical abilities used in the discovery and creation of meaning through drawing by giving students extensive experience with materials, keeping in mind developmental guidelines, and planning lessons with clearly defined objectives and carefully sequenced.

Spodek, B., L. Gandini, C. Weisman Topal, & G. Forman. 1996. Art experiences. *Child Care Information Exchange* (Beginnings Workshop suppl.) March/April (108): 39–46, 51–58.

Highlights art as a creative, expressive, social, and cognitive activity.

Stinson, W.J., ed. 1990. *Moving and learning for the young child.* Reston, VA: American Alliance for Health, Physical Education, Recreation, and Dance.

Discusses the linkage between movement and learning in the lives of young children. Informs about the young child as an active learner, becoming physically educated, linking dance with physical education, international physical education programs, assessing children's movement, and the challenges of linking movement and learning.

Sullivan, M. 1982. *Feeling strong, feeling free: Movement exploration for young children.* Washington, DC: NAEYC.

Describes techniques and activities appropriate for children in age groups 3 to 4 and 5 to 8. Furnishes techniques and a format for teaching movement exploration to make the experience fulfilling and joyful for both teachers and children.

Tegano, D.W., J.D. Moran III, & J. Sawyers. 1991. *Creativity in early childhood classrooms.* Washington, DC: National Education Association.

Discusses the developmental characteristics of creative potential in the young and how to optimize creativity in preschool and kindergarten curriculum. Teacher attitudes and teaching styles that foster the creative process are elaborated.

Thompson, C. 1994. *Art image preschool: Introducing 3–5 year old children to art and artists.* Champlain, NY: Art Image.

Five packets of selected artwork reproductions represent varied interpretations of a theme to engage the attention and curiosity of preschool children. Accompanying teacher guides offer suggestions for introducing children to and encouraging them to explore the works of art in varied ways in the classroom.

Thompson, C.M. 1995. Transforming curriculum in the visual arts. *Reaching potentials: Transforming early childhood curriculum and assessment, volume 2,* eds. S. Bredekamp & T. Rosegrant, 81–98. Washington DC: NAEYC.

Discusses development and learning in early childhood art, selecting content for the art curriculum, the National Standards for Visual Arts Education K–4, and evaluating art learning.

Thompson, C.M., ed. 1995. *The visual arts and early childhood learning.* Reston, VA: National Art Education Association.

Comprehensive look at early childhood art education in 21 chapters. Some important topics include socialization through art experiences, developmentally appropriate practices, narrative qualities of young children's art, historical and critical understanding, interdisciplinary and museum approaches, artistically gifted young children, and multiculturalism in early childhood.

Language and literacy

Allington, R.L. 1998. *Teaching struggling readers: Articles from* The Reading Teacher. Newark, DE: International Reading Association.

A compilation of articles from *The Reading Teacher* focused specifically on helping children with reading problems.

Armington, D. 1997. *The living classroom: Writing, reading, and beyond.* Washington, DC: NAEYC.

The work in one first-grade teacher's classroom conveys the power of children's writing in their learning to read and in many areas of their intellectual, emotional, and social development.

Barclay, K., C. Benilli, & A. Curtis. 1995. Literacy begins at birth: What caregivers can learn from parents of children who read early. *Young Children 50* (4): 24–28.

Describes how to structure the environment and support interactions in the child care center so as to give infants and toddlers the advantages often found in the homes of children who read early.

Barnes, D. 1992. *From communication to curriculum.* 2d ed. Portsmouth, NH: Heinemann.

"Exploratory talk"—how children talk to make connections and rearrange, reconceptualize, and internalize new experiences and ideas—is the crux of this book. Describes how teachers can set up, develop, and support this kind of talking for learning.

Barrs, M., & A. Thomas, eds. 1993. *The reading book.* Portsmouth, NH: Heinemann.

A primary teacher's guide. Part I covers what we know about learning to read, one chapter profiling "The Day in the Life of a Reader." Amply illustrated with photos and drawings and includes practical teaching ideas on topics such as book making, reading media, and using computers, plus help on working with parents and keeping track of children's progress.

Beginnings Workshop: Building literacy. 1999. *Child Care Information Exchange* (129): 43–62.

A collection of five articles by early childhood educators, each discussing an aspect of promoting literacy. Topics include literacy events in the classroom, using the project approach, family literacy, and selecting books.

Bos, B. 1990. *Before the basics: Creating conversations with children.* St. Paul, MN: Redleaf.

Offers unique ideas to encourage genuine interchanges with preschool children—conversations that take their cues from children and proceed "from the inside out." Teaching approaches are illustrated with examples throughout the curriculum.

Burns, M.S., P. Griffin, & C. Snow, eds. 1999. *Starting out right: A guide to promoting children's reading success.* Washington, DC: National Academy Press.

For parents, child care providers, teachers, and policymakers, this book offers specific strategies, activities, and resources for preparing young children to read. It also identifies the key elements that all children need to become good readers and the factors that often put children at risk of reading failure.

Calkins, L.M. 1994. *The art of teaching writing.* New ed. Portsmouth, NH: Heinemann.

Describes the writing workshop in elementary classrooms, including chapters on assessment, thematic studies, writing throughout the day, reading-writing relationships, publication, curriculum development, non-fiction writing, and home-school connections.

Campbell, R., ed. 1998. *Facilitating preschool literacy.* Newark, DE: International Reading Association.

Addresses three important themes in the literacy learning of preschool children: children are active constructors of their own learning, families provide invaluable support in the early literacy learning of children, and preschool settings should reflect the literacy learning that occurs in many homes and should provide opportunities for children to further develop their literacy.

Carbo, M. 1996. Whole language vs. phonics: The great debate. *Principal* 75 (3): 36–8.

This article discusses the benefits of whole language and phonics and stresses the importance of developing a curriculum that includes both.

Carr, J. 1999. *A child went forth: Reflective teaching with young readers and writers.* Portsmouth, NH: Heinemann.

Takes the reader into a large multiethnic combination first- and second-grade classroom where the teacher grapples with a year-round schedule and controversial state-curriculum frameworks. The author describes in detail how she met these challenges, beginning with the process of getting her classroom and materials ready through the first two months of school and establishing routines and structures, as the children become readers and writers.

Christie, J.F., C. Vukelich, & B.J. Enz. 1997. *Teaching language and literacy: Preschool through the elementary grades.* New York: Addison Wesley Longman.

Addresses the acquisition and promotion of language and literacy with special features on such topics as facilitating reciprocal discussions and conversations, bilingual and second-language learners, and creating and using portfolios to assess language and literacy.

Clay, M. 1993a. *Reading recovery: A guidebook for teachers in training.* Portsmouth, NH: Heinemann.

Describes the Reading Recovery Program that originated with the author in New Zealand in the early 1960s. Designed for teachers of primary-school children who have difficulty reading and writing. Specific procedures and teaching steps for implementing reading recovery are introduced.

Clay, M. 1993b. *What did I write? Beginning writing behavior.* Portsmouth, NM: Heinemann.

Examines the child's first attempts to write. By tracing patterns of development in actual samples of children's work, this book provides invaluable insight for teachers who are supporting early writing in kindergarten

Clay, M. 1998. *By different paths to common outcomes.* York, ME: Stenhouse.

Brings together new, previously unpublished works that call for changes in how primary teachers think about literacy awareness as it develops before and after children's transition to school. Clay reiterates the importance of sensitive observation and the challenge in how teachers put language down in print, adapt to diversity, and introduce storybooks. Shows conversation as a tool for improving teaching interactions. Practical examples accompany reasoned discussion.

Collins, R., & P. Collins. 1997. *The power of story: Teaching through storytelling.* 2d ed. Scottsdale, AZ: Goruch Scarisbrick.

Describes the value of telling stories and discovering personal narratives. The authors detail how teachers can prepare and tell stories and explore the art of storytelling through dramatization and other activities. An appendix includes short lists of essentials for good stories and storytelling.

Cooper, P. 1993. *When stories come to school: Telling, writing, & performing stories in the early childhood classroom.* New York: Teachers and Writers Collaborative.

Describes the role of children's personal stories in the reading-writing process. In her explanation of how to make stories central to the early childhood curriculum, Cooper addresses such issues as readiness, misuses of whole language, and invented spelling in preschool and kindergarten.

Cunningham, P., & R. Allington. 1994. *Classrooms that work: They can all read and write.* New York: HarperCollins.

Theory and practice of reading instruction for primary classrooms. Presents a balanced approach, including phonics.

Davidson, J.I. 1996. *Emergent literacy and dramatic play in early education.* Albany, NY: Delmar.

This resource presents a comprehensive view of the link between dramatic play and language development. Real-life stories and pictures illustrate how dramatic play enhances literacy.

de Villiers, P.A., & J.G. de Villiers. 1979. *Early language.* Cambridge, MA: Harvard University Press.

Documents how the toddler learns language, with a focus on infants, toddlers, and preschoolers. Vivid examples illustrate the course of learning to talk and communicate, with attention to how the adult learns what a child knows about language.

Dombey, H., M. Moustafa, & Staff of the Centre for Language in Primary Education. 1998. *W(hole) to part phonics: How children learn to read and spell.* Portsmouth, NH: Heinemann.

Summarizes the research on letter-sound relationships and how the traditional phonics instruction ignores the complexity of children's natural learning processes. In easy-to-read language, the authors trace the multi-level process of learning to read and spell and illustrate how it translates into classroom practice for children ages 4 to 6, and children ages 6 to 8.

Dyson, A.H. 1997. *Writing superheroes: Contemporary childhood, popular culture, and classroom literacy.* New York: Teachers College Press.

Graphically portrays the ways that classroom literacy is intimately related to children's personal lives, popular culture in the form of superheroes, and the social relationships in the classroom.

Edelsky, C., B. Altwerger, & B. Flores. 1991. *Whole language: What's the difference?* Portsmouth, NH: Heinemann.

A comprehensive discussion of the meaning of a whole-language philosophy, its roots from Dewey and early childhood educators such as Caroline Pratt, Lucy Sprague Mitchell, and others in progressive education. Vignettes portray whole-language classrooms, especially the writing process.

Ericson, L., & M.F. Juliebo. 1998. *The phonological awareness handbook for kindergarten and primary teachers.* Newark, DE: International Reading Association.

A practical and comprehensive means of teaching and monitoring children's development of phonological awareness, including a possible teaching sequence and activities to encourage children's playing with sounds in natural word play and more formal tasks. Pre-and post-teaching tests are included in the appendix.

Ewart, F. 1998. *Let the shadows speak: Developing children's language through shadow puppetry.* Staffordshire, England: Trentham.

Intended for preschool and primary teachers who are looking for effective ways to help children express themselves—be it a bilingual child, a child with learning difficulties, a bored or shy child—as a means of discussing sensitive social problems or furthering curriculum projects. A Scottish primary school teacher introduces techniques for making imaginative and magical puppets and screens, writing plays, and using shadow puppetry in a variety of ways in the classroom. (Distributed by Stylus Publishing, Herndon, Virginia.)

Fisher, B. 1991. *Joyful learning: A whole language kindergarten.* Portsmouth, NH: Heinemann.

Interweaves theory and practical strategies for creating a kindergarten classroom environment that supports joyful, natural learning in language arts as well as other content areas.

Fisher, B. 1996. *Inside the classroom: Teaching kindergarten and first grade.* Portsmouth, NH: Heinemann.

Describes how to set up a classroom environment conducive to learning, specifically in the area of reading and writing. The author discusses ways of assisting the emergent and initial reader.

Fountas, I., & G.S. Pinnell. 1996. *Guided reading: Good first teaching for all children.* Portsmouth, NH: Heinemann.

Focused on K–3 classrooms but applicable to all elementary grades, this works demonstrates how to create a balanced, student-centered classroom while attending to a range of needs and strengths within a single classroom.

Fountas, I.C., & G.S. Pinnell. 1999a. *Matching books to readers: Using leveled books in guided reading, K–3.* Portsmouth, NH: Heinemann.

Supports teachers in selecting appropriate books for guided, independent, and home reading. Features 7,500 simple one-sentence caption books, natural language texts, series books, and children's literature organized by difficulty, title, and word counts to assist teachers as they take running records. Ten chapters are devoted to acquiring books and creating a classroom collection and using leveled book lists in a guided reading program.

Fountas, I.C., & G.S. Pinnell, eds. 1999b. *Voices on word matters: Learning about phonics and spelling in the literacy classroom.* Portsmouth, NH: Heinemann.

Highlights phonics and spelling in a variety of primary-grade interactive reading, writing, and oral-language contexts. The "voices" are those of literacy educators who address curricular topics such as word solving, assessing spelling knowledge, language delights, and word walls. Concludes with suggestions for professional growth—learning conversations that can take place among teachers. (This book is Part 2 to an earlier work listed later in this section as Pinnell & Fountas 1998.)

Friedberg, J.B. 1995. *Super storytimes: A guide for caregivers—Why, how and what to read to young children.* Pittsburgh, PA: Carnegie Library of Pittsburgh, Beginning with Books.

Designed especially for caregivers in family day care and child care centers serving infants, toddlers, and preschoolers. Read-aloud techniques fit busy settings and suggest books appropriate for newborns to 4-year-olds.

Gaffney, J., & B.J. Askew, eds. 1999. *Stirring the waters: The influence of Marie Clay.* Portsmouth, NH: Heinemann.

Twenty experts pay tribute to Clay's work with papers highlighting her principles about the acquisition of literacy. Content includes topics such as developmental diversity and beginning literacy instruction, what reading achievement really means, creating independent learners, the gift of story, the socialization of attention in learning to read and write, and the meaning of good first teaching.

Gibson, L. 1989. *Literacy learning in the early years: Through children's eyes.* New York: Teachers College Press.

Uses theory and anecdotes to present the process of learning to read and write from birth to age 8. Emphasizes holistic teaching strategies for literacy acquisition.

Glover, M.K. 1999. *A garden of poets: Poetry writing in the elementary classroom.* Urbana, IL: National Council of Teachers of English.

Designed to help teachers nurture the art of poetry in their classroom. The author uses a garden project as a metaphor for gaining insight into writing poetry and more broadly into the teaching/learning process. Practical strategies are accompanied by many poems by children and professional writers.

Goodman, K.S. 1986. *What's whole in whole language?* Portsmouth, NH: Heinemann.

Describes the essence of the whole-language movement—its basis, features, and future. Provides criteria that parents and teachers can use in helping children develop literacy.

Goodman, K., ed. 1998. *In defense of good teaching: What teachers should know about the reading wars.* York, ME: Stenhouse.

Collection of articles that articulate the current situation on the teaching of reading: the sequence of events that led up to the phonics/whole language debate, the real meaning behind the decisions, and proposed perspectives and strategies for primary-school teachers.

Graves, D.H. 1994. *A fresh look at writing.* Portsmouth, NH: Heinemann.

Examines the details of teaching conventions and spelling, record keeping, portfolios, and how to use data to help both parents and administrators understand the approaches to teaching writing.

Hall, N., & A. Robinson, eds. 1994. *Keeping in touch: Using interactive writing with young children.* Portsmouth, NH: Heinemann.

An overview of interactive writing with 5- through 9-year-olds. Case studies illustrate the varied ways interactive writing can be implemented. Gives practical advice about getting started with interactive writing and details the benefits to teachers.

Hart, B., & T.R. Risley. 1999. *The social world of children learning to talk.* Baltimore, MD: Brookes.

Describes in storytelling style the findings of a longitudinal study that examined the early experiences of typically developing children and their families. Specifically, the book discusses the amount of opportunities children have to speak, as shaped by their interactions with their families, and how this affects children's learning to talk.

Harwayne, S. 1999. *Lasting impressions: Weaving literature into the writing workshop.* Portsmouth, NH: Heinemann.

Examines the writing workshop structures of minilessons, conferences, author studies, and reader-response groups and adds several ways to weave literature into children's writing lives.

Heard, G. 1989. *For the good of the Earth and Sun: Teaching poetry.* Portsmouth, NH: Heinemann.

Offers the newcomer a chance to see poetry through the eyes of a poet, teacher, and student; a method of teaching poetry that is not formulaic but gives step-by-step suggestions, enabling teachers to become more familiar with and comfortable at engaging in teaching poetry in K–6 classrooms.

Heath, S.B. 1983. *Ways with words: Language, life, and work in communities and classrooms.* New York: Cambridge University Press.

Documents two communities of children learning to use language at home and in school whose deep cultural differences—and ways with words—had far reaching implications when they entered school. A rich explanation of language use between teachers and children provides insight into the teaching processes of those working with young children today.

Hindley, J. 1996. *In the company of children.* York, ME: Stenhouse.

Offers specific suggestions for creating rigorous and efficient reading and writing workshops. Based on work with her third graders, author makes realistic recommendations for teaching such as how to manage a productive workshop setting in a crowded classroom or improve your conferences with individual children.

Howard, S., A. Shaughnessy, D. Sanger, & K. Hux. 1998. Let's talk! *Young Children* 53 (3): 34–39.

Discussions of support oral language skills in preschool and primary classrooms is the common thesis of these two articles. Strategies for optimizing language interactions include such techniques as extensions and parallel talk, dramatic reenactments, metalinguistic analysis and modifying teacher expectations for language participation.

Kratcoski, A., & K. Katz. 1998. Conversing with young language learners in the classroom. *Young Children* 53 (3): 30–33.

Teachers have many opportunites during the day to facilitate language learning and use. These authors describe how to use these opportunities.

Kuball, Y.E. 1995. Goodbye dittos: A journey from skill-based teaching to developmentally appropriate language education in a bilingual kindergarten. *Young Children* 50 (2): 6–14.

Discusses how the author began to use developmentally appropriate practices to teach reading and writing, what she does and why, and the developmental stages she has observed in children learning to write.

Laminack, L.L. 1998. *Volunteers working with young readers.* Urbana, IL: National Council of Teachers of English.

Discusses the theoretical foundations for literacy development as well as the practical details that help a volunteer understand a child's literacy development. Describes scenarios and situations with real children in authentic classrooms. Much of the information is also useful to parents of beginning readers.

Lindfors, J.W. 1999. *Children's inquiry: Using language to make sense of the world.* New York: Teachers College Press.

Explores the purpose and nature of the inquiry process and how children develop and use the language of inquiry in preschool and elementary school settings. The author explains how to recognize and participate in authentic inquiry events and the nature of expressive forms and styles used in these classroom dialogues.

Lynn, L. 1997. Language-rich home and school environments are key to reading success. *Of Primary Interest* 4 (3): 1–4.

Published by the Colorado (Denver) Department of Education, Early Childhood Initiatives. Discusses the importance of giving children the chance to develop and practice oral language skills. Offers a wide variety of ideas and suggestions for both parents and teachers about how to engage children in environments that stimulate language growth.

Machado, J.M. 1999. *Early childhood experiences in language arts.* 6th ed. Albany, NY: Delmar.

Reports on the development of oral language and emergent literacy skills, with special focus on planning programs and activities for infants, toddlers, and preschoolers that promote individual language background and consider teachers' conversational styles.

Makin, L., J. Campbell, & C.J. Diaz. 1995. *One childhood, many languages: Guidelines for early childhood education in Australia.* Sydney, Australia: HarperEducational.

Explores language learning in educational settings for children from birth to 8 years. The authors provide both an explanation of how early language and literacy develop and a set of guidelines for developing children's skills in all their languages. (Distributed by the Australian Early Childhood Association, Watson, ACT, 011-61-262416900.)

McCarrier, A., G.S. Pinnell, & I.C. Fountas. 2000. *Interactive writing: How language and literacy come together, K–2.* Portsmouth, NH: Heinemann.

Asserts that for children to become writers whose "voices radiate from the paper," they need to begin with interactive writing—a collaborative literacy event in which children actively compose together, considering appropriate words, phrases, and the organization of text and layout. The authors discuss the elements of interactive writing, how to get it going, and a step-by-step process by grade levels, including charts, examples, and assessment.

Ministry of Education, New Zealand. 1994a. *Dancing with the pen: The learner as a writer.* Katonah, NY: Richard C. Owen.

A handbook on writing for primary-school teachers to develop their understanding of how children learn to write and how they can facilitate this process. Helps teachers create teaching environments in which learners feel confident to develop their writing.

Ministry of Education, New Zealand. 1994b. *Reading in junior classes.* Katonah, NY: Richard C. Owen.

Bright photographs of children working with teachers and print-rich classrooms with children's work convey the respected New Zealand style of teaching reading to 4- to 7-year-olds. Guidelines for implementing a balanced program for emergent, early, and fluent readers include the integration of writing and language and techniques for monitoring children's progress as they learn about print.

Mooney, M. 1990. *Reading to, with, and by children.* Katonah, NY: Richard C. Owen.

Presents four levels of reading instruction: read aloud, shared reading, guided reading, and independent reading.

Morrow, L.M. 1997. *Literacy development in the early years: Helping children read and write.* Boston: Allyn & Bacon.

Presents an integrated language arts perspective and an interdisciplinary approach to literacy development as it addresses developing writing, reading, and oral language in the home and total school curriculum. Using children's literature is emphasized as the most important instructional material. Stresses the joy of early literacy experiences to ensure lifelong reading habits.

Morrow, L.M., D.S. Strickland, & D. Gee Woo. 1998. *Literacy instruction in half- and whole-day kindergarten: Research to practice.* Newark, DE: International Reading Association.

Looks at the effect of half- and whole-day kindergarten programs on children in an urban school district and addresses a number of questions significant to literacy professionals: What is the best way to begin early literacy instruction? How much time should be spent on literacy instruction in kindergarten classrooms? and Should kindergarten meet for a full school day? Methodology details and assessment results are given to suggest plans for designing the curriculum and organizing kindergarten classrooms for both half- and whole-day.

Moustafa, M. 1997. *Beyond traditional phonics.* Portsmouth, NH: Heinemann.

Update on the research on language learning and the reading process that challenges the recent return to isolated phonics and skills instruction. Offers an alternative approach toward supporting the development of graphophonic understanding within a meaning-centered model of reading.

Muse, D. 1997. *The New Press guide to multicultural resources for young readers.* New York: New Press.

Contains over 1,000 books for the K–3 reader organized by grade level and theme to assist teachers in using culturally diverse materials across the curriculum. Extensive reviews and multiple indexes enable users to access resources by type—multimedia, bilingual, and curriculur packets—or by broad cultural group, title, author name, and subject matter topic.

Neuman, S.B., C. Copple, & S. Bredekamp. 2000. *Learning to read and write: Developmentally appropriate practices for young children.* Washington, DC: NAEYC.

Translates into everyday teaching practice the key points of the position statement from NAEYC and the International Reading Association on learning to read and write. Includes the text of the position statement, dozens of teaching ideas, and chapters on assessment and policy.

Neuman, S.B., & K.A. Roskos, eds. 1998. *Children achieving: The best practices in early literacy.* Newark, DE: International Reading Association.

Each chapter in this book highlights a critical issue in early literacy, examines what is known about it, and describes literacy practices suggested from this existing knowledge base. Focuses on issues of theory and practice appropriate for children ages 2 through 8 in classrooms ranging from prekindergarten settings through third grade.

Pinnell, G., & I.C. Fountas. 1997. *Help America read: A handbook for volunteers.* Portsmouth, NH: Heinemann.

For both new and experienced volunteers who work with young children learning to read and write in schools and centers. Easy-to-read format, with basic information on the development of literacy combined with concrete suggestions, such as how to gain children's trust, for making the most of one's tutoring time.

Pinnell, G.S., & I.C. Fountas. 1998. *Word matters: Teaching phonics and spelling in the reading/writing classroom.* Portsmouth, NH: Heinemann.

The goal of this book is to teach children to become word solvers. The authors explain what it means to become a word solver and word explorer and how to create a dynamic classroom environment. Practical tools for setting up a word-study system or a writing workshop are cited, such as spelling minilessons and word lists with frequently used words, antonyms, and synonyms. (Part 1 to a work listed earlier in this section as Fountas & Pinnell 1999b.)

Raines, S.C, & R. Isbell. 1999. *Tell it again: Easy-to-tell stories with activities for young children.* Beltsville, MD: Gryphon House.

Describes ideas from expert storytellers and discusses how to capture the attention and imagination of young children through retellings of familiar stories. Includes ways to extend a story with activities that are specifically created to fit the story.

Raison, G., with J. Rivalland. 1994. *Writing: Developmental continuum.* Portsmouth, NH: Heinemann.

One of eight in a series developed by the Education Department of Western Australia to provide a framework for linking assessment to teaching and learning (a second is Rees 1997 listed below). The continuum describes six phases of a child's writing development, beginning in preschool years with role-play writing. Serves as a tool to map children's progress, report to parents, and help teachers make informed decisions about what to do next in supporting a child's writing development. Another book, *Writing Resource Book,* complements this and gives preschool and primary teachers additional ideas for working with children on six different forms of writing.

Rand, D., T. Parker, & S. Foster. 1998. *Black books galore! Guide to great African American children's books.* New York: John Wiley.

Consists of annotations of 500 books—board books, story and picture books, fiction, nonfiction, poetry, history, biography, fables—including 115 books for babies and preschoolers and 200 titles for the K–3 age group. Organized by age level, title, topic, author and illustrator, the resource includes guidelines for encouraging young readers and portraits of selected authors.

Rees, D. 1997. *Spelling developmental continuum.* Portsmouth, NH: Heinemann.

A comprehensive description of the five phases of learning to spell from preliminary spelling to independent spelling. Explains what is known about spelling and gives key indicators in each phase to assist teachers in knowing what children can do and how they do it so as inform their practice and monitor children's progress through an ongoing collection of data and consultation with and involvement of parents. Based on the philosophy that spelling is a thinking process, not a rote learning task.

Reutzel, D.R., & R.B. Cooter. 1996. *Teaching children to read: From basals to books*. 2d ed. Englewood Cliffs, NJ: Merrill.

Concentrates on transition approaches to teaching reading, with extensive coverage of all reading teaching methods. Shows future teachers how balanced literacy programs can be developed to draw upon the most important and successful ideas from both whole-language and traditional, direct-instruction philosophies.

Rice, M.L., K.A. Wilcox, & B.H. Bunce. 1995. *Building a language-focused curriculum for the preschool classroom, vol. 1: A foundation for lifelong communication*. Baltimore, MD: Brookes.

Highlights ways to incorporate a rich infusion of language stimulation into children's centers. A companion volume (Bunce, B.H. 1995. *A Planning Guide, vol. 2*. Baltimore, MD: Brookes) provides examples from preschool settings that illustrate teaching suggestions.

Routman, R. 1994. *Invitations: Changing as teachers and learners K–12*. Portsmouth, NH: Heinemann.

Discusses shared reading and shared writing for 4- through 18-year-olds, guided reading, developing literature extension activities, setting up an independent reading program, journal writing, teaching phonics and skills strategically, integrating spelling into the reading-writing classroom, getting the publishing process going, and managing the whole-language classroom.

Routman, R. 1999. *Conversations. Strategies for teaching, learning and evaluating*. Portsmouth, NH: Heinemann.

This monumental volume (656 pages) reflects Routman's current thinking about the literacy landscape and is a comprehensive guide to reading, writing, and teaching in the primary years. Grounded in the idea that the best educational tool we have is the human mind—given time to ponder, inquire, analyze, debate, suggest, share, and reason—relevant research (both classroom-based and scientific) is presented to support the author's beliefs about teaching and learning. Many examples and anecdotes portray the realization of "best practice" as well as the literacy problems and pitfalls. Includes a 200-page list of annotated professional resources.

Schickedanz, J.A. 1998. *Much more than the ABCs: The early stages of reading and writing*. Washington DC: NAEYC.

This revised volume offers a rich picture of children's early steps toward literacy. The author offers concrete suggestions, grounded in research and expert practice, on topics such as reading aloud with children, setting up a book corner and writing center, and introducing the alphabet in meaningful ways. Book lists assist in choosing good books for children at different ages.

Smith, F. 1997. *Reading without nonsense*. 3d ed. New York: Teachers College Press.

Based on the idea that reading and reading instruction must make sense to the learner to be effective. Provides information on phonics and meaningful reading, comprehension and learning, the act and the range of reading, and teaching reading to children with special needs.

Smith, J., & W. Elley. 1997. *How children learn to read: Insights from the New Zealand experience* and *How children learn to write.* Katonah, NY: Richard C. Owen.

The first book offers a comprehensive discussion of reading instruction, encompassing the philosophy underlying whole language. The second includes a focus on learning to write, why writing is taught the way it is, and chapters on the Graves' process approach and Cambourne's model of literacy learning the natural way.

Stewig, J.W., & M. Jett-Simpson. 1995. *Language arts in the early childhood classroom.* Boston: Wadsworth.

Focuses on all facets of language arts—reading, speaking, listening, writing—and the study of literature for grades K–3. Emphasizing literature as the approach to all aspects of language, this book encourages an integrated curriculum to facilitate learning.

Strickland, D.S. 1998. *Teaching phonics today: A primer for educators.* Newark, DE: International Reading Association.

Reports on the phonics controversy and shows how changes in literacy instruction have influenced the teaching of phonics. Examples of curriculum frameworks for K–2 levels are balanced between intensive, code-driven phonics and holistic meaning-driven approaches.

Strickland, D.S., & L.M. Morrow, eds. 1989. *Emerging literacy: Young children learn to read and write.* Newark, DE: International Reading Association.

Contributors to this award-winning book share practical ideas promoting reading and writing with 2- through 8-year-olds.

Sulzby, E. 1991. Emergent literacy: All young children read and write. *Creating the learning environment: A guide in early childhood education,* ed. D. Strickland, 36–45. Orlando, FL: Harcourt Brace Jovanovich.

Presents the research supporting the belief that early childhood literacy emerges in environments in which children are allowed to interact with books and writing materials. Information about how both parents and teachers can support emergent literacy is included. Work samples illustrate varying stages of emerging literacy.

Taylor, D, & C. Dorsey-Gaines. 1988. *Growing up literate.* Portsmouth, NH: Heinemann.

Focuses on children who successfully learn to read and write despite extraordinary economic hardship. Presents images of the strengths of the family as educator and the ways personal biographies and educative styles of families shape the literate experiences of children.

Weitzman, E. 1992. *Learning language and loving it: A guide to promoting children's social and language development in early childhood settings.* Toronto, Canada: Hanen Centre.

Designed to help practitioners promote the language learning of all children, birth through five 5 years old, but particularly children whose communication skills are less developed than those of their peers.

Wells, G. 1986. *The meaning makers: Children learning language and using language to learn.* Portsmouth, NH: Heinemann.

Follows the development of a representative sample of children from their first words to the end of their elementary education. Contains many examples of language experience, both spoken and written, recorded in naturally occurring contexts in homes and classrooms, and shows the active role that children play in their own learning as they construct both an internal model of the world and a linguistic system for communicating about it.

Whitmore, K.F., & Y.M. Goodman. 1995. Transforming curriculum in language and literacy. In *Reaching potentials: Transforming early childhood curriculum and assessment, volume 2,* eds. S. Bredekamp & T. Rosegrant, 145–63. Washington, DC: NAEYC.

Discusses how children develop language and literacy, the developmental continuum of language and literacy learning, and language and literacy at school.

Wilson, L. 1994. *Write me a poem: Reading, writing and performing poetry.* Portsmouth, NH: Heinemann.

Children's experience of poetry is typically one of using rhythm; consequently when they start to compose, they frequently sacrifice meaning so as to make the verse rhyme. Strategies here help address this problem as teachers encourage children to explore reading, writing, and performing many different types of poetry.

Wolf, D., C. Genishi, A.H. Dyson, J.S. Bloch, J.L. Friedman, & D. Addock. 1996. Talking. *Child Care Information Exchange* (110): 43–62.

Describes the importance of children's conversations and guides teachers on respecting differences in speech patterns of children birth through 5 years old.

Mathematics

Baker, A., & J. Baker. 1991. *Counting on a small planet: Activities for environmental mathematics.* Portsmouth, NH: Heinemann.

Uses mathematics to explore how actions affect the world. Topics have an introductory activity designed to present the material and suggested investigations that provide ideas and structure for further action. Math Fact Files at the end of each topic relate the local to the global situation. Activities encourage children to pose questions about the environment and offer solutions.

Baker, D., C. Semple, & T. Stead. 1990. *How big is the moon? Whole math in action.* Portsmouth, NH: Heinemann.

Based on natural learning theories, this book for elementary teachers aims to integrate math into the broader curriculum through the exploration of facts, skills, and concepts in relevant and meaningful contexts. Encourages creation of a collaborative learning environment and provides innovative evaluation methods that depart from traditional means of testing.

Baratta-Lorton, M. 1995. *Mathematics their way (20th anniversary edition).* Saratoga, CA: Center for Innovation in Education.

Provides a complete range of activities essential for kindergarten and primary-grade students' development of mathematical understanding. The author includes a rationale that assists teachers in incorporating activities in a meaningful way. Beyond the Book includes actual projects from K–4 teachers who have successfully applied the Mathematics their Way philosophy.

Baron, J., & H.P. Ginsburg. 1993. Cognition: Young children's construction of mathematics. In *Research ideas for the classroom: Early childhood mathematics*, ed. R.J. Jenson, 3–21. Reston, VA: National Council for Teachers of Mathematics.

Provides a review of research on young children's construction of mathematics. Authors indicate that children as young as 2 or 3 years old understand such abstract concepts as addition and subtraction if presented in concrete situations.

Baroody, A.J. 1987. *Children's mathematical thinking: A developmental framework for preschool, primary, and special education.* New York: Teachers College Press.

Part 1 provides a framework, including a research-based rationale, for meaningful math instruction, plus examples of children's surprising informal knowledge, key points for designing a developmentally appropriate curriculum, a rationale for going beyond standard tests, and practical advice for overcoming math anxiety. Part 2 discusses research on children's informal knowledge of counting, number, and arithmetic, and Part 3, what research reveals about formal, school-taught mathematics.

Baroody, A.J. 1991. Living mathematics. In *Creating the learning environment: A guide in early childhood education,* ed. D. Strickland, 76–83. Orlando, FL: Harcourt Brace Jovanovich.

Begins by describing 4-year-olds' typical day in relation to the various mathematical concepts used. Presents information about ways teachers and parents can use mathematical games and activities to enhance a young child's basic counting, matching, sorting, and comparison skills.

Baroody, A.J., with R.T. Coslick. 1998. *Fostering children's mathematical power: An investigative approach to K–8 mathematics instruction.* Mahwah, NJ: Erlbaum.

A clear rationale for a purposeful, meaningful, and inquiry-based approach for elementary-level mathematics teaching, plus practical advice for implementing this approach recommended by the National Council of Teachers of Mathematics. General guidelines and specific lesson ideas included.

Barrett, K., E. Blinderman, B. Boffen, J. Ecols, P. House, K. Hosoume, & J. Kopp. 1999. *Science and math explorations for young children.* (GEMS/PEACHES Handbook for Early Childhood Educators, Childcare Providers, and Parents.) Berkeley: University of California–Berkeley.

Developed with early childhood practitioners and the Lawrence Hall of Science, this handbook is framed by the math and science national standards and describes lively, integrated activities for curriculum planning and gives clear explanations about the way exploratory learning develops. Topics include relationships of play, creativity, language, and equity to math and science, and also the role of the parent. Another teacher guide developed by this group, *Mother Opossum and Her Babies,* highlights math strands of logic and language, number measurement and statistics, and concepts of the behavior and life cycle of marsupials in projects piloted in pre-K–1 classrooms.

Bloom, L., L. Burrell, & J.C. Perlmutter. 1993. Whole math through investigations. *Childhood Education* 70 (1): 20–24.

Provides a description of how children in a K–2 combination class learn mathematics in real, sensible, and interesting ways. The similarities to whole-language instruction are described.

Burns, M. 1992. *About teaching mathematics: A K–8 resource.* Sausalito, CA: Marilyn Burns Education Associates.

Demonstrates how to replace traditional math teaching with strategies that focus on children's thinking and reasoning. Presents the case for teaching mathematics through problem solving.

Burns, M. 1998. *Math: Facing an American phobia.* Sausalito, CA: Math Solutions.

Examines why so many people in the United States are fearful of—and actively avoid—mathematics. Captivating in both its message and tone, this book describes ways in which traditional math programs have failed and how teachers and parents can reverse this trend. Invites the reader to thoughtfully entertain ideas about what children truly need to become skilled, confident, and prepared for the math needs of today's world.

Carpenter, T.P., E. Fennema, M.L. Franke, L. Levi, & S.B. Empson. 1999. *Children's mathematics: Cognitively guided instruction.* Portsmouth, NH: Heinemann.

Explains how numerical understanding develops throughout the 4- to 8-year-olds period, with examples of teachers connecting with children's intuitive math thinking. Includes two CDs showing primary teachers in classrooms leading math discussions and implementing the recommended strategies. A workshop leader's kit and guide are also available.

Charlesworth, R. 1997. Mathematics in the developmentally appropriate curriculum. *Integrated curriculum and developmentally appropriate practice birth to age eight,* eds. C.H. Hart, D.C. Burts, & R. Charlesworth, 51–73. Albany: State University of New York Press.

Opens with a brief description of the current view of mathematics for young children as defined by the NAEYC and the National Council of Teachers of Mathematics. Includes an explanation of the theoretical foundations of mathematics education and information on how the classroom and curriculum can be organized for developmentally appropriate, integrated mathematics instruction.

Charlesworth, R. 2000. *Experiences in math for young children.* 4th ed. New York: Delmar.

Based on theories of child development and learning, this book is compatible with NAEYC guidelines and those of the National Council of Teachers of Mathematics. Stresses developmentally appropriate curriculum as well as language and literature.

Contestable, J., S. Regan, & L. Robertson. 1999. *Number power: A cooperative approach to mathematics and social development, Kindergarten.* Oakland, CA: Developmental Studies Center.

Designed to engage children in cooperatively exploring addition and subtraction, number relationships, grouping, and counting, with a focus on using mathematical reasoning to develop number sense. Experiences include partner work, class discussion, role play, sample charts, suggested manipulatives, and teacher facilitation and performance assessment techniques.

Contestable, J., C. Westrich, S. Regan, S. Alldredge, & L. Robertson. 1999. *Number power: A cooperative approach to mathematics and social development, grade two, Vols. 1 & 2.* Oakland, CA: Developmental Studies Center.

Units in each volume include an overview of the math concepts, suggestions for implementation, a team-building lesson, conceptual lesson, and a transition lesson. Volume 1 addresses grouping, place value, and informal computation. Volume 2 covers informal computation and number relationships. (First- and third-grade volumes are also 1999, by L. Robertson and others.)

Corwin, R.B., with J. Storeygard & S. Price. 1996. *Talking mathematics: Supporting children's voices.* Portsmouth, NH: Heinemann.

Based on a project exploring how teachers can support children's communication of their math ideas such as invented strategies, this book provides both the rationale for having math, with discussions from Eleanor Duckworth, David Hawkin, and Vivian Paley, as well as practical suggestions for primary-classroom implementation from teachers. (See "Videorecordings/Teaching and Curriculum for Preschool and Primary" for an accompanying video by the same title.)

Dacey, L.S., & R. Eston. 1999. *Growing mathematical ideas in kindergarten.* Sausalito, CA: Math Solutions.

The authors present their vision of a kindergarten classroom that nurtures the growth of all students' mathematical understanding. They provide specific guidelines for how to create a thoughtful classroom environment, including planning for a full year of teaching and learning mathematics, choosing mathematical tasks, and assessing for understanding.

Developmental Studies Center. 2000. *Homeside math.* Oakland, CA: Author.

Supports parent involvement in mathematics through a series of activities introduced in kindergarten and first grade classrooms and sent home for children and a home partner to do together. Activities are designed to foster discussion and exploration between children and their families in the areas of number, geometry, and measurement, and to culminate in a class discussion or project.

Edwards, D. 1990. *Maths in context: A thematic approach.* Portsmouth, NH: Heinemann.

Designed to help teachers develop a mathematics program based on real-life situations. Explains how to encourage children to think divergently and creatively in the mathematics classroom.

Ervin, C., S. Travis, & N.N. Vacc. 1995. Beyond the classroom. *Teaching Children Mathematics* 1: 494–97.

Uses a trip to the zoo to provide problem-solving opportunities for first-through fifth-graders. Incorporates measurement and pattern activities as well as collaboration.

Ginsburg, H.P., S.F. Jacobs, & L.S. Lopez. 1989. *The teacher's guide to flexible interviewing in the classroom: Learning what children know about math.* Boston: Allyn & Bacon.

Designed to help primary-grade teachers understand and use flexible interviewing to uncover children's thinking about math and other subjects. The methods described were developed and tested by classroom teachers.

Headington, R. 1997. *Supporting numeracy.* London, England: David Fulton.

Provides explanations of mathematics in the early years and puts them into action through practical activities. The author aims to reduce the fear factor of mathematics and increase the confidence of those who assist in early childhood settings by providing knowledge of mathematic learning, language, and equipment.

Hiebert, J., T.P. Carpenter, E. Fennema, K.C. Fuson, D.Wearne, H. Murray, A. Olivier, & P. Human. 1997. *Making sense: Teaching and learning mathematics with understanding.* Portsmouth, NH: Heinemann.

An exploration of different approaches to teaching math with primary-school children in the United States and South Africa that led to a set of essential features characterizing classrooms in which all children are making sense of mathematics. Sections address the nature of tasks, mathematical tools, and the teacher's roles such as orchestrating mathematical discussions.

Hohmann, C. 1991. *Mathematics.* Ypsilanti, MI: High/Scope.

Discusses how math relates to children's stages of thinking and the adult's role. Presents High/Scope's key experiences for math.

Jensen, R.J. 1992. *Research ideas for the classroom: Early childhood mathematics.* Reston, VA: National Council of Teachers of Mathematics.

Explores the issues of how children learn and how to implement effective arithmetic instruction in the primary grades. In addition to containing information about analyzing, synthesizing, and interpreting mathematics research, this book gives a wide variety of practical ideas in an accessible format.

Kamii, C., with L.L. Joseph. 1989. *Young children continue to reinvent arithmetic, 2nd grade: Implications of Piaget's theory.* New York: Teachers College Press.

Describes a constructivist process of learning in which children are encouraged to do their own thinking about math problems and approaches for supporting children's natural ways of thinking about number from the teacher's perspective.

Kamii, C, with S.J. Livingston. 1994. *Young children continue to reinvent arithmetic, 3rd grade: Implications of Piaget's theory.* New York: Teachers College Press.

Describes a program that encourages children to use math in real ways that stimulate them to reinvent arithmetic. Includes an evaluation of teaching practices consistent with constructivist theory and documents how children with three years in constructivist classrooms were able to reason better than children who had more traditional instruction.

Mills, H., T. O'Keefe, & D. Whitin. 1996. *Mathematics in the making: Authoring ideas in primary classrooms.* Portsmouth, NH: Heinemann.

Demonstrates how you can help children become respected authors of their own ideas by emphasizing mathematics as a way of thinking. A range of math experiences shows teachers how to help children become empowered, mathematical thinkers through such activities as yearlong investigations and establishing certain math rituals. Ideas for working with parents and meeting district goals are included.

Moomaw, S., & B. Hieronymus. 1999. *Much more than counting: More math activities for preschool and kindergarten.* St. Paul, MN: Redleaf.

Through photographs and text, shows how teachers can increase children's participation in mathematical thinking by imbedding opportunities for mathematical reasoning in their plans for each activity area of the classroom. Following a section describing how math concepts develop and can be nurtured, are suggested activities. They include the math concepts, children's potential age-level responses and comments, and questions to extend children's thinking.

Moon, J. 1997. *Developing judgment: Assessing children's work in math.* Portsmouth, NH: Heinemann.

Reports on the findings of a group of elementary teachers who discussed children's mathematical work in relation to alternative assessments. Describes the process of developing professional judgement by improving teachers' abilities to analyze student work according to performance indicators and by practicing the art of making judgements in collaboration with colleagues.

Moon, J., & L. Schulman. 1995. *Finding the connections: Linking assessment, instruction, and curriculum in elementary mathematics.* Portsmouth, NH: Heinemann.

Using performance-based techniques, the authors provide a model for integrating assessment and guided opportunities for teachers' practice in developing their own documentation and creating process folios.

Neugebauer, B., & D.P. Wolf. 1996. *More than numbers: Mathematical thinking in the early years.* Redmond, WA: Exchange Press.

Offers methods and strategies for presenting mathematics to young children as a way of thinking through practical, hands-on, real-world experiences.

O'Connell, S.R. 1995. Newspapers: Connecting the mathematics classroom to the world. *Teaching Children Mathematics* 1: 268–74.

Discusses ways in which newspapers provide opportunities to apply mathematics, such as product costs in advertisements, weather data, and sports' statistics. Newspaper activities can also provide practice in reading, thinking, discussing, writing, and applying mathematical skills and concepts.

Overholt, J., J. White-Holtz, & S. Dickson. 1999. *Big math activities for young children.* Albany, NY: Delmar.

Provides a wide selection of activities and investigations for young children. Multilevel activities provide increasingly advanced skills for preschool through third grade and have been designed to promote mathematical reasoning, communications and problem-solving skills.

Payne, J., ed. 1990. *Mathematics for the young child.* Reston, VA: National Council of Teachers of Mathematics.

Helps teachers make important decisions about the mathematics curriculum and provides effective ways to help children attain the mathematical power needed both for everyday use and future careers in the twenty-first century.

Richardson, K., & L. Salked. 1995. Transforming mathematics curriculum. *Reaching potentials: Transforming early childhood curriculum and assessment, volume 2*, eds. S. Bredekamp & T. Rosegrant, 23–42. Washington, DC: NAEYC.

Presents the National Council of Teachers of Mathematics standards and information about how to apply the NAEYC framework of teaching in developmentally appropriate ways to these standards. Discusses the link between symbols and the concepts the standards represent, the teacher's role in engaging children in mathematical tasks and in assessing growth in the learning of mathematics, the age at which it is best to teach various mathematical concepts, and how to plan developmentally appropriate mathematics experiences.

Rowan, T.E., & B. Bourne. 1994. *Thinking like mathematicians: Putting the K–4 NCTM Standards into practice*. Portsmouth, NH: Heinemann.

Applies the NCTM *Standards* to integrated curriculum and assessment in the early grades, stressing mathematics as thinking, not just correct answers. Through graphics and vignettes, many suggestions are given for involving children in building on their prior knowledge, exploring mathematical concepts and experiences, and documenting their discoveries through concrete materials and representation.

Schifter, D. 1996. *What's happening in math class: Envisioning new practices through teacher narratives, volume 1*. New York: Teachers College Press.

Teachers' stories of teaching mathematics in ways that are based on how children learn. Offers readers opportunities to see and hear what happens in developmentally appropriate elementary classrooms.

Shaw, J., & S. Blake. 1998. *Mathematics for young children*. Upper Saddle River, NJ: Merrill/Prentice Hall.

Provides an overview of math teaching and developmental expectations for children in K–4 settings. Teaching strategies include consideration of equity issues, parent involvement, and a wide variety of authentic assessment tools of mathematical ability. Covers specific math content and includes materials, activities, classroom vignettes, adaptations for advanced learners, and a list of suppliers of math materials.

Skinner, P. 1991. *What's your problem?* Portsmouth, NH: Heinemann.

Details a mathematics program for kindergarten and primary-grade children that begins with a modeling of teacher-written story problems and progresses to dictated and child-written problems. Each story problem is written, illustrated, and presented in book style.

Smith, S.S. 1997. *Early childhood mathematics.* Needham Heights, MA: Allyn & Bacon.

Covers the early math concepts of matching, classification, comparing, ordering, patterning, graphing, and other math relationships and problem solving in the preschool years. Teacher techniques are reported for building math into thematic units, assessing children's learning, and identifying software resources.

Stolberg, J., & E. Daniels. 1998. *Creating child-centered materials for math and science.* Washington, DC: Children's Resources International.

Demonstrates the use of inexpensive or free household or outdoor materials that can be used to support math and science activities for preschool children. Explanations of the math and science concepts accompany each activity as well as follow-up activities that link the child's family to classroom learning experiences.

Teaching Committee of the Mathematical Association (United Kingdom). 1987. *Math talk.* Portsmouth, NH: Heinemann.

Members of the committee created this book to demonstrate that the skills of spoken language are as important in mathematics as they are in other areas of the curriculum. They prove that learning mathematics is not just a case of mastering concepts and applying rules but of using the same abilities children employ in developing language skill.

Thiessen, D., & M. Matthias. 1992. *The wonderful world of mathematics: A critically annotated list of children's books in mathematics.* Reston, VA: National Council of Teachers of Mathematics.

Reviews each book's content and accuracy, illustrations and their appropriateness, the author's writing style, and the included activities. Each book is rated for its usefulness in teaching mathematical concepts.

Thompson, I., ed. 1997. *Teaching and learning early number.* Philadelphia: Open University Press.

Citing recent research into how mathematical knowledge develops, the authors suggest an alternative approach to the way number concepts are usually introduced to young children. Practical activities and current thinking are included on such topics as preschool children's beliefs and abilities in counting and the role of counting and children's informal knowledge in number development.

Trafton, P.R., & D. Thiessen. 1999. *Learning through problems: Number sense and computational strategies. A resource for primary teachers.* Portsmouth, NH: Heinemann.

Weaves the strands of math (addition, subtraction, place value, and problem solving) together into a teaching plan that demonstrates how to launch a new year, deal with basic facts, use hundreds of charts and base-ten blocks, and develop standard algorithms. Each page has sample problems, photos of children that demonstrate materials and working arrangements, or teacher reflections that complement the author's guidance in developing both invented and familiar computational approaches.

Wakefield, A. 1997. Supporting math thinking. In *Annual editions: Early childhood education, 1999/2000, 20th edition,* eds. K. Panciorek & J. Munro. Guilford, CT: Dushkin/McGraw-Hill.

Discusses how opportunities for constructing mathematics knowledge through problem-solving activities allow children to devlop a better grasp of the concepts to be learned. The author demonstrates how to make problem-solving activities in math education available through the use of manipulatives and games.

Wakefield, A. 1998. *Early childhood number games: Teachers reinvent math instruction, pre-K through 3rd grade.* Boston: Allyn & Bacon.

Shows how playing math games not only enables young children to develop their own natural abilities to think but also encourages interaction that is necessary for the development of logical-mathematical thinking.

Whitin, D.J., H.T. Mills, & T. O'Keefe. 1990. *Living and learning mathematics.* Portsmouth, NH: Heinemann.

Brings readers into the world of the 6-year-old and shows the kinds of strategies young children are capable of devising when they solve mathematical problems. Shows children helping to shape the mathematical curriculum according to their own interests, questions, and observations.

Whitin, D.J., & S. Wilde. 1992. *Read any good math lately? Children's books for mathematical learning, K–6.* Portsmouth, NH: Heinemann.

Focuses on the opportunities that children's literature can provide to encourage children to think mathematically. Techniques for fostering math conversations and following children's leads are presented.

Whitin, D.J., & S. Wilde. 1995. *It's the story that counts: More children's books for mathematical learning, K–6.* Portsmouth, NH: Heinemann.

Highlights the voices of children, teachers, and authors, then focuses on the books themselves to show opportunities that children's literature can provide children to think mathematically. Includes techniques for fostering math conversations and following children's leads.

Physical development and movement

Altman, R. 1992. Movement in early childhood. In *Explorations with young children,* eds. A. Mitchell & J. David, 229–40. Beltsville, MD: Gryphon House.

Connects movement to children's learning. Movement activities in the form of practical skills, games, and creative movement, and framed by themes are presented for settings including 2- to 8-year-olds.

Andress, B. 1991. Research in review. From research to practice: Preschool children and their movement responses to music. *Young Children* 47 (1): 22–27.

This research has implications for the manner in which we provide movement experiences that will more effectively help children express the music they hear.

Barlin, A. L. 1979. *Teaching your wings to fly: The nonspecialists guide to movement activities for young* children. Santa Monica, CA: Goodyear.

Presents a program of dance movement activities for teachers of 3- to 12-year-olds with a large selection of music and instruments. Specific techniques communicate how to introduce the activities and support children's natural instincts and imagination.

Barrett, K.R. 1992. What does it mean to have a developmentally appropriate physical education program? *Physical Educator* 49 (3): 114–18.

Addresses three issues regarding developmentally appropriate physical education: what it means; what teachers must know (change occurs in an orderly, sequential fashion and is age and experience related); and how teachers can implement it (be skilled observers of movement and be clear about the purpose of the task).

Block, M. 1994. *A teacher's guide to including students with disabilities in regular physical education.* Baltimore, MD: Brookes.

Two chapters in this practical book are particularly helpful for preschool teachers: one provides ways to adapt activities for specific disabilities, the other discusses how to draw young children with disabilities into active physical participation.

Block, M.E., & T.D. Davis. 1996. An activity-based approach to physical education for preschool children with disabilities. *Adapted Physical Activity Quarterly* 13 (3): 230–46.

The concept of an activity-based intervention model is introduced and examples provided of how the model can be implemented within motor development/physical education contexts for preschool children with disabilities.

Brown, B., & R. Prideaux. 1998. Children with movement learning difficulties. A collaborative initiative with 4- to 5-year-old mainstreamed children and their parents. *British Journal of Physical Education* 19: 186–89.

Describes a collaborative approach among teachers, parents, and support staff for diagnosing, assessing, intervening, monitoring, and reevaluating young children's movement skill. A justification for a physical curriculum within the overall preschool curriculum is described using a developmental model. The link between early movement experiences and their successful integration in playground, classroom, and movement settings are illustrated.

Chenfeld, M.B. 1993. *Teaching in the key of life.* Washington, DC: NAEYC.

Gives examples of the author's own experiences in the classroom and how she uses creative movement to provide an engaging learning environment. She describes many hands-on experiences to emphasize the value of tuning in to what children like.

Cryer, D., T. Harms, & A.R. Ray. 1996. *Active learning for fives.* Menlo Park, CA: Addison Wesley.

Consists of a planning guide and four activity sections: listening and talking, physical development, creativity, and learning about the world. Includes strategies for learning design, implementation, and follow-up.

Engstrom, G., ed. 1971. *The significance of the young child's motor development.* Washington, DC: NAEYC.

Discusses the importance of physical activity in early childhood development. Chapters include information on the significance of motor development, learning to observe and observing to learn, and what movement means to the young child.

Gallahue, D.A. 1995. Transforming physical education curriculum. In *Reaching potentials: Transforming early childhood curriculum and assessment, volume 2,* eds. S. Bredekamp & T. Rosegrant, 125–44. Washington, DC: NAEYC.

Introduces the concept of developmental physical education and offers suggestions on how to incorporate it in the early childhood curriculum. Discusses the categories of movement, how movement skills are learned, and how to plan movement skill themes and program strands and to assess progress.

Gallahue, D.A. 1996. *Developmental physical education for today's children.* 3d ed. Madison, WI: Brown & Benchmark.

Designed for college students taking a first course in children's physical education. It provides a framework to approach the teaching of movement activities to children based on a developmental perspective.

Gerhardt, L.A. 1973. *Moving and knowing: The young child orients himself in space.* Englewood Cliffs, NJ: Prentice Hall.

In addition to developing a conceptual framework built on analysis and synthesis of movement and conceptualization, the book links this framework to teaching and learning through analyses of selected classroom observations of children's seeming development of spatial ideas through their body movement. Describes ways of designing a facilitating curriculum.

Graham, G., ed. 1992. Developmentally appropriate physical education for children. *Journal of Physical Education, Recreation and Dance* 63 (6), 29–60.

Nine articles in this feature discuss persistent physical education practices that are not in the best interest of children, suggesting developmentally appropriate alternatives. Some topics discussed are the sequence of instruction in games, developmentally appropriate dance and gymnastics, social-emotional components, and activities with questionable value.

Graham, G., S.A. Holt/Hale, & M. Parker. 1998. *Children moving: A reflective approach to teaching physical education.* Mountain View, CA: Mayfield.

Designed for teachers wanting to implement a quality elementary physical education program. The book describes the skill-theme approach to teaching physical education and includes information on child development, appropriate instruction, curriculum, and assessment of elementary children in the movement setting.

Grant, J.M. 1995. *Shake, rattle, and learn: Classroom-tested ideas that use movement for active learning.* York, ME: Stenhouse.

Movement based learning activities for pre-K through sixth grade are tied to nine content areas: practicing communication; experiencing stories and poetry; interpreting the environment, human relationships and societal issues; working with visual design and spatial relationships; and investigating rhythm.

Griss, S. 1998. *Minds in motion: A kinesthetic approach to teaching elementary curriculum.* Portsmouth, NH: Heinemann.

Offers support for teachers who have no experience with movement as well as those who already use movement and are looking for new and imaginative ways to transform lessons into creative kinesthetic experiences. Specific examples illustrate how movement makes learning tangible and accessible in subjects like math, language arts, science, and history.

Hammett, C.T. 1992. *Movement activities for early childhood.* Champaign, IL: Human Kinetics.

Includes developmentally appropriate movement activities based on the use of skill themes. Learning tasks are divided into locomotor, ball handling, gymnastics, and rhythmic activities. Lesson plans provide information about the objective, vocabulary, equipment, safety, and organizational procedures in presenting activities to children.

Helion, J.G., & F. Fry. 1995. Modifying activities for developmental appropriateness. *Journal of Physical Education, Recreation, and Dance* 66 (7): 57–59.

Physical educators need to modify activities in ways that will increase each student's chance of successful participation. Examples are provided of how to modify activities to make them more appropriate.

Helm, J.H., & S. Boos. 1996. Increasing the physical educator's impact: Consulting, collaborating, and teacher training in early childhood programs. *Journal of Physical Education, Recreation and Dance* 67 (3): 26–32.

Focuses on an early childhood education center that recognized a need for a structured movement curriculum and invited physical educators to act as consultants. Interactive workshops for teachers provided training in movement principles and skills and information on lesson planning, evaluation, and developmentally appropriate equipment.

Ignicio, A. 1996. Early childhood physical education: Providing the foundation. In *Annual editions: Early childhood education, 17th edition,* eds. K.M. Paciorek & J.H. Munro, 205–07. Guilford, CT: Dushkin/Brown & Benchmark.

Discusses the ways that developmentally appropriate motor skill instruction and the introduction of movement concepts in preschool build a foundation for successful participation in later childhood and adult physical activities.

Johnson, M. 1997. Can marching be developmentally appropriate? *Teaching Elementary Physical Education* 8 (6): 25–26.

Attempts to make the case for use of marching in a developmentally appropriate movement program for children, suggesting that this locomotor skill provides movement and conceptual knowledge activities that can be considered appropriate objectives for children.

Morford, L., ed. 1997. Developmentally appropriate physical education. *Teaching Elementary Physical Education* 8 (2): 3–11, 25–31.

Provides four articles that provide examples of how to apply developmentally appropriate national guidelines to elementary physical education programs. The feature provides a program evaluation checklist to assist teachers in determining the developmental appropriateness of their physical education programs and takes an objective commonsense approach to implementing developmentally appropriate standards.

National Association for Sport and Physical Education (NASPE). 1995. *Developmentally appropriate practice in movement programs for young children ages 3 to 5: A position statement of the NASPE Council on Physical Education for Children.* Reston, VA: American Alliance for Health, Physical Education, Recreation, and Dance.

Defines quality physical education in terms of developmentally and instructionally appropriate practices that recognize children's changing capacities to move, accommodate a variety of individual characteristics, and maximize opportunities for learning and success by all children. A guide for teaching physical education is also available.

National Association for Sport and Physical Education (NASPE). 1998. *Physical activity for children: A statement of guidelines.* A position statement of the National Association for Sport and Physical Education developed by the Council on Physical Education for Children. Reston, VA: American Alliance for Health, Physical Education, Recreation & Dance.

Summaries of the health benefits of regular physical activity and meaningful activity guidelines for all adults dedicated to promoting physically active lifestyles among children.

Olds, A.R., C.S. Kranowitz, R. Porter, & M. Carter. 1994. Building in opportunities for gross motor development. *Child Care Information Exchange* (96): 31–50.

Describes children's needs to move indoors and outdoors and instructs teachers on how to adapt experiences for children's differing abilities. Focuses on children from infancy through age 5.

Payne, G., & J.E. Rink. 1997. Physical education in the developmentally appropriate integrated curriculum. In *Integrated curriculum and developmentally appropriate practice: Birth through age eight,* eds. C.H. Hart, D.C. Burts, & R. Charlesworth, 145–70. Albany: State University of New York Press.

Describes the importance of creating high-quality physical education programs specifically designed for young children. Includes the National Association for Sport and Physical Education's definition of a physically fit person as well as the organization's national standards for physical education.

Pica, R. 1997. Beyond physical development: Why young children need to move. *Young Children* 52 (6): 4–11.

Explores how movement promotes development in the following areas: social/emotional, creative, and cognitive. Discusses how movement promotes development in areas of the mind as well as the body.

Pica, R. 1999. *Moving and learning across the curriculum.* New York: Delmar.

Includes activities designed to make movement part of the early childhood curriculum by integrating movement with art, language arts, mathematics, music, science, and social studies.

Pica, R. 2000. *Experiences in movement with music, activities, and theory.* 2d ed. New York: Delmar.

Provides knowledge for all that would like to understand and utilize movement curriculum in early childhood education. Includes information on the benefits of movement, lesson planning, creating and maintaining a positive learning environment, and bringing movement education outdoors.

Poest, C.A., J.R. Williams, D.D. Witt, & M.E. Atwood. 1990. Challenge me to move: Large muscle development in young children. *Young Children* 45 (5): 4–10.

A well-defined program for large-muscle development (or motor development). Addresses three major categories: fundamental movement skills, physical fitness, and perceptual motor development.

Pugmire-Stoy, M.C. 1991. *Spontaneous play in early childhood.* Albany, NY: Delmar.

Emphasizes the setting up of environments in which children can express themselves through movement. The primary focus is that children should be encouraged to explore and solve problems while the teacher nurtures this process.

Rodger, L. 1996. Adding movement throughout the day. *Young Children* 51 (3): 4–6.

Explains how movement can be added to the classroom throughout the day and how it can enhance learning.

Sanders, S. 1993. Developmentally appropriate movement practices for 3- to 5-year-olds. *Teaching Elementary Physical Education* 4 (5): 1,7,11,16.

Written after the 1992 developmentally appropriate physical education practices document was published and makes the case that this document does not go far enough in outlining appropriate practice for preschool children. Presents some examples of components for an early childhood document, with the intent of soliciting national debate and discussion during the time the paper "Developmentally Appropriate Practice in Movement Programs for Young Children Ages 3–5" was being developed.

Sanders, S. 1994. Preschool physical education: Challenges for the profession. *Journal of Physical Education, Recreation and Dance* 65 (6): 25–56.

Eight articles in this feature discuss developmentally appropriate practices in movement programs for young children. Some topics discussed are skill themes and movement concepts as a curricular foundation, playgrounds, class organization, integrated learning, and providing movement experiences for preschool children with disabilities. Also included is an article on the role of teacher preparation in providing developmentally appropriate movement experiences for young children.

Sanders, S., & B. Yongue. 1998. Challenging movement experiences for young children. *Dimensions of Early Childhood* 26 (1): 9–18.

Provides a review of developmentally appropriate practices related to child development, teaching strategies, curriculum, and assessment in early childhood movement programs. The authors provide background information for teachers in selecting appropriate teaching strategies, curriculum, and assessment tools.

Stinson, W.J., ed. 1990. *Moving and learning for the young child.* Reston, VA: American Alliance for Health, Physical Education, Recreation, and Dance.

Contains presentations from an early childhood conference in Washington, D.C., on "Forging the Linkage between Moving and Learning for Preschool Children." Presentations highlighted the integration of children's affective, motor, and cognitive development through movement experiences focused on the process of learning to move and moving to learn.

Stinson, W.J., H.H. Mehrof, & S. Thies. 1993. *Quality daily thematic lesson plans for classroom teachers: Movement activities for pre-K and kindergarten.* Dubuque, IA: Kendall Hunt.

The authors present ideas for the development of themes in the classroom and movement setting. Collaborative themes created by the classroom teacher and movement specialist are included.

Torbert, M., & L.B. Schneider. 1993. *Follow me too*. Reading, MA: Addison-Wesley.

Includes research as background support for using movement games in early childhood settings. A perceptual motor chart indicating the skills involved in suggested activities, suggestions for parent involvement, and directions for making inexpensive equipment are also given.

Werner, P., S. Timms, & L. Almond. 1996. Health stops: Practical ideas for health-related exercise in preschool and primary classrooms. *Young Children* 51 (6): 48–55.

Argues that educators of young children need to prioritize exercise in their students' lives to enhance physical and psychological health. Guides teachers in creating developmentally appropriate exercise, creative movement activities, movement, and make-believe activities.

Wessel, J.A., & B.V. Holland. 1992. The right stuff: Developmentally appropriate physical education for early childhood. *ERIC Digest*. ED348784. Urbana-Champaign, IL: ERIC Clearinghouse on Early Childhood Education.

Focuses on physical education for students in preschool (3 to 5 years old) and primary grades K–2 (5 to 7 years old). Describes developmentally appropriate practices as a set of indicators for high-quality play and motor skills programs for all children, including children with special needs. Also describes and recommends an outcome-driven decisionmaking model to integrate the identified quality program indicators for making instructional and curricular decisions to serve all children.

Yongue, B., & K. Kelly. 1997. Developmentally appropriate use of equipment. *Teaching Elementary Physical Education* 8 (5): 13.

Provides a few examples of the types of equipment that should be provided for children in a developmentally appropriate movement program.

Science

American Association for the Advancement of Science. 1993. *Benchmarks for science literacy*. New York: Oxford University Press.

Guidelines for the science children should know and be able to do by the end of specific grade levels. This volume (software version also available) contains goals and content standards teachers can use in organizing their science curriculum and outlines ways of achieving them.

Atkinson, S., & M. Fleer, eds. 1995. *Science with reason*. Portsmouth, NH: Heinemann.

In suggested approaches to teaching and learning science, collected authors highlight the role of children's intuitive ideas and offer techniques for enhancing and building upon children's often unanticipated spontaneous responses. Unique content areas and science projects are included.

Barrett, K., E. Blinderman, B. Boffen, J. Ecols, P. House, K. Hosoume, & J. Kopp. 1999. *Science and math explorations for young children.* (GEMS/PEACHES Handbook for Early Childhood Educators, Childcare Providers, and Parents.) Berkeley: University of California–Berkeley.

Developed with early childhood practitioners and the Lawrence Hall of Science, this handbook is framed by the math and science national standards and describes lively, integrated activities for curriculum planning and clear explanations about the way exploratory learning develops. Topics include the relationships of play, creativity, language, and equity to math and science and the role of the parent. Another teacher guide developed by this group, *Mother Opossum and Her Babies,* highlights math strands of logic and language, number measurement and statistics, and concepts of the behavior and life cycle of marsupials in projects piloted in pre-K–1 classrooms.

Bell, E., D. Gee, & M. Mathews. 1995. Science learning with a multicultural emphasis. *Science and Children* 32 (6): 20–23, 54.

The authors use Wasserman's and Ivany's play-debrief-replay technique to integrate science and multicultural literature in kindergarten and primary grades.

Burnett, R. 1992. *The pillbug project: A guide to investigation.* Arlington, VA: National Science Teachers Association.

An inquiry project on docile pill bugs demonstrates how to do investigations of natural habitats with primary-school children, including using cooperative learning and a variety of assessment techniques.

Carroll, K. 1999. *Sing a song of science.* Tucson, AZ: Zephyr.

This book-audiocassette set contains student-tested methods designed to help teachers synthesize a hands-on approach to science. Contains information about how to use stories, songs and raps, visualization, mind mapping, and kinesthetic learning to enhance the science curriculum.

Chaillé, C., & L. Britain. 1997. *Young child as scientist: A constructivist approach to early childhood science education.* Boulder, CO: HarperCollins.

Describes children as theory builders learning to predict their world and provides a picture of real science curriculum in preschool classrooms.

Cornell, J. 1998. *Sharing nature with children.* 2d ed. Nevada City, CA: Dawn Publications.

Describes how teachers can engage children in appreciating natural objects and events. The nature walks and games are indexed by age (beginning with 3-year-olds), according to the concepts and attitudes they engender in children and the environments in which they can best be used.

Doris, E. 1991. *Doing what scientists do: Children learn to investigate their world.* Portsmouth, NH: Heinemann.

Contains practical, commonsense guidelines that even science-phobic elementary teachers can implement in their classrooms. Examples are given of classroom dialogue and illustrations of children's work.

Duckworth, E. 1996. *The having of wonderful ideas and other essays on teaching and learning.* New York: Teachers College Press.

In this revised second edition of her indispensable classic on Piaget and teaching, renowned educator and scholar Eleanor Duckworth provides a new introduction to her wide-ranging writings and adds a chapter on children's approaches to science.

Fleer, M. 1991. *Why won't my torch work? Physics for 4 to 8 year olds.* Australian Early Childhood Resource Booklets, no. 1. Watson, ACT: Australian Early Childhood Association.

Illustrates the topic of electricity and provides an example in easily read format of how science education can be fostered in early childhood using an interactive approach. Activities, materials that can be constructed and teaching techniques necessary to investigate circuitry are covered.

Fleer, M., & C. Leslie. 1992. *The light side of darkness: Helping children understand the concept of light and colour.* Australian Early Childhood Resource Booklets, no. 4. Watson, ACT: Australian Early Childhood Association.

The second in a series designed to show how physics topics can be introduced to preschool children. Booklet provides basic information about light, including simple nonfiction and fiction books for young children. A four-step teaching sequence is described.

Gallas, K. 1995. *Talking their way into science: Hearing children's questions and theories, Responding with curricula.* New York: Teachers College Press.

Presents strategies of a first-grade teacher for helping children bring their personal ideas about science into classroom discussions. The author discusses the nature of science for young children and the role of science talks in the curriculum, with concrete examples from the classroom.

George, Y.S., S.M. Malcom, V.L. Worthington, & A.B. Daniel, eds. 1995. *In touch with preschool science.* Washington, DC: American Association for the Advancement of Science.

Includes information on starting a preschool science program and a wide selection of activities for young children and their families. In Spanish and English.

Hall, J.S., with C. Callahan, P. O'Brien, H. Kitchel, & P. Pierce. 1998. *Organizing wonder: Making inquiry science work in the elementary school.* Portsmouth, NH: Heinemann.

Offers lots of suggestions about initiating an inquiry-based science program in elementary classrooms. The book includes case studies and strategies for guiding and supporting children in their investigations. Samples of children's work are included to show how students reflect on and record their learning. A teaching approach that is aligned with the concepts and strategies outlined in the national science standards.

Harlan, J.C., & M.S. Rivkin. 2000. *Science experiences for the early childhood years: An integrated approach.* 7th ed. Columbus, OH: Merrill/Prentice Hall.

Focuses on weaving science experiences throughout the curriculum in a way that reduces fragmentation and creates harmonious teaching as well as learning for children. The authors acknowledge the socioemotional underpinnings of cognitive learning when planning activities and emphasize the teacher's sensitive role. A section tells how to transform schoolyards into natural settings for children's exploration of the environment.

Harlen, W., & S. Jelly. 1990. *Developing science in the primary classroom.* Portsmouth, NH: Heinemann.

Designed for teachers who may lack confidence for teaching science; presents ways to start, structure, and manage classroom activities on any topic, giving attention to concepts and content as well as process skills.

Holt, B-G. 1989. *Science with young children.* Rev. ed. Washington, DC: NAEYC

Designed for preschool teachers, this guide explains how to tune into children and plan science experiences as well to create an environment that respects children's special qualities.

Howe, A.C., & L. Jones. 1998. *Engaging children in science.* 2d ed. Columbus, OH: Merrill/Prentice Hall.

Describes how children learn science and explains how certain teaching strategies in primary-school classrooms capitalize on the way children learn best. Different planning methods, sample unit plans, and a case study are included.

Kellough, R. 1996. *Integrating mathematics and science for kindergarten and primary children.* Columbus, OH: Merrill/Prentice Hall.

Introduces the appropriate math and science content according to national standards and then emphasizes the rationale and methods of integrating the curriculum. Examines Science/Technology/Society (STS)—one of the most promising approaches to curriculum integration—as the primary theme for a K–4 curriculum design. Includes activities that encourage interaction and collaboration.

Kilmer, S.J., & H. Hofman. 1995. Transforming science curriculum. In *Reaching potentials: Transforming early childhood curriculum and assessment, volume 2,* eds. S. Bredekamp & T. Rosegrant, 43–64. Washington DC: NAEYC.

Discusses developmentally appropriate "sciencing" goals for early childhood. Provides information about facilitating sciencing; assessing sciencing attitudes, skills, and knowledge; and gaining an overview of developmentally appropriate sciencing.

Kokoski, T.M., & M.M. Patton. 1996. How good is your early childhood science, mathematics, and technology program? Strategies for expanding your curriculum. *Young Children* 51 (5): 38–44.

Guidelines for evaluating the strength of science, mathematics, and technology curricula. The authors include examples of integration with other content areas, places to take the curriculum outside of the classroom, and connections with parents.

Lind, K. 1997. *Science in the developmentally appropriate integrated curriculum. Integrated curriculum and developmentally appropriate practice birth to age 8.* Albany: State University of New York Press.

Describes how the early childhood science curriculum can be built on constructivist and developmental foundations. Provides an overview of the current view of teaching and learning science in the early years, with an emphasis on the importance of selecting science content that matches the cognitive capacities of children at different stages of their development.

Lind, K. 2000. *Exploring science in early childhood: A developmental approach.* 3d ed. Albany, NY: Delmar.

Covers how young children develop concepts about science; units and activities for planning science curricula for preschool and primary classrooms.

National Science Resources Center, National Academy of Sciences, & Smithsonian Institution. 1996. *Resources for teaching elementary school science.* Washington, DC: National Academy Press.

Annotated bibliography containing information about hands-on, inquiry-centered curriculum materials and sources of help for teaching science from kindergarten to sixth grade. Information is grouped by scientific area and type of material. Also includes a listing by region of science centers, museums, and zoos.

National Science Teachers Association. 1997. *Pathways to the science standards: Guidelines for moving the vision into practice, elementary school edition.* Arlington, VA: Author.

Practical guidebook has specific recommendations and examples that guide teachers in implementing each of the science standards in the real world of the classroom.

Neugebauer, B., ed. 1996. *The wonder of it: Exploring how the world works.* Redmond, WA: Exchange Press.

Offers methods and strategies for teaching and conveying the excitement of scientific pursuit to young children. Articles speak to supporting children's curiosity, teaching them to ask good questions, stimulating their thinking, and sharing their joy of discovery.

Olien, R. 1998. *Walk this way: Classroom hikes to learning.* Portsmouth, NH: Heinemann.

Tells how to plan an outdoor education program for K–3 children to enrich projects on ecological concepts and an aesthetic appreciation of the environment and to complement the math and science learning in the classroom. Strategies for conducting minihikes in the community surrounding the school (both urban and rural) encompass topics such as questioning techniques and keeping nature notebooks.

Pearce, C.R. 1999. *Nurturing inquiry: Real science for the elementary classroom.* Portsmouth, NH: Heinemann.

Takes the reader into author's science inquiry classroom to view students investigating and discovering, based on their own questions, and learn about the choices and values that shape a climate of inquiry. Content addresses how to prepare the classroom, the children, and the teacher for introducing inquiry, to sustain interest throughout the school year, and to assess inquiry through surveys, checklists, and dialogue journals.

Saul, W., & J. Reardon, eds. 1996. *Beyond the science kit.* Portsmouth, NH: Heinemann.

Demonstrates the potential of science inquiry in the classroom by having teachers and children become the producers as well as the consumers of scientific knowledge. Primary-school teachers propose a frame of reference to guide classroom science experiences.

Sprung, B., M. Froschl, & P.B. Campbell. 1985. *What will happen if...: Young children and the scientific method.* New York: Educational Equity Concepts.

Shows how science can revitalize play, expand thinking, and encourage children to investigate their world in new ways. The activities, which include experiments designed to explore concepts such as flow, density and viscosity, and momentum focus on the physical sciences and emphasize visual-spatial, problem-solving, and creative thinking abilities.

Stolberg, J., & E. Daniels. 1998. *Creating child-centered materials for math and science.* Washington, DC: Children's Resources International.

Demonstrates use of inexpensive or free household or outdoor materials that can be used to support math and science activities for preschool children. Explanations of the math and science concepts accompany each activity as well as follow-up activities that link the child's family to classroom learning experiences.

Wassermann, S., & J.W.G. Ivany. 1996. *Teaching elementary science: Who's afraid of spiders?* 2d ed. New York: Teacher's College Press.

Features a model of inquiry-based teaching—play-debrief-replay—that incorporates elements of investigative play with critical thinking skills. Includes activities and suggestions for leading reflective discussions.

Wilson, R.A. 1996. Starting early: Environmental education during the early childhood years. *ERIC Digest.* ED402147. Columbus, OH: ERIC Clearinghouse for Science, Mathematics, and Environmental Education.

Presents the argument that environmental education based on life experiences should begin during the earliest years of life, such experiences playing a critical role in shaping lifelong attitudes, values, and patterns of behavior toward natural environments. Guidelines are given for appropriate experiences.

Periodicals—Offering teaching strategies and science activities for ages 3 through 8.

Science and Children. Arlington, VA: National Science Teachers Association.

Magazine contains articles for teaching kindergarten through sixth grade, including science activities, teaching techniques, reviews of software resources, and topic-related resources. *Dragonfly* magazine focuses on science activities for preschool.

Ranger Rick and *Zoobooks.* Washington, DC: National Wildlife Federation.

Resources help children learn about animals and their habitats and provide activities and content information for teachers of young children. Another resource, *Your Big Backyard,* focuses on protecting the environment and offers ideas for prekindergarten, kindergarten, and first-grade teachers on outdoor activities, setting up a science corner in the classroom, and developing nature crafts.

Social studies

Billman, J. 1992. The Native American curriculum: Attempting alternatives to tepees and headbands. *Young Children* 47 (6): 22–25.

Highlights the need for child development specialists and Native Americans to work together to help early childhood professionals provide a more accurate portrayal of Native American cultures.

Bisson, J. 1997. *Celebrate! An anti-bias guide to enjoying holidays in early childhood programs.* St. Paul, MN: Redleaf.

Provides strategies for implementing culturally and developmentally appropriate holiday activities. Information is included on developing a holiday policy, selecting holidays, and evaluating holiday activities.

Cordeiro, P., ed. 1995. *Endless possibilities: Generating curriculum in social studies and literacy.* Portsmouth, NH: Heinemann.

Defines what it means to generate a curriculum that reflects the developmental strengths of children it affects. Documents with many practical ideas the progress of a social studies curriculum through four primary-school classrooms, one third/fourth- grade multiage environment, and two fifth-grade classrooms.

Dimidjian, V.J. 1989. Holidays, holy days, and wholly dazed: Approaches to special days. *Young Children* 44 (6): 70–75.

This article clarifies the value of holidays in the preschool and elementary-school curriculum based on children's needs, traditions, and values.

Feeney, S., & E. Moravik. 1995. *Discovering me and my world.* Circle Pines, MN: American Guidance Service.

Provides an integrated curriculum for four-, five-, and six-year-olds, based on a framework that weaves together the social sciences and social-emotional themes of children's lives. Includes four books of activities: Self,

Family, Community, and Environment, with extensive bibliographies of multicultural children's literature in each.

Fredericks, A., A. Meinbach, & L. Rothlein. 1993. *Thematic units: An integrated approach to teaching science and social studies.* New York: Delmar.

Provides approaches to integrate literature and language arts with teaching science and social studies in the primary grades.

Graves, D. 1999. *Bring life into learning: Create a lasting literacy.* Portsmouth, NH: Heinemann.

History, art, science—indeed all disciplines are created by people. The author shows us how to explore and develop curriculum through a focus on and study of people. In doing so, he maintains that we discover and understand the world through the lives of those who had a role in shaping and creating it.

Haas, M., & M. Laughlin. 1997. *Meeting the standards: Social studies readings for K–6 educators.* Washington, DC: National Council for the Social Studies.

A collection of carefully selected articles on the best of developmentally appropriate social studies issues. Useful in the implementation of national social studies standards.

Hansen, K.A., R.K. Kaufmann, & S. Saifer. 1997. *Education and the culture of democracy: Early childhood practice.* Washington, DC: Children's Resources International.

Contends that there are subtle yet effective techniques that encourage choice, creativity, equality, and appreciation of individual needs while keeping group needs in focus. Describes an educational initiative that introduced developmentally appropriate teaching and the connections to democracy well-established early childhood programs in Eastern and Central Europe.

Hinitz, B. 1992. *Teaching social studies to the young child: A research and resource guide.* New York: Garland.

Provides references to resources and research in the field of early childhood social studies education. With essays and annotations on selected areas of early childhood social studies education and chapters about geography, economics, and history for young children. Also highlights teacher education texts in the fields of early childhood and elementary-school social studies and student texts and teacher manuals for kindergarten to grade 3.

Hopkins, S., & J. Winters. 1990. *Discover the world: Empowering children to value themselves, others, and the earth.* Gabriola Island, B.C., Canada: New Society.

Provides a holistic framework for integrating personal, social, and environmental responsibility into the developmental experience of children from ages 3 through 12. Activities are organized to encourage understanding and appreciation of cultural diversity and respect for the Earth through art, music, science, large- and fine-muscle activities, and language.

Mitchell, L.S. 1971. *Young geographers: How they explore the world and how they map the world.* New York: Bank Street College of Education.

Shows teachers of 3- to 6-year-olds how to incorporate geography (both the concepts and skills) into the curriculum through timeless techniques such as trips into the community that are represented back in the classroom through such activities as mapping with blocks and other found materials.

Roberts, P. 1996. *Integrating language arts and social studies for kindergarten and primary children.* Columbus, OH: Merrill/Prentice Hall.

Presents a broad view of what integrated curriculum and learning is really like from the teacher's point of view. Advance organizers help teachers prepare to integrate language arts and social studies. A range of techniques and activities show how to integrate the two subjects with each other and across the curriculum.

Rogovin, P. 1998a. *Classroom interviews in action.* Portsmouth, NH: Heinemann.

Views of classroom interviews inside the author's classroom and outside the school will help primary teachers understand how to make the content of interviews a regular part of classroom life. Children are portrayed interviewing a range of community workers, taking notes represented by pictures and invented spelling. Examples are shown of a planning session and ways to incorporate the interview content into all parts of the curriculum.

Rogovin, P. 1998b. *Classroom interviews: A world of learning.* Portsmouth, NH: Heinemann.

Shares self-proven techniques of conducting class interviews with family members, neighbors, peers, and community people, and turning the children's interview journals into a centerpiece for learning reading, writing, and social studies.

Seefeldt, C. 1995. Transforming curriculum in social studies. In *Reaching potentials: Transforming early childhood curriculum and assessment, volume 2,* eds. S. Bredekamp & T. Rosegrant, 109–24. Washington DC: NAEYC.

Discusses ways in which teachers can introduce children to important geographic and civic concepts. Includes the national standards for teaching geography, history, and civics, as well as information on how to incorporate these standards into curriculum.

Seefeldt, C. 1997a. Social studies in the developmentally appropriate integrated curriculum. In *Integrated curriculum and developmentally appropriate practice birth to age 8,* eds. C.H. Hart, D.C. Burts, & R. Charlesworth, 171–99. Albany: State University of New York.

Describes the process of planning an integrated, meaningful social studies curriculum that will extend and expand children's understanding of their social and physical world. Emphasizes that children's experiences cannot be separated into different subjects or disciplines.

Seefeldt, C. 1997b. *Social studies for the preschool/primary child.* 5th ed. Upper Saddle River, NJ: Prentice Hall.

Based on a solid, theoretical and research foundation on child growth, development, and learning. Also presents practical ideas, suggestions, and guides for introducing young children to social studies. With an integrated focus on family and community as classroom, the book introduces student teachers to both traditional and cutting-edge early childhood social studies education.

Seefeldt, C., & A. Galper. 2000. *Active experiences for active children: Social studies.* Columbus, OH: Merrill/Prentice Hall.

Puts John Dewey's theory into practice through constructing participatory democracies in the classroom. Social studies curricula include history, geography, economics, and civics as well as social relationships. Vignettes illustrate the key concepts, and photos and charts demonstrate how to make materials and complete the activities for 4- though 8- year old children.

Sobel, D. 1998. *Mapmaking with children: Sense of place education for elementary years.* Portsmouth, NH: Heinemann.

Opens new possibilities that extend far beyond the boundaries of traditional geography education. Because this text ties mapmaking to all content areas and offers many instructional suggestions, children learn to see it as a relevant and necessary skill for life. Many photographs, drawings, and examples enrich the book.

Swiniarski, L., M. Breitborde, & J. Murphy. 1999. *Educating the global village: Including the young child in the world.* Columbus, OH: Prentice Hall.

Demonstrates the need for global education and how to expand the early childhood curriculum to include the world. Vignettes, models, photographs, curriculum themes and discussion questions are some of the ideas offered for implementing a global education that infuses the early childhood curriculum.

Winston, L. 1997. *Keepsakes: Using family stories in elementary classrooms.* Portsmouth, NH: Heinemann.

Demonstrates how elementary-school teachers can draw on family stories to enliven and enrich the curriculum, giving children a direct connection with the past and an immediate sense of history. An uplifting look at a truly multicultural curriculum—one that celebrates differences and similarities and strengthens the bonds between families and schools.

Using technology in the classroom

The recommended and available resources in this category are dominated by computer technology, with just a few that address use of television, video, and multimedia. Because both hardware and software become obsolete so rapidly, we sought resources that discuss relationships to children's learning and advise teachers in integrating computers in developmentally appropriate ways. Many of the recent books cited under the broad heading of "Teaching and Curriculum for Preschool and Primary" include chapters dedicated to technology. One 1984 reference is included in this section because it provides details on the young child's developing perception and understanding of technology.

American Academy of Pediatrics (AAP). 1995. Position paper: Children, adolescents, and television. *American Academy of Pediatrics* 96 (4): 786–87.

Reviews hazards of exposure to television for children and makes recommendations for caregivers.

Association for Supervision and Curriculum Development (ASCD). 1997. *Only the best: The annual guide to the highest-rated educational software and multimedia 1997.* Alexandria, VA: Author.

Identifies educational software and multimedia programs that have met the ASCD standards for excellence in the past year. Each product description includes grade-level subject area, hardware requirements, cost, and tips from educators.

Beginnings workshop: Young children and technology. 1998. *Child Care Information Exchange* (123): 43–62.

The Beginnings Workshop series contains four articles written by early childhood educators that discuss varying perspectives on using technology. For teachers of children who span the age range from infancy through school-age. One article evaluates software for children.

Bolinski, D., ed. 1997. *Family Internet companion.* Upper Saddle River, NJ: Prentice Hall.

Provides a basic introduction to the Internet, assuming no prior knowledge and keeping jargon to a minimum. An interactive guide, the user will navigate screen by screen trying out the activities displayed. Includes examples of websites from around the world created by people of all ages.

Caine, T. 1998. Getting the most out of technology in the classroom. *Exceptional Parent* 28 (11): 44–46.

A fresh perspective on using technology for children with special needs. Includes real-life examples of creative application of assistive technology. The adaptive products discussed allow for the creation of customized activities for individual student's needs.

Clements, D.H., B.K. Nastasi, & S. Swaminathan. 1993. Young children and computers: crossroads and directions from research. *Young Children* 48 (2): 56–64.

Discusses what exactly children learn when using computers and how best to incorporate computer use into various curriculum areas. Provides examples of appropriate and inappropriate computer use within early childhood and primary-school classrooms.

Clements, D.H., & S. Swaminathan. 1995. Technology and school change: New lamps for old? *Childhood Education* 71: 275–81.

Discusses research that can help early childhood educators use computers in new ways to lead to new ways of understanding for young children, and not simply as a tool to teach old material in the same way. Suggests ways that teachers can design curriculum and learning experiences to successfully accompany appropriate use of technology.

Dowling, C. 1999. *Writing and learning with computers.* Melbourne, Victoria: Australian Council for Educational Research Press.

Explores the types of computer-mediated writing that can occur in elementary classrooms and the many ways computers can help children enjoy writing. Addresses the relationship of word processing to writing, questions about spelling and handwriting, word processing activities, and using hypertext, multimedia, and the Internet to support literacy goals such as collaboration and ownership of work. (Distributed by Stylus Publishing, Herndon, Virginia.)

Downes, T., & C. Fatouros. 1996. *Learning in an electronic world: Computers and the language arts classroom.* Portsmouth, NH: Heinemann.

Focusing on the role the computer can play in language learning, this practical text carefully considers ways to enhance talking, listening, reading, and writing with children ages 5 through 12. More advanced topics include databases, multimedia texts, and telecommunications. Teachers are challenged to move beyond viewing the computer as a word processor and discover multiple modes of improving communication.

Elkind, D. 1996. Young children and technology: A cautionary note. *Young Children* 51 (6): 22–23

Cautions against using a child's computer competence to measure developmental and intellectual abilities and levels. Argues that education is a social experience that computers cannot simulate.

Elliott, A. 1996. *Learning with computers.* AECA Resource Book Series, vol. 3, no. 2. Watson, ACT: Australian Early Childhood Association.

Contains the basic information for setting up a computer-active classroom beginning with a glossary of terms and advice on selecting computers and software. Especially useful for teachers who are just beginning to use computers in their early childhood classrooms, this short booklet details the kinds of educational application appropriate for young children.

Gatewood, T., & S. Conrad. 1997. Is your school's technology up-to-date? *Childhood Education* 73 (4): 249–51.

Helps educators assess elementary schools' technology programs and determine their needs. The authors describe how to conduct a needs assessment, taking into consideration such components as computer workstations and technology resource centers.

Greenfield, P.M. 1984. *Mind and media: The effects of television, video games, and computers.* Cambridge, MA: Harvard University Press.

Presents research that examines how various media can be used to promote social growth and thinking skills. Findings show that each medium can make a contribution to development and the ideal childhood environment includes multimedia approaches to learning.

Haugen, K. 1995. Using technology to help children with diverse needs participate and learn. *Child Care Information Exchange* (105): 58–62.

Discusses how children with disabilities are discovering through technology new ways to communicate, learn, and interact with their peers and environment. The author specifically describes adaptations and activities that demonstrate how computers and adaptive technologies can enhance (rather than replace) the repertoire of materials and strategies in many early childhood settings. Also provides resource information to assist in planning adaptations for individual students.

Haugland, S. 1999. What role should technology play in young children's learning? *Young Children* 54 (6): 26–31.

Discusses the role of computers in young children's lives. Author explains that ways of using computers with threes and fours are different from the ways computers should be used in kindergarten and the primary grades. Also explores models for computer integration across curriculum areas.

Haugland, S.W., & J.L Wright. 1997. *Young children and technology: A world of discovery.* Boston: Allyn & Bacon.

Contains information on the potential dangers and benefits of using computers with young children ages 2 through 14. Discusses how computer use affects development and provides guidelines for selecting computers, ideas for using computers, and reviews of developmentally appropriate computer software.

Healy, J.M. 1998. *Failure to connect: How computers affect our children's minds—for better and worse.* New York: Simon & Schuster.

Examines the advantages and drawbacks of computer use for children at home and in school, exploring the effects on children's health, creativity, brain development, and social and emotional growth. The author explains how computers can be used successfully with children of different age groups as a supplement to classroom curricula, research tools, or in family projects.

Hohmann, C., B. Carmody, & C. McCabe-Branz. 1995. *High/Scope buyer's guide to children's software.* 11th ed. Ypsilanti, MI: High/Scope.

A guide to software for children from 3 to 7 years of ages; designed to help teachers and parents evaluate and choose computer software for home or classroom use. Includes software descriptions, ratings of educational software programs, listings of award-winning programs, a glossary, and a national directory of software producers.

Jody, M., & M. Saccardi. 1998. *Using computers to teach literature: A teacher's guide.* Urbana, IL: National Council of Teachers of English.

Reviews the multiple ways telecommunications can link to language arts. The authors invite readers to launch computer conversations, students and teachers to discuss questions and ideas about a book and then share their ideas online with a class in another school. Covers computer, and tips for going online and using the World Wide Web.

Levin, D.E., & N. Carlsson-Paige. 1994. Developmentally appropriate television: Putting children first. *Young Children* 49 (5): 38–44.

Examines the effects of the 1984 deregulation of children's television and outlines what early childhood educators can do to counteract these effects. The authors outline a series of emotional and social attitudes, explain what children need and what children see on commercial TV, and then draw conclusions. Provides a developmental framework for assessing TV.

Morton, J.G. 1998. *Kids on the 'net: Conducting Internet research in K–5 classrooms.* Portsmouth, NH: Heinemann.

A teacher of first- and second-graders demonstrates how her curriculum is enriched by the spontaneous conversations her children have with experts around the globe via the Internet. Using examples such as her year-long study of birds, Morton offers techniques for teaching children how to use e-mail for research and to connect the information gained through the search back to classroom talk, reading, and writing about the topic.

NAEYC position statement: Technology and young children—Ages three through eight. 1996. *Young Children* 51 (6): 11–16.

Encourages educators to address the following issues related to the use of technology: role of teacher evaluation, benefits of appropriate use, integration into learning environments, equitable access and especially for children with special needs, role of teachers and parents as advocates, and implications for professional development.

PACER Center. 1997. *Kids included through technology are enriched: A guidebook for teachers of young children.* Minneapolis, MN: Author.

This illustrated book suggests practical strategies for integrating computers, communication aids, and other devices to help children with disabilities at school and at home. Resource lists as well as reproducible forms and questionnaires will help both parents and professionals choose and use technology effectively.

Papert, S. 1986. *Mindstorms: Children, computers, and powerful ideas.* New York: Basic.

Lays a foundation for future work in elementary schools. A collaborative model of computers and children provides the background on how children can use the computer to think. Tells the story of the invention of LOGO, the first child-friendly computer programming language.

Papert, S. 1996. *The connected family: Bridging the digital generation gap.* Marietta, GA: Longstreet.

Raises issues regarding the use and misuse of computers. Focusing on the creative ways that families can explore technology together, the author describes specific software and Internet projects that are rooted in the "culture of children." Will challenge teachers and families to consider the computer as a versatile tool for all ages to use in the collaborative construction of knowledge.

Shade, D.D. 1996. Software evaluation. *Young Children* 51 (6): 17–21.

A guide for evaluating software for use with children in early childhood programs, including child features, teacher features, and technical features.

Shade, D., & B. Davis. 1997. The role of computer technology in early childhood education. In *Trends and issues in early childhood education: Challenges, controversies and insights,* eds. J. Isenberg & M. Jalongo, 90–103. New York: Teachers College Press.

Based on the premise that much information about computers learned today will be obsolete tomorrow. What children need to learn is the habit of using the technology as a tool for accomplishing whatever learning task is at hand. The authors discuss computer technology in relation to developmental appropriateness and issues of equity.

Snider, S.L., & T. L. Badgett. 1995. "I have this computer, what do I do now?" Using technology to enhance every child's learning. *Early Childhood Education Journal* 23 (2): 101–04.

Acquaints early childhood educators with available basic, as well as adaptive, technological hardware and software and provides an overview of technology transfer in young learners. Provides specific strategies for children with special needs.

Von Blanckensee, L. 1999. *Technology tools for young learners.* Larchmont, NY: Eye on Education.

Illustrates how graphic images, word processing, e-mail, the Internet, videoconferencing, and multimedia techniques can be integrated into the learning process of 4- to 8-year-olds. The author shows how children can control these tools and enhance their own creative ideas through activities such as using digital photography to document a science project and record their observations of the real world.

Wright, J.L., & D.D. Shade, eds. 1994. *Young children: Active learners in a technological age*. Washington, DC: NAEYC.

Focuses on the young child as an active user of technology, including computers and audio- and videocassettes. Includes the role of the teacher in carefully selecting software and in integrating technological tools into the curriculum so as to enhance children's development and learning.

Integrating curriculum

Included in this category are those resources that offer explanations of the meaning of an integrated curriculum, the rationale for integrating curriculum across subject matter disciplines, and concrete strategies for accomplishing an integrated curriculum. Different models and approaches for the preschool years and primary grades are described, but all focus on the interrelatedness of children's social, emotional, physical, and cognitive abilities and highlight techniques for bringing the content areas together in classrooms in ways that are meaningful to children yet meet reasonable subject matter requirements.

Barrett, K., E. Blinderman, B. Boffen, J. Ecols, P. House, K. Hosoume, & J. Kopp. 1999. *Science and math explorations for young children*. (GEMS/PEACHES Handbook for Early Childhood Educators, Childcare Providers, and Parents.) Berkeley: University of California–Berkeley.

Developed with early childhood practitioners and the Lawrence Hall of Science, this handbook is framed by the math and science national standards and describes lively, integrated activities for curriculum planning and gives clear explanations about the way exploratory learning develops. Topics include the relationships of play, creativity, language, and equity to math and science and the role of the parent. Another teacher guide developed by this group, *Mother Opossum and Her Babies,* highlights math strands of logic and language, number measurement and statistics, and concepts of the behavior and life cycle of marsupials in projects piloted in pre-K–1 classrooms.

Bickmore-Brand, J., ed. 1990. *Language in mathematics.* Portsmouth, NH: Heinemann.

Discusses the dangers in both the traditional approach to teaching mathematics and current trends. Offers constructive ways to maximize the contribution that language can make in generating, comprehending, and expressing mathematical ideas and mathematical knowledge.

Cecil, N.L., & P. Lauritzen. 1996. *Literacy and the arts for the integrated classroom: Alternative ways of knowing.* New York: Longman.

Advocates integrated programs of drama, song, dance, photography, art, and poetry to promote children's literacy development. Based on Howard Gardner's theory of multiple intelligences.

Charlesworth, R., & K.K. Lind. 1999. *Math and science for young children.* 3d ed. Albany, NY: Delmar.

Provides teachers with the knowledge and skills needed to effectively integrate mathematics and science curriculums in a developmentally appropriate manner. Appropriate assessment strategies are integrated throughout.

Davidson, J.I. 1996. *Emergent literacy and dramatic play in early education.* Albany, NY: Delmar.

Presents a comprehensive view of the link between dramatic play and language development. Real-life stories and pictures illustrate how dramatic play enhances literacy.

Edwards, L.C. 1996. *Affective development and the creative arts: A process approach to early childhood education.* Columbus, OH: Merrill.

Shows teachers how to tap into their own creativity to foster children's creative growth; grounded in research and theory. Supports a constructivist view of the creative arts, moving learners away from prescribed activities and projects and instead encouraging the creative potential in all children.

Ernst, K. 1994. *Picturing learning: Artists and writers in the classroom.* Portsmouth, NH: Heinemann.

Offers a framework for integrating reading and writing in art programs in kindergarten to fourth- grade classrooms. A teacher documents how the children use writing and picturing to express their thinking and how teachers can use such elements as choice of subject and medium, minilessons, conferences, and connections to children's literature.

Forston, L., & J. Reiff. 1995. *Early childhood curriculum. Open structures for integrative learning.* Needham, MA: Allyn & Bacon.

Reflects a genuine grasp of the richness and interconnectedness of learning. Focuses on a change in understanding of what learning is, how children learn, and the role of the teacher. Includes numerous examples, suggestions, and attention to instructional design.

Fraser, J., & D. Skolnick. 1994. *On their way: Celebrating second graders as they read and write.* Portsmouth, NH: Heinemann.

Second-grade teachers depict how to organize a classroom that captures the dynamic nature of 7- and 8-year-olds working on projects and how to help children read, write, engage in collective dialogue, and evaluate their own learning.

Fredericks, A., A. Meinbach, & L. Rothlein. 1993. *Thematic units: An integrated approach to teaching science and social studies.* New York: Delmar.

Provides approaches to integrate literature and language arts with teaching science and social studies in the primary grades.

Goldberg, M. 1997. *Arts and learning: An integrated approach to teaching learning in multicultural and multilingual settings.* Boston: Addison Wesley Longman.

Illustrates how teaching and learning can be enhanced by the arts. Specific examples of drama, the visual arts, dance, music, poetry, and all forms of literature used in multiple ways in all the curriculum content areas in the elementary school.

Hart, C.H., D.C. Burts, & R. Charlesworth. 1997. *Integrated curriculum and developmentally appropriate practice: Birth through age 8.* Albany: State University of New York Press.

Explains how content areas can serve as the focal points for an integrated curriculum, with specific examples for each area. The author also details the developmental theory underlying the foundations of the early childhood curriculum and provides each content area's national professional standards.

Johnson, P. 1997. *Picture and words together: Children illustrating and writing their own books.* Portsmouth, NH: Heinemann.

Shows how preschool and primary-school children can be taught to create books that fuse their writing and drawing in profound ways. Offers advice on helping children think about the most effective way to blend text and pictures, draw the characters and settings for their narratives, and publish their book, using simple cutting, folding, and binding techniques.

Kellough, R. 1996. *Integrating mathematics and science for kindergarten and primary children.* Columbus, OH: Merrill/Prentice Hall.

Introduces the appropriate math and science content according to national standards and then emphasizes the rationale and methods of integrating the curriculum. Examines Science/Technology/Society (STS)—one of the most promising approaches to curriculum integration—as the primary theme for a K–4 curriculum design. Includes activities that encourage interaction and collaboration.

Kohl, M., & C. Gainer. 1996. *Math arts: Exploring math through art for 3 to 6 year-olds.* Beltsville, MD: Gryphon House.

Uses an integrated approach to introduce preschoolers to early math concepts. Each of the hands-on projects is designed to help children discover essential math skills through a creative process unique for every individual.

Kostelnik, M.J., A.K. Soderman, & A.P. Whiren. 1999. *Developmentally appropriate curriculum: Best practices in early childhood education.* 2d ed. Upper Saddle River: Merrill/Prentice Hall.

Brings together the best information currently available for developing an integrated approach to curriculum and instruction in the early years. Designed for current and future early childhood professionals working in group settings with young children ranging in age from 3 to 8.

Krogh, S.L. 1995. *The integrated early childhood curriculum.* 2d ed. New York: McGraw-Hill.

Begins by introducing the definition and general theory underlying the integrated approach, then presents a chapter on each major content area such as mathematics, science, and language arts. Each chapter reviews the content development and gives examples of that area's integration with others.

Lawler-Prince, D., J.L. Altieri, & M.K. Cramer. 1996. *Moving toward an integrated curriculum in early childhood education.* Washington, DC: National Education Association.

Readers learn how webbing helps bridge the gap between the use of basal readers and a completely integrated, thematic curriculum. Sample thematic units and webs and an annotated bibliography provide plenty of ideas to help teachers make learning meaningful, real, and relevant for children.

Lubinski, C.A., & A.D. Otto. 1997. Literature and algebraic reasoning. *Teaching Children Mathematics* 3 (6): 290–95.

Through Pat Hutchin's *The Doorbell Rang,* children have the opportunity to develop algebraic reasoning. After children read the book, the teacher guides them through activities that enable them to discover the number patterns exemplified in the story.

Peterson, E. 1996. *Early childhood planning, method, and materials.* Boston: Allyn & Bacon.

Focuses on helping teachers organize their ideas, methods, and materials into effective plans for young children. The author's suggestions support individual choices and teaching styles and help teachers document the good work they are already doing.

Pica, R. 1999. *Moving and learning across the curriculum.* New York: Delmar.

Includes activities designed to make movement part of the early childhood curriculum by integrating movement with art, language arts, mathematics, music, science, and social studies.

Pigdon, K., & M. Woolley. 1993. *The big picture: Integrating children's learning.* Portsmouth, NH: Heinemann.

Through examples of classroom practice and planning models, this work portrays what integrated curriculum is and how it is accomplished. Techniques for translating the model into practice incorporate evaluation and the need to meet subject requirements.

Raines, S.C. 1995. *Whole language across the curriculum: Grades 1, 2, 3.* New York: Teachers College Press.

The first part describes how several primary-school teachers implemented whole language in their classrooms. The second part connects whole language to other content areas and to portfolio assessment.

Reutzel, D.R. 1997. Integrating literacy learning for young children: A balanced literacy perspective. In *Integrated curriculum and developmentally appropriate practice: Birth to age eight,* eds. C.H. Hart, D.C. Burts, & R. Charlesworth, 225–54. Albany: State University of New York Press.

Presents information about the different stages of reading and writing development. Offers suggestions on how to create a developmentally appropriate reading and writing curriculum and a literacy learning classroom as well.

Roberts, P. 1996. *Integrating language arts and social studies for kindergarten and primary children.* Columbus, OH: Merrill/Prentice Hall.

Presents a broad view of what integrated curriculum and learning is really like from the teacher's point of view. Advance organizers help teachers prepare to integrate language arts and social studies, and a range of techniques and activities show how to integrate the two subjects with each other and across the curriculum.

Rogovin, P. 1998. *Classroom interviews in action.* Portsmouth, NH: Heinemann.

Views of classroom interviews inside author's classroom and outside the school will help primary teachers understand how to make the content of interviews a regular part of classroom life. Children are portrayed interviewing a range of community workers, taking notes representing by pictures and invented spelling early in the year. Examples are shown of a planning session and ways to incorporate the interview content into all parts of the curriculum.

Rowen, B. 1994. *Dance and grow: Developmental activities for three- through eight-year-olds.* Pennington, NJ: Princeton.

Combines play activities with basic dance instruction in an accessible format for teachers of young children. Discusses how the basic elements of dance—rhythm, space, and quality of movement are used in teaching concepts in language, math, social studies, science, art, and music.

Schickedanz, J.A., M.L. Pergantis, J. Kanosky, A. Blaney, & J. Ottinger. 1997. *Curriculum in early childhood: A resource guide for preschool and kindergarten teachers.* Boston: Allyn & Bacon.

Takes an integrated, theme-based approach to curriculum rather than a focus on specific subject matter or activity areas. The combination textbook/curriculum guide features activities and themes strongly grounded in early childhood theories.

Schwartz, S., & M. Pollishuke. 1991. *Creating the child-centered classroom.* Katonah, NY: Richard C. Owen.

Features classroom set-up, flexible timetabling, whole language and integrated units of study, and learning centers. Includes many photos, sample forms such as tracking sheets for children to use, and sample letters to parents.

Smith, J. 1994. Threading mathematics into social studies. *Teaching Children Mathematics* 1: 438–44.

    Discusses V. Flournoy's *The Patchwork Quilt*, which provides many ideas for integrated learning experiences through a patchwork-quilt project.

Tchudi, S., ed. 1993. *The astonishing curriculum: Integrating science and humanities through language.* Urbana, IL: National Council of Teachers of English.

    Discusses the meaning of integrated curriculum and interdisciplinary learning. Portrays teaching settings in which kindergarten and first- and third-graders are learning science, language arts, and math through group talks and other integrated language-based activities.

Walmsley. S. 1994. *Children exploring their world: Theme teaching in elementary school.* Portsmouth, NH: Heinemann.

    Focuses on the principles of developing themes and on practical approaches for carrying out themes in integrating the curriculum across content areas in the primary-school classroom.

Welchman-Tischler, R. 1992. *How to use children's literature to teach mathematics.* Reston, VA: National Council of Teachers of Mathematics.

    Suggests ways to present thought-provoking math experiences related to literature, using a manipulative context in kindergarten through sixth-grade classrooms. Sample activities organized by age level lay the groundwork for developing math concepts and promote experimentation with reasoning and problem-solving ideas.

White, C.S., & M. Coleman. 2000. *Early childhood education: Building a philosophy for teaching.* Columbus, OH: Merrill/Prentice Hall.

    Designed to help beginning teachers and student teachers develop a sense of professional identity by understanding the development and diversity of childhood life experiences and social contexts that influence the care and education of children birth through age 8. Content includes historical precedents and current trends in early childhood education, extensive examination of family development and involvement in schools, organizing the classroom, and integrating curriculum.

Whitin, D.J., & S. Wilde. 1992. *Read any good math lately? Children's books for mathematical learning, K–6.* Portsmouth, NH: Heinemann.

    Focuses on the opportunities that children's literature can provide to encourage children to think mathematically. Techniques for fostering math conversations and following children's leads are presented.

York, S. 1998. *Big as life: The everyday inclusive curriculum.* Vol. 1. St. Paul, MN: Redleaf.

    Provides an approach to developing a curriculum that incorporates multicultural perspectives and integrates content areas. Includes a listing of resource books.

Assessing children's learning and development

This resource category covers evaluation issues such as the use of standardized tests and readiness tests, grading policies, and the validity of assessment tools for measuring all children's abilities. Many kinds of assessment tools are described: observation guides, portfolio assessment systems, tests that evaluate specific skills such as reading and math, or assessment tools for specific kinds of settings such as mixed-age classes. Details are provided on linking assessment to curriculum, families, and the children.

Allen, D. 1998. *Assessing student learning: From grading to understanding.* New York: Teachers College Press.

Represents K–12 educational projects that demonstrate a range of assessment processes that enable teachers to reflect on the ideas and patterns in children's ongoing work in school. Models such as the Collaborative Assessment Conference protocol give teachers feedback on children's thinking as well as teachers' own practices.

Anthony, R.J., T.D. Johnson, N.I. Mickelson, & A. Preece. 1991. *Evaluating literacy: A perspective for change.* Portsmouth, NH: Heinemann.

Explores the essential connection between educational aims, curriculum implementation, and assessment-evaluation processes in literacy learning. Authors describe and provide examples of how to gather, interpret, and evaluate assessment information.

Barr, M.A., D.A. Craig, D. Fisette, & M.A. Syverson, eds. 1999. *Assessment literacy with the learning record: A handbook for teachers, grades K–6.* Portsmouth, NH: Heinemann.

The instrument is designed to record the progress of students from kindergarten on and to provide a portfolio of information for administrators, teachers, children, and parents. Student performance is measured by a variety of authentic language and literacy tasks and in consultations with students and parents.

Beaty, J.J. 1998. *Observing development of the young child.* 4th ed. Upper Saddle River, NJ: Merrill/Prentice Hall.

Offers a comprehensive guide to the observation of young children in all developmental domains and in early academic areas, as well as suggestion for sharing the observational data with parents. The book details steps and methods of observation and recording and provides guidance in interpreting assessment information gathered through direct observation and samples of children's work.

Bentzen, W.R. 1997. *Seeing young children: A guide to observing and recording behavior.* Albany, NY: Delmar.

Designed to provide essential background information on many aspects of child development and recording techniques. Individuals may use the information within this text to observe and record young children's behavior in child care centers, early childhood classrooms, homes, public schools, and various other settings.

Billman, J., & J.A. Sherman. 1996. *Observation and participation in early childhood settings.* Boston: Allyn & Bacon.

Gives preparing teachers some experience with effective methods for observing young children's development and documenting their observations. It is designed to guide student teachers' participation with children of different age groups in a variety of early childhood settings.

Boehm, A.E., & R.A. Weinberg. 1997. *The classroom observer: Developing observation skills in early childhood settings.* New York: Teachers College Press.

Focuses on skills that will enable the observer to make appropriate, valid inferences and arrive at decisions based on objective observation data gathered in natural learning environments and diverse educational settings.

Calkins, L., K. Montgomery, & D. Santman with B. Falk. 1998. *A teacher's guide to standardized reading tests: Knowledge is power.* Portsmouth, NH: Heinemann.

Helps teachers confront the current pressures for high test scores and commensurate curriculum mandates to teach to the test by becoming better informed and articulate about test lingo, learning what tests do and do not measure, and discovering demonstrated ways in which reading and writing workshops can be adapted to help children develop the capabilities they need to meet future challenges.

Clay, M. 1993. *An observation survey of early literacy achievement.* Portsmouth, NH: Heinemann.

Introduces K–3 teachers to ways of observing children's progress in the early years of learning in literacy and oral language development. The observation survey is designed to help teachers determine which children need extra support, improve their teaching plans, and monitor children's progress.

Cohen, D.H., V. Stern, & N. Balaban. 1997. *Observing and recording the behavior of young children.* 4th ed. New York: Teachers College Press.

Provides a classic manual on getting to know children and their behavior through carefully described methods of observation and recording. It updates earlier editions with information on children's cognitive functioning, observing infants and toddlers, and children with special needs.

Courtney, A., & T. Abodeeb. 1999. Diagnostic-reflective portfolios. *The Reading Teacher* (April): 708–14.

Shows the kind of guidance and support that is necessary from the teacher for second-graders to learn how to use portfolios in self-assessment, continually setting and monitoring appropriate learning goals, and using the process to reflect on their own learning.

Dichtelmiller, M.L., J.R. Jablon, D.B. Marsden, & S.J. Meisels. 1994. *Omnibus guidelines: Preschool through third grade*. Ann Arbor, MI: Rebus.

Describes the Work Sampling System of assessing children's development and learning. Gives educators information about child development, discusses the content of several disciplines, helps teachers align curriculum with state and other external standards, gives curriculum-embedded examples of active learning, provides a tool for implementing standards, and enhances teacher's understanding of integrated and applied practices.

Fleege, P.O. 1997. Assessment in an integrated curriculum. In *Integrated curriculum and developmentally appropriate practice: Birth through age 8*, eds. C.H. Hart, D.C. Burts, & R. Charlesworth, 313–34. Albany, NY: State University of New York Press.

Presents the criticisms of traditional testing and provides an excellent overview of alternative means of assessment. The authors discuss documentation strategies such as checklists, rating scales, anecdotal records, running records, time sampling, and event sampling. Brief assessment snapshots provide examples of how assessment can be integrated with curriculum for infants and toddlers, preschoolers, and primary-grade children. Resources for developing an assessment plan are also described.

Forsten, C., J. Grant, & I. Richardson. 1999a. *The looping evaluation book*. Peterborough, NH: Crystal Springs.

Helps teachers or administrators identify and consider all the factors that will lead to a thriving looping classroom. Part 1 explains looping and the kinds of instructional practices associated with it; Part 2 details the steps necessary to implementing looping; Part 3 identifies which elements need to be evaluated (includes checklists) and how results should be used; Part 4 has resources, sample surveys, letters, forms, and charts.

Forsten, C., J. Grant, & I. Richardson. 1999b. *The multiage evaluation book*. Peterborough, NH: Crystal Springs.

Contains detailed checklists for understanding the concept of preparing multiage programming and the reason for implementing it. Gives teachers help in designing, implementing, and assessing a multiage classroom. For educators already engaged in multiage practice, provides help finding out which components are working well and which need revising. Includes sample parent questionnaires in English and Spanish.

Genishi, C., ed. 1992. *Ways of assessing children and curriculum*. New York: Teachers College Press.

Essays written by early childhood teachers provide a look at the ways these teachers document the development of children from diverse cultural backgrounds in various contexts. The alternative ways of assessing, some traditional and some novel, include observing, note taking, role-playing, and keeping portfolios of children's work over time.

Goodman, K.S., Y.M. Goodman, & W.J. Hood. 1989. *The whole language evaluation book*. Portsmouth, NH: Heinemann.

The section "School Beginnings" describes classroom environments and practices with 5- through 8-year-olds that integrate oral and written language learning with assessment and evaluation. Vignettes of assessment are given for typical English-speaking children and those with Hispanic backgrounds.

Graves, D., & B. Sunstein. 1998. *Portfolio portraits*. Portsmouth, NH: Heinemann.

Recounts the experiences of teachers as they develop portfolios in a variety of subject areas. Techniques are explained for using portfolios effectively, integrating them into teaching, managing time, and coping with other problems through the portfolio method.

Gredler, G.R. 1992. *School readiness: Assessment and educational issues*. Brandon, VT: Clinical Psychology Publishing.

Presents contrasting views of school readiness in light of contemporary knowledge of child development and prevalent practices in readiness testing. It discusses problems associated with extra-year programs and summarizes the major issues educators and parents face in ensuring appropriate educational programs and assessment.

Gronlund, G. 1998. Portfolios as an assessment tool: Is collection of work enough? *Young Children* 53 (3):4–10.

Provides recommendations for collecting and storing informative samples of children's work, distinguishing among differing types of portfolios and their uses. The author stresses that teacher analysis and commentary are essential to understanding what the children's work samples are demonstrating about their progress.

Gullo, D.F. 1994. *Understanding assessment and evaluation in early childhood education*. New York: Teachers College Press.

Explains different assessment techniques, when and how they should be applied, and their strengths and limitations so that early childhood professionals can make informed decisions about assessment and evaluation.

Helm, J.H., S. Beneke, & K. Steinheimer. 1997. Documenting children's learning. *Childhood Education* 73 (4): 200–05.

Illustrated with graphics and narratives of practical classroom approaches, this article describes ways to collect, analyze, interpret, display, and communicate evidence of children's learning so that administrators and parents can recognize progress.

Helm, J.H., S. Beneke, & K. Steinheimer. 1998. *Windows on learning: Documenting young children's work.* New York: Teachers College Press.

Shows that children, teachers, and parents learn more from school projects that involve documentation techniques such as using photographs, narratives, drawings, videocassettes, and captions. Children gain a deeper understanding of what they've been studying; parents become aware of children's school experiences; and teachers gain insight into what children know, where their interests lie, and how to further their understanding. An accompanying guide, *Teacher Materials for Documenting Young Children's Work: Using "Windows on Learning,"* describes the lists, shortcuts, handouts, and forms that the authors developed as they worked with teachers who were learning to document children's work.

Hills, T.W. 1992. Reaching potentials through appropriate assessment. In *Reaching potentials: Appropriate curriculum and assessment for young children, volume 1,* eds. S. Bredekamp & T. Rosegrant, 43–63. Washington, DC: NAEYC.

Applies NAEYC and NAECS/SDE (National Association of Early Childhood Specialists in State Departments of Education) curriculum and assessment guidelines to assessing young children's progress. It illustrates the principles with graphics and examples of children's work that can be used to document children's development and learning.

Hills, T.W. 1993. Assessment in context—Teachers and children at work. *Young Children* 48 (5): 20–28.

Assessment serves the best interests of children when it functions as an integrated part of an overall program, contributes positively to children's self-esteem and developmental process, recognizes children's individuality, and respects individual family and community backgrounds.

Jablon, J.R., A.L. Dombro, & M.L. Dichtelmiller. 1999. *The power of observation.* Washington, DC: Teaching Strategies.

Explores the key connection between observing and effective teaching. Also offers guidelines for effective observation and specific strategies to help teachers and caregivers refine their observation skills and transform observing into an integral part of their practice.

Kamii, C. 1990. *Achievement testing in the early grades: The games grown-ups play.* Washington, DC: NAEYC.

Explains how test mania does not tell teachers what they need to know about children's progress, encourages bad teaching, and harms children.

Katz, L.G. 1997. *A developmental approach to assessment of young children.* Urbana-Champaign, IL: ERIC Clearinghouse on Elementary and Early Childhood Education.

Applies the concept of developmental appropriateness to the assessment of children and children's learning during the early years.

Leonard, A.M. 1997. *I spy something! A practical guide to classroom observations of young children.* Little Rock, AR: Southern Early Childhood Association.

Explains how observation helps one understand what children know and are learning. Encourages the teacher to make educational decisions while reflecting on observations of the children.

Leslie, L., & M. Jett-Simpson. 1997. *Authentic literacy assessment: An ecological approach.* New York: Longman.

Offers variety of classroom-based literacy assessments that are easily integrated into instruction for elementary school children. Emphasizes portfolio assessment and how teachers can observe children's reading and organize observations for the portfolio. Also addresses issue of reliability and validity.

MacDonald, S. 1996. *Portfolio and its use: A road map for assessment.* Little Rock, AR: Southern Early Childhood Association.

Describes using portfolio assessment as a means of evaluating children's progress. Samples of real portfolios illustrate the benefits and steps involved in using this method. Also explains how to involve families in the assessment process.

Martin, R.A. 1997. Everything I ever needed to know about assessment I can learn in kindergarten. *Science and Children* (September): 50–53.

The author observes in visiting a kindergarten class in which the children are doing a project on trees that the activities provide opportunities for assessment. The children's involvement and interactions call for children to perform or create something, invoke real-world applications, demonstrate that there is more than one answer, and provide a holistic picture of student progress.

Martin, S. 1994. *Take a look: Observation and portfolio assessment in early childhood.* Ontario, Canada: Addison Wesley/Longman.

Explains the range of methods that can be used for recording observations. Data concerning assembling and analyzing portfolios are also provided so that the reader can make informed choices about early childhood assessments.

McAfee, O., & D. Leong. 1997. *Assessing and guiding young children's development and learning.* 2d ed. Boston: Allyn & Bacon.

Covers a wide range of approaches to assessment and includes an appendix listing examples of behaviors related to many aspects of the child's various selves. The author also includes developmental chronologies.

McLean, M., D. Bailey, & M. Wolery. 1996. *Assessing infants and preschoolers with special needs.* Columbus, OH: Merrill/Prentice Hall.

Included is a focus on family-centered assessment and suggested procedures for ensuring assessment that is nonbiased. The authors discuss assessment tools and devote individual chapters to assessment in key curriculum/developmental areas in natural environments rather than solely in clinical settings. One chapter addresses assessment of family concerns, resources, and priorities.

Meisels, S.J. 1993. Remaking classroom assessment with the Work Sampling System. *Young Children* 48 (5): 34–40.

The purpose of the Work Sampling System is to assess and document children's skills, knowledge, behavior, and accomplishments as displayed across a wide variety of classroom domains and as performed on multiple occasions.

Meisels, S.J., & S. Atkins-Burnett. 1994. *Developmental screening in early childhood: A guide.* 4th ed. Washington, DC: NAEYC.

Explains how to organize and conduct an exemplary early childhood screening program. Also includes advice on selecting an appropriate screening instrument, sample forms, and NAEYC's position statement on standardized testing.

Meisels, S., & E. Fenichel. 1996. *New visions for the developmental assessment of infants and young children.* Washington, DC: ZERO TO THREE.

Provides guidelines for assessing infants and young children through ongoing processes that build on family strengths, are sensitive to cultural and family contexts, engage families as partners, and draw out the infant or child's competencies through play and naturalistic observation.

Mindes, G., H. Ireton, & C. Mardell-Czudnowski. 1996. *Assessing young children.* St. Paul, MN: Redleaf.

Illustrates how to draw useful developmental information from parents, teachers, and the assessment process to make effective decisions regarding children birth to age 8 and the programs that serve them.

Moon, J., & L. Schulman. 1995. *Finding the connections: Linking assessment, instruction, and curriculum in elementary mathematics.* Portsmouth, NH: Heinemann.

Using performance-based techniques, the authors provide a model for integrating assessment and guided opportunities for teachers' practice in developing their own documentation and creating process folios.

NAEYC & NAECS/SDE (National Association of Early Childhood Specialists in State Departments of Education). 1991. Guidelines for appropriate curriculum content and assessment in programs serving children ages 3 through 8. *Young Children* 46 (3): 21–38.

This position paper of NAEYC and NAECS/SDE sets forth guidelines for developing appropriate curriculum and assessment procedures complementing NAEYC's developmentally appropriate practice materials. The assessment guidelines include principles and steps for assessment that can help teachers plan instruction and communicate with parents, identify children with special needs and disabilities, and evaluate early childhood programs.

Nilsen, B. 1997. *Week by week: Plans for observing and recording young children.* Albany, NY: Delmar.

Acquaints the reader with many observation methods, reviews child development, and presents an organized week-by-week plan for building comprehensive developmental portfolios on each child in the group.

Parker, D.L., & A.J. Picard. 1997. Portraits of Susie: Matching curriculum, instruction, and assessment. *Teaching Children Mathematics* 3 (7): 376–82.

Two assessment portraits of Susie illustrate the contrast between assessment based on problem-solving activities in the classroom and assessment based on standard test performance.

Pelligrini, A. 1996. *Observing children in their natural world.* Mahwah, NJ: Erlbaum.

Thoughtful and understandable guide for using observational methods in working with young children.

Puckett, M.B., & J.K. Black. 2000. *Authentic assessment of the young child: Celebrating development and learning.* Upper Saddle River, NJ: Merrill.

Presents assessment techniques that focus on collecting authentic information about individual children and a developmental continuum to help teachers focus on emerging development rather than on perceived deficits in children. Considers brain development research, the standards movement, and approaches that engage children in the assessment process and support the interconnectedness between learning, planning, and assessment.

Rencken, K.S., S. Cartwright, N. Balaban, & G. Reynolds.1996. Observing children. *Child Care Information Exchange* (112): 43–62.

Describes ways to support children's play and to use observation as an assessment tool.

Richardson, K. 1997. Too easy for kindergarten and just right for first-grade. *Teaching Children Mathematics* 3 (8): 432–37.

By noticing children's levels of enthusiasm and engagement, teachers can assess the appropriateness of a particular task. A hierarchy of development is described.

Schweinhart, L.J. 1993. Observing young children in action: The key to early childhood assessment. *Young Children* 48 (5): 29–33.

States that the assessment field must develop new practices, such as performance-based assessment, that are consistent with the early childhood profession's process goals.

Sharman, C., W. Cross, & D. Vennis. 1995. *Observing children: A practical guide.* New York: Cassell.

A short, user-friendly guide to observation techniques ideal for beginning teachers—it looks at why child care workers need to observe and gives clear instruction on how to record, interpret, and use observations for promoting children's developmental progress from birth through age 8..

Shepard, L.A. 1994. The challenges of assessing young children appropriately. *Phi Delta Kappan* 76 (3): 206–12.

Calls for assessment procedures consistent with knowledge of how young children 4 through 6 years old develop and learn. It emphasizes that testing and other assessment means must be matched with the purposes of assessment and the ways the information will be used.

Shepard, L., S.L Kagan, & E. Wurtz. 1998. *Principles and recommendations for early childhood assessments.* Washington, DC: National Education Goals Panel.

Takes a look at recent issues surrounding assessment with young children. Presents several principles to guide assessment policies and practices. Outlines purposes of assessment for young children: promoting learning and development, identifying services and health needs, evaluating programs, and assessing academic achievement. Includes a chart that details the appropriate uses and accuracy of assessments as they change through the early childhood years.

Shores, E.F., & C. Grace. 1998. *The portfolio book: A step-by-step guide for teachers.* Beltsville, MD: Gryphon House.

Provides a step-by-step guide on creating, maintaining, and interpreting portfolios, as well as an in-depth explanation about how portfolios support child-centered learning. Includes a wide variety of different types of children's work as examples of what to include in portfolios.

Strickland, K., & J. Strickland. 1999. *Making assessment elementary.* Portsmouth, NH: Heinemann.

Grounded in the philosophy that part of authentic assessment means being able to trust children to be able to evaluate their own work, set realistic goals, and make decisions for themselves. For teachers, it means being able to give up control. Principles such as these are translated into practice in chapters that describe techniques such as keeping anecdotal records and creating rubrics, reading and writing assessment, portfolios, tests, and grades. Useful for K–3.

Voss, M.M. 1992. Portfolios in first-grade: A teacher's discoveries. In *Portfolio portraits,* eds. D.S. Graves & B.S. Sunstein, 17–33. Portsmouth, NH: Heinemann.

Recounts the experience of a teacher as she begins developing portfolios as a means of record keeping and assessment of her first-graders. Describes how she solved the problems she faced in using portfolios effectively, integrating them into her teaching, and managing her time.

Wason-Ellam, L. 1994. *Literacy moments to report cards.* Portsmouth, NH: Heinemann.

Uses "literacy moments" with 5- through 8-year-olds, drawn from the teacher's own journal, to illustrate ways to plan instruction, collect and organize assessment information, and arrive at informed judgments about children's progress. It presents a variety of checklists, interview questions, and examples of children's work.

Wilson, L.C., L. Watson, & M.A. Watson. 1995. *Infants and toddlers: Curriculum and teaching.* 3d ed. New York: Delmar.

Based on the Child Development Associate Competency Standards, this book provides age-specific curriculum from birth to age 3. Includes information on designing infant and toddler curriculum with appropriate caregiver strategies for different stages of child development.

Woodward, H. 1994. *Negotiated evaluation: Involving children and parents in the process.* Portsmouth, NH: Heinemann.

Provides practical suggestions for creating a classroom evaluation system that is part of the continuum of day-to-day events, with a focus on how to involve parents and primary-school children. Included are topics such as classroom organization, interviewing and reporting to parents, and observation grids for children and parents to use.

Wortham, S.C. 1997. Setting up meaningful portfolios. *Early Childhood Today* (August/September): 52–54.

Provides the rationale for portfolio assessment with 4- through 8-year-olds, the criteria for selecting material, and a clearly outlined list of potential categories and types of materials. Suggestions are included for storage of material and for using the portfolios as the basis for reporting to parents, child self-evaluation, and teacher self-evaluation.

Creating physical environments

The reader will find help in this section in designing both indoor and outdoor spaces in a wide variety of preschool settings and elementary classrooms. The powerful impact of the daily environment on teachers, children, and the quality of the education is evident throughout these resources.

Many resources provide practical suggestions for purchasing or creating materials and equipment, displaying learning materials, arranging rooms and setting up learning centers (including children's suggestions), and setting up outdoor play spaces. Criteria for assessing and designing physical environment are also included. Techniques for teachers conducting field trips are placed in this section because they serve to extend the curriculum into the broader community.

Ard, L., & M. Pi, eds. 1995. *Room to grow: How to create early childhood environments*. Rev. ed. Austin: Texas Association for the Education of Young Children.

> Teachers and caregivers will obtain criteria, including checklists for evaluating classroom space, both indoors and out, to best plan the use of space and materials.

Brett, A., R.C. Moore, & E. Provenzo, Jr. 1993. *The complete playground book*. Syracuse, NY: Syracuse University Press.

> An examination of the history and purpose of outdoor play areas. Addresses how adventure, designer, and creative playgrounds support play. Photographs portray playgrounds all over the world.

Bronson, M.B. 1995. *The right stuff for children birth to 8: Selecting play materials to support development*. Washington, DC: NAEYC.

> Provides a guide for the selection of play materials for infants, toddlers, preschool, kindergarten, and primary-school children, giving age-appropriate principles, criteria for selection, and concrete suggestions.

Browning, K.G. 1991. Setting up the learning environment. In *Creating the learning environment: A guide in early childhood education,* ed. D. Strickland, 10–19. Orlando, FL: Harcourt Brace Jovanovich.

> Discusses the importance of a well-planned learning environment in the early childhood classroom and offers examples of different interest centers. Includes sample classroom floor plans and suggestions about making inexpensive materials.

Bruya, L.D., ed. 1991. *Playspaces for children: A new beginning*. Reston, VA: American Alliance for Health, Physical Education, Recreation, and Dance.

> Offers many innovative designs for arranging spaces and rooms that reflect the needs of preschool children. Also gives ideas for planning space and rearranging centers and schools creatively.

Bunnet, R., & N. Davis. 1997. Getting to the heart of the matter. *Child Care Information Exchange* (114): 42–44.

Describes a classroom that has been designed with the young learner in mind. Includes questions teachers can ask themselves when evaluating their own classrooms and planning new designs.

Church, E.B. 1997. Creating a welcoming classroom. *Early Childhood Today* (August–September): 46–47.

Contains ideas about some of the elements that make an environment stimulating and safe for children as well as ideas for teachers to use to keep their rooms fresh and special.

Cooper, H., P. Hegarty, & N. Simco. 1996. *Display in the classroom: Principles, practice, and learning theory.* London: David Fulton.

Discusses the role of the kindergarten through third-grade teacher in setting up the classroom environment; reflects on the effect of that environment on teaching and learning.

Ebensen, S. 1990. Designing the setting for the early childhood education program. In *Child care and education: Canadian dimensions,* ed. I.M. Doxey, 49–68. Toronto: Nelson.

Focuses on the preschool child and offers suggestions for setting up indoor spaces that can be easily implemented by teachers of children in the expanded 4- to 8-year-olds age group.

Ellison, G. 1975. *Play structures: Questions to discuss, designs to consider, directions for construction.* Pasadena. CA: Pacific Oaks College.

A practical and philosophical guide to planning and building outdoor play structures for preschool and primary children. Although written years ago, the imaginative designs are current today. Accompanied by good photographs and architectural drawings and design specifications for over 30 school and park play structures.

Feldman, J.R. 1997. *Wonderful rooms where children can bloom.* Peterborough, NH: Crystal Springs.

Designed for the teacher of K–second grade. Shows how to enhance the ambiance of the school, beginning with how it looks from the road and progressing to the lobby and halls, the parent's place, and outdoors. Classroom designs focus on learning centers, children's art, literacy space, and games.

Gandini, L. 1991. Not just anywhere: Making child care centers into "particular" places. *Child Care Information Exchange* (78): 5–9.

Uses the Reggio Emilia classroom as an example of how to design a physical environment that reflects the personalities of the inhabitants—children. Discusses the importance of personal space, a sense of community, and an awareness of space.

Gandini, L. 1994. Educational and caring spaces. Chapter 8. In *The hundred languages of children: The Reggio Emilia approach to early childhood education,* eds. C. Edwards, L. Gandini, & G. Forman. Norwood, NJ: Ablex.

With numerous illustrations done by young children, displays how the physical environment in the Reggio Emilia schools becomes the "third teacher." Discussion of how the schools are structured and key elements of the philosophy that dictate design and organization of the children's environment (including surrounding community).

Gareau, M., & C. Kennedy. 1991. Structure time and space to promote pursuit of learning in the primary grades. *Young Children* 46 (4): 46–51.

Argues that to be effective teachers must understand developmental characteristics of children and use these as a basis for designing their programs. Rather than imposing a structure that is counter to children's natural ways of learning, teachers must design timetables and classroom environments to accommodate and capitalize on these.

Greenman, J. 1988. *Caring spaces, learning places: Children's environments that work.* Redmond, WA: Exchange Press.

Provides a comprehensive look at the ways child care providers can design and create indoor and outdoor spaces that are appropriate for both children and staff. The author offers practical advice on acoustics, room arrangement, aesthetics, buildings, groups, outdoor environments, storage, and the process of change.

Hart, C. 1993. *Children on playgrounds: Research perspectives and applications.* Albany, NY: State University of New York Press.

Focuses on key issues and current research evidence of links between children's behavior in outdoor play environments and children's development. Specific attention is given to the ways that outdoor play environments are extensions of other developmental settings like the classroom or family.

Hewes, J. 1975. *Build your own playground! A sourcebook of play sculptures, designs, and concepts from the work of Jay Beckwith.* Boston: Houghton Mifflin.

This text, schematic drawings, and sequential photographs help early educators learn how to use parents and community to build creative playground or innovative structures that delight children. Special attention is given to play theory, environmental planning, and safety.

Hohmann, C., & W. Buckleitner. 1992. *Learning environment.* Ypsilanti, MI: High/Scope.

A comprehensive guide that offers useful information on the physical setting, daily schedule, and teacher-child interaction strategies for active learning classrooms. Describes how to arrange and equip the learning environment and set up a daily schedule to support a balanced range of individual, small-group, and large-group learning experiences.

Ingraham, P.B. 1997. *Creating and managing learning centers: A thematic approach.* Peterborough, NH: Crystal Springs.

An experienced teacher of 3- to 8-year-olds sets forth a framework for supporting child-directed learning through a large variety of centers. Ways to keep track of children's work in learning centers and to create a physical environment, materials, and center-based activities are illustrated by sample charts, contracts, assessment tools, and forms for children's use.

Isbell, R. 1995. *The complete learning center book: An illustrated guide to 32 different early childhood centers.* Beltsville, MD: Gryphon House.

Encourages teachers to enrich their classroom environments with unique learning centers and gives new ideas for traditional centers. Clear illustrations provide a layout of each center with suggestions on setting up the classroom environment. Each center includes an introduction, learning objectives, a letter to the parents, a list of topic-related vocabulary, and a web of integrated learning diagramming the curriculum areas taught.

Jackson, B.R. 1997. Creating a climate for healing in a violent society. *Young Children* 52 (7): 68–70.

Explores the trauma a violent society creates for young children and how an early childhood program can be a safe haven. Discusses how trauma can affect a child's sense of self, relationships with others, and world view.

Jackson, M. 1993. *Creative display and environment.* Portsmouth, NH: Heinemann.

Explores the whole school and classroom environment and any part of the natural or made world that can be brought into it. Designed to help teachers provide children with both firsthand experiences using objects and items as stimuli for a wide range of learning experiences as well as a sound, practical, and interesting environment in which education can effectively take place.

Jones, E., & E. Prescott. 1984. *Dimensions of teaching-learning environments: A handbook for teachers in elementary schools and day care centers.* Pasadena, CA: Pacific Oaks College.

Translates research concepts into ideas that can be used by teachers to informally analyze their own classroom environments. Physical setting and teacher behavior are evaluated based on the following values: open/closed, soft/hard, simple/complex, intrusive/seclusive, and high/low mobility.

Kritchevsky, S., E. Prescott, & L. Walling. 1977. *Planning environments for young children: Physical space.* Washington, DC: NAEYC.

Explains characteristics of high-quality physical environments and provides strategies for evaluating environments. Authors also show how the organization of space can diminish discipline problems.

Meek, A., ed. 1995. *Designing places for learning.* Alexandria, VA: Association for Supervision and Curriculum Development & Council for Educational Facility Planners/International.

Several authors provide convincing evidence of the link between architecture and academic success. Presents facts about the conditions of schools across the nation along with suggestions for improving the design of existing and future buildings. A cost analysis of school building neglect provides information for persuading community members to invest in school improvements.

Moore, G.T. 1996. Addressing center size: A village of interconnected houses for very large centers. *Child Care Information Exchange* (111): 77–81.

Author discusses some of the important ways the size of the physical building affects children's and teacher's behavior and the quality of the program, whether in a private facility or public school.

Moore, R.C., S.M. Goltsman, D.S. Iacofano, & S. McIntyre. 1992. *Play for all guidelines: Planning settings for all children.* 2d ed. Berkeley, CA: MIG Communications.

Within this basic reference is a treasure trove of playground design, including information on how to comply with the Americans with Disabilities Act.

Moore, R.C., & H.H. Wong. 1997. *Natural learning: Creating environments for rediscovering nature's way of teaching.* Berkeley, CA: MIG Communications.

Describes a collaboration between a field naturalist, landscape architect, local businesses such as a seed company, and an elementary school and its neighbors to convert an urban schoolyard into a joyful space for learning. Authors detail the transformation of the curriculum both inside the school and out as children studied and wrote about such things as the garden ecosystem, the watershed, the butterflies, birds, and pond life or the personal joy and peace that they and their teachers experienced in their relationships with each other.

Moyer, J., ed. 1995. *Selecting educational equipment and materials for school and* home. Wheaton, MD: Association for Childhood Education International.

Collection of articles on creating the learning environment, including such topics as room arrangement. A comprehensive discussion of materials and resources includes suggestions for collecting, compiling, and constructing materials and equipping a child care center or school for infant/toddlers, preschoolers, kindergartners, and early elementary-school grades.

Olien, R. 1998. *Walk this way: Classroom hikes to learning.* Portsmouth, NH: Heinemann.

Tells how to plan an outdoor education program for K- to third-grade children to enrich projects on the aesthetic appreciation of the environment and to complement the math and science learning. Strategies for conducting minihikes in the community surrounding the school (both urban and rural) encompass topics such as questioning techniques and keeping nature notebooks.

Sanoff, H. 1995. *Creating environments for young children.* Mansfield, OH: Bookmaster's.

Addresses all the conditions necessary for creating appropriate environments for young children, such as the need for privacy, soft space, aesthetic use of color, and an adequate amount of space for various learning activities.

Schwartz, S., & M. Pollishuke. 1991. *Creating the child-centered classroom.* Katonah, NY: Richard C. Owen.

Features many ways to set up the classroom to support child-centered learning and discusses the use and organization of materials or graphic displays of children's work. Illustrated with photographs and drawings of learning centers.

Shepherd, W., J. Eaton, E. Prescott, A.R. Olds, & E. Eisenberg. 1997. Room arrangement. *Child Care Information Exchange* (117): 41–56.

Focuses on creating environments that intrigue and delight children and adults. The authors provide insight into room arrangement and mood creation.

Skrupskelis, A. 1990. Going places with young children. *Dimensions* 18 (3): 3–6.

Examines reasons for incorporating field trips into the curriculum, ways to plan successful expeditions, and appropriate field trip experiences for young children. (Distributed by ERIC Document Reproduction Service; EJ410771.)

Stine, S. 1997. *Landscapes for learning: Creating outdoor environments for children and youth.* New York: John Wiley.

Explores the vital and growing movement that is transforming schoolyards, day care facilities, and museum grounds around the world. The author presents detailed analyses of a wide variety of outdoor environments for children and the principles and processes that enabled their design, creation, and ongoing operation.

Stolberg, J., & E. Daniels. 1998. *Creating child-centered materials for math and science.* Washington, DC: Children's Resources International.

Demonstrates use of inexpensive or free household or outdoor materials that can be used to support math and science activities for preschool children. Explanations of the math and science concepts accompany each activity as well as follow-up activities that link the child's family to classroom learning experiences.

Trawick-Smith, J. 1992. The classroom environment affects children's play and development. *Dimensions* 20 (2): 27–31.

Discusses the influence of the classroom environment on children's play and development. The author suggests that physical design changes can resolve classroom problems and enhance program outcomes and argues for the theory that planned space is a critical aspect of developmentally appropriate practice.

Weinstein, C., & T.G. David, eds. 1987. *Spaces for children: The built environment and child development.* New York: Plenum.

Examines the impact that physical spaces such as child care settings, large and small schools, infant/toddler settings, and home environments have on the quality of life and the development of the young child. The implications for teachers and administrators include such aspects as location, boundaries, pathways, storage space, and outdoor and indoor space adapted to the nature of the children's activity.

Wiseman, A.S. 1997. *Making things: The handbook of creative discovery.* New York: Little, Brown.

Features creative activities that emphasize learning by doing and using everyday objects to help children represent their environment. Clear diagrams, simple instructions, and appealing illustrations make these projects and teaching materials easy to construct.

Youcha, V., & K. Wood. 1997. Enhancing the environment for all children. *Child Care Information Exchange* (114): 45–47.

Discusses ways to make adaptions to a classroom's physical environment to serve the needs of all children. Provides information about the Americans with Disabilities Act and the concept of universal access; gives specific examples of how to make activities accessible for a wide range of special needs.

Promoting health and safety

This wide range of resources familiarizes practitioners with issues concerning children's health and safety in child care settings. Readers also will find different perspectives on increasing young children's awareness of safe environments and descriptions of good nutrition and health.

Adams, G. 1995. *How safe? The status of state efforts to protect children in child care.* Washington, DC: Children's Defense Fund (CDF).

Updates the state licensing policies examined in *Who Knows How Safe?* (CDF 1990) and includes new information on state policies as of November 1993. The five sections include a summary of state policies and state-by-state charts on exempting certain family child care providers from state licensing or regulation, selected health and safety regulations, state policies on the number of children allowed per caregiver and maximum group sizes, and the extent to which states inspect regulated programs.

Aronson, S. 1991. *Health and safety in child care.* New York: HarperCollins.

Designed as an introduction to all aspects of children's health and safety in child care settings. Topical organization facilitates its use as a reference guide, and suggested activities are included as a help to instructors using the book as a course text.

Casamassimo, P. 1996. *Bright futures in practice: Oral health.* Vienna, VA: National Maternal and Child Health Clearinghouse.

> Contains current oral health promotions and disease prevention guidelines for children of all ages.

Clark, M., K. Holt, & D. Sofka, eds. 1998. *Early childhood nutrition resource guide.* Arlington, VA: National Center for Education in Maternal and Child Health.

> A valuable resource in planning and providing nutrition services for young children between the ages of 2 and 6. (Distributed free from National Maternal and Child Health Clearinghouse, 2070 Chain Bridge Road, Suite 450, Vienna, VA 22182-2536; 703-356-1964. An electronic version is available from the National Center for Education in Maternal and Child Health's Website, http://www.ncemch.org)

Early Childhood Committee of the Pennsylvania Chapter of the American Academy of Pediatrics. *Preparing for illness: A joint responsibility for parents and caregivers—Revised.* 1997. Washington, DC: NAEYC.

> Makes clear the important role shared by parents and child care providers in keeping children healthy. This booklet is of special interest to directors, family child care providers, and parents, detailing information on signs, symptoms, and causes of specific conditions of illness, including when to seek medical advice and guidelines for determining exclusion of an ill child from a child care center.

Early Childhood Education Linkage System (ECELS). 1997. *Model child care health policies.* Rev. ed. Washington, DC: NAEYC.

> Contains model health policies that can be adapted or used selectively in any type of child care setting. Also includes guidelines and forms to support health policies and resources for health education materials.

Edelstein, S. 1992. *Nutrition and meal planning in child-care programs. A practical guide.* Chicago, IL: American Dietetic Association.

> Based on Department of Agriculture guidelines, this resource highlights important basic nutrition information and takes into account diverse cultural food preferences.

Graves, D., & C. Suitor, eds. 1997. *Making food healthy and safe for children: How to meet the National Health and Safety Performance Standards—Guidelines for out-of-home child care Programs.* Arlington, VA: National Center for Education in Maternal and Child Health.

> Developed to help caregivers provide children with healthy and safe food and meet the identified nutrition standards. Includes information about all of the nutrition-based standards in *Caring for Our Children* and practical recommendations on each topic to help meet the standards.

Green, M. 1994. *Bright futures: Guidelines for health supervision of infants, children, and adolescents.* Vienna, VA: National Maternal and Child Health Clearinghouse.

Includes comprehensive health supervision guidelines for children of all ages.

Healthy Child Care America Campaign (HCCAC). 1997. *Blueprint for action: 10 steps that communities can take to promote safe and healthy child care.* Elk Grove Village, IL: American Academy of Pediatrics (AAP).

Includes strategies, examples, and resources for promoting healthy child care in communities by determining needs and setting priorities. (Distributed by AAP or available on the Website, http://nccic.org/hcca/abthcca.html)

Hendricks, C., & C.J. Smith. 1995. Transforming health curriculum. In *Reaching potentials: transforming early childhood curriculum and assessment, volume 2,* eds. S. Bredekamp & T. Rosegrant, 65–79. Washington, DC: NAEYC.

Provides national health education standards for grades K–4, describes a comprehensive health education program, and argues that health education must also be integrated into other curriculum areas. Includes explanation of 10 topics of health education that educators should consider.

Kaiser, B., & J.S. Rasminsky. 1993. *HIV/AIDS and child care: Fact book and facilitator's guide.* Washington, DC: NAEYC.

The Canadian Child Care Federation in partnership with Health Canada produced this book of user-friendly information on HIV/AIDS. Serves as a guide for preparing staff and parents to welcome children with HIV into child care and for developing policies that serve the best interests of all children in the program.

Kendrick, A.S., R. Kaufmann, & K.P. Messenger, eds. 1995. *Healthy young children: A manual for programs.* Washington, DC: NAEYC.

Intended for early childhood programs, this basic manual is used to promote and protect the health and safety of children, staff, and families. This edition represents a comprehensive review that includes the most current information related to health and safety policies and practices and replaces all earlier editions of this publication.

Marotz, L.R., J. Rush, & M. Cross. 1997. *Health, safety, and nutrition for the young child.* Albany, NY: Delmar.

Addresses some of the most important issues related to the health and safety of children's environments, including common illnesses; emergency care; the organization of quality environments; assessment of children's health status; child abuse; and health, safety, and nutrition education for children. In addition, the authors provide comprehensive information about the nutritional needs of infants, toddlers, and preschoolers, including feeding concerns, food safety alerts, menu planning, and educational lesson plans.

Mohay, H., & L. Holzheimer. 1997. *Understanding asthma in young children.* Australian Early Childhood Education Association Resource Book Series, vol. 4, no. 3. Watson, ACT: Australian Early Childhood Association.

Reports on the symptoms, diagnosis and causes of asthma and what can trigger an attack. This short booklet, written in layman's terms will be helpful for caregivers and teachers in knowing what to do to care for a child with asthma.

National Resource Center for Health and Safety in Child Care. 1997. *Stepping stones to using* Caring for Our Children. Vienna, VA: National Maternal and Child Health Clearinghouse.

Contains information about the 182 health and safety standards that most affect the spread of infection in child care settings. The standards are taken from the larger *National Health and Safety Performance Standards* (American Academy of Pediatrics & American Public Health Association 1992) for out-of-home child care.

Robertson, C. 1998. *Safety, nutrition, and health in early education.* Albany, NY: Delmar.

Discusses issues of children's safe environments and good nutrition and health in a practical and realistic manner. The book includes health assessment tools and describes ways of setting up and managing a safe environment in child care.

Smith, C.J., C.M Hendricks, & B.S. Bennett. 1997. *Growing, growing strong: A whole health curriculum for young children.* St. Paul, MN: Redleaf.

Makes health an interactive, fun part of the curriculum. Eight themes weave together dozens of topics and hundreds of activities. Authors provide staff and parent information, evaluation guides, and resources.

Taylor, B. 1997. *Early childhood program management: People and procedures.* Columbus, OH: Merrill.

Provides a comprehensive view of administrative child care issues and includes chapters on procedures for ensuring children's health and safety.

Supporting children's play

Play, in its many forms and qualities, is highlighted in these materials. Primary among the themes is the role of play in children's development and learning in preschool and primary school settings, outdoors, and in the home. The roles of teachers in planning for play, during play, and after play has occurred are linked to the benefits for children. Issues and controversies surrounding play are also discussed in this section.

Burrell, L., & J.C. Perlmutter. 1995. Learning through *play* as well as *work* in the primary grades. *Young Children* 50 (5): 14–21.

Discusses the concepts of work and play in a mixed-age (K–2) primary-school classroom. Topics include a comparison of preschool and primary-school play, how children classify work and play, the kinds of work and play in which the children engage, and how the teacher integrates work and play and assesses progress in both.

Carlsson-Paige, N., & D.E. Levin. 1987. *The war play dilemma: Balancing needs and values in the early childhood classroom.* New York: Teachers College Press.

The authors examine the effects of war play in preschool classrooms and present approaches and guidelines for teachers confronted with specific situations.

Casey, M.B., & M. Lippman. 1991. Learning to plan through play. *Young Children* 46 (4): 52–58.

Gives suggestions on helping children become better planners through play. Shows that when children take responsibility for control of what goes on in the classroom, they feel proud and successful.

Catron, C., & J. Allen. 1999. *Early childhood curriculum: A creative play model.* 2d ed. Columbus, OH: Merrill/Prentice Hall.

Presents a creative play model in which curriculum for infants, toddlers, and preschoolers is organized around developmental goals for children. Some features include teaching approaches for helping children cope with stress, integrate computers into the curriculum, and developmental checklists for observing and assessing.

Christie, J.F., & F. Wardle. 1992. How much time is needed for play? *Young Children* 47 (3): 28–32.

Suggests that programs serving preschool and kindergarten not only recognize the critical importance of constructive and group dramatic play but also realize that these forms of play are more likely to occur in play periods of 30 minutes or more.

Cuffaro, H.K., S. Cartwright, K. Stritzel, S. Reifel, & K. Stephens. 1995. Block play. *Child Care Information Exchange* (103): 33–56.

Discusses how block building provides opportunities for learning, fosters cooperative living and learning, and offers suggestions on enriching block play and helping teachers become block partners with children.

Fromberg, D.P. 1998. Play issues in early childhood education. In *Continuing issues in early childhood education,* eds. C. Seefeldt & A. Galper, 190–212. Upper Saddle River, NJ: Merrill/Prentice Hall.

Presents the idea that, for children, play is voluntary, meaningful, active, symbolic, rule-bound, and pleasurable. Discusses the relationship between play and work, how play influences other development, equity in play, and implications for teachers.

Frost, J.L. 1992. *Play and perspectives.* Albany, NY: Delmar.

Includes an overview on providing play for children with disabilities, along with a particularly strong discussion of good outdoor play equipment.

Heidemann, S., & D. Hewitt. 1992. *Pathways to play: Developing play skills in young children.* St. Paul, MN: Redleaf.

Overview on the development of play, with a checklist for observations and a step-by-step guide for teacher intervention and support.

Henniger, M.L. 1994. Planning for outdoor play. *Young Children* 49 (4): 10–15.

Discusses the importance of children playing outside and gives ideas for creating creative outdoor play spaces. Focuses on the importance of healthy risk taking and graduated challenges, promoting a variety of play types, and manipulation of the environment.

Hirsch, E.S., ed. 1996. *The block book.* 3d ed. Washington, DC: NAEYC.

Expanded and updated, this classic helps teachers discover exciting possibilities for block play and recognize the rich contributions of blocks, not only to creativity and dramatic play but to science, math, social studies, and other learning domains. Includes practical tips for equipping and organizing a block area, plus a new chapter on large blocks.

Isenberg, J.P., & M.R. Jalongo. 1997. *Creative expression and play in early childhood.* Upper Saddle River, NJ: Merrill.

Describes ways to facilitate children's creative expression in early childhood classrooms and explains the importance of creative expression in the developing person. One chapter depicts the characteristics, development, and controversy surrounding play in the preschool and primary school curriculum and defines specific roles and responsibilities.

Jones, E. 1989. Inviting children into the fun: Providing enough activity choices outdoors. *Child Care Information Exchange* (70): 15–19.

Presents the idea that in environments that offer the possibility of discovery and inventiveness, children's play sustains itself.

Jones, E., & G. Reynolds. 1992. *The play's the thing: Teachers' roles in children's play*. New York: Teachers College Press.

Describes why play is a fundamentally important part of children's development and shows how adults can support and promote play. The authors offer systematic descriptions and analyses of the different roles a teacher adopts toward this end.

Kamii, C., & R. DeVries. 1980. *Group games in early education: Implications of Piaget's theory*. Washington, DC: NAEYC.

Suggests ways to select or adapt both new and familiar games to make them more appropriate for children's development. Chapters include information about good group games, the issue of competition, and the principles of teaching.

Klugman, E., ed. 1995. *Play, policy, and practice*. St. Paul, MN: Redleaf.

Features selections from international experts on such topics as media, culture, and the undermining of play in the United States; the teacher's role in enabling play; and the importance of play in human development.

Mulligan, V. 1996. *Children's play*. New York: Addison Wesley Longman.

Provides practitioners with an excellent introduction to creating developmentally, individually, and locally appropriate play environments for children from infancy through school age.

Owocki, G. 1999. *Literacy through play*. Portsmouth, NH: Heinemann.

With many glimpses of children and teachers, this book portrays play-based curricula in a preschool and first-grade classroom and explains how children come to know about the functions, forms, genres, and features of written language through play. Gives practical tips for identifying children's concepts of print and creating literate play environments.

Paley, V. 1986. *Mollie is three: Growing up in school*. Chicago: University of Chicago Press.

Provides insightful, highly readable teacher observations of a year in the life of Mollie's preschool classroom. Paley relates that "Mollie is 3, in a place called school, a place she needs to make sense of quickly lest she feel too small and disconnected." "Fantasy play," she says, "is the most compelling and useful aspect of preschool life" and "Playing together, young children construct shared understandings of their lives."

Paley, V. 1992. *You can't say you can't play*. Cambridge, MA: Harvard University Press.

The author interweaves her reflections and conversations with children to tell what happened when she instituted a new rule in her class that prohibited children from excluding someone who wanted to play. The implications of such a nonexclusion rule were profound; most of the children resisted at first but with discussion began to adjust their behavior and truly experience the benefits of "making no one a stranger."

Phillips, A.L., ed. 1996. *Topics in early childhood education: Playing for keeps.* St. Paul, MN: Redleaf.

The author uses a variety of contexts such as research, teaching, theory, and practice to examine ways of supporting children's play. Selected papers by members of the Four-College Consortium—Bank Street College, Erikson Institute, Pacific Oaks College, and Wheelock College—are included.

Reynolds, G., & E. Jones. 1997. *Master players: Learning from children at play.* New York: Teachers College Press.

A companion volume to *The play's the thing,* this book defines and analyzes the concept of master player based on videotaped observations of preschool children at play. By interweaving sequences of play with dialog about them, the authors model how teachers can work as a team to develop their understanding of a particular child and the value of children's quality of play and how they can support both.

Rivkin, M. 1995. *The great outdoors: Restoring children's right to play outside.* Washington, DC: NAEYC.

Makes a compelling argument for restoring children's birthright to outdoor play and learning. Gives examples of exciting playgrounds in the United States and other countries and provides practical information on topics that include safety, accessibility, and curriculum.

Sawyers, J.K., & C.S. Rogers. 1988. *Helping young children develop through play: A practical guide for parents, caregivers, and teachers.* Washington, DC: NAEYC.

An overview of why play is so important to children's learning. Contains practical suggestions on how adults can foster play with infants, toddlers, preschoolers, and school-agers.

Segal, M. 1997, 1998. *Birth to 1, 1 to 2, 2 to 3, 3 to 5,* and *5 to 8.* Your Child at Play series. New York: Newmarket.

Accessible, anecdotal, and fun to read, these books provide insight into the child's emerging capacities and help adults to understand what's happening from the child's viewpoint. Filled with play ideas for enhancing children's development and making everyday routines fun for children and parents.

Sheridan, M.K., G.M. Foley, & S.H. Radinski. 1995. *Using the supportive play model: Individualized intervention in early childhood practices.* New York: Teachers College Press.

Filled with specific suggestions on using play to integrate children with disabilities into the life of the school.

Shipley, D. 1998. *Empowering children: Play-based curriculum for lifelong learning.* Ontario, Canada: Nelson.

Covers an enormous breadth of theory and practice on play and the necessity of open choices and personal empowerment. Spans the developmental stages from infancy through the primary-school years.

Stone, S.J. 1995. Wanted: Advocates for play in the primary grades. *Young Children* 50 (6): 45–54.

Includes information on the benefits of play so that advocates for play can describe them to others. Also included are ways of integrating play into the curriculum, working with parents, and creating time for play.

Trawick-Smith, J. 1994. *Interactions in the classroom: Facilitating play in the early years.* New York: Merrill/Prentice Hall.

Focuses on teacher-child interactions and the role of teachers in children's play. Shows future teachers of children aged 3 to 8 how to construct a play-based curriculum in which children guide their own learning with informal assistance from skilled play facilitators.

Van Hoorn, J., P. Nourot, B. Scale, & K. Alward. 1998. *Play at the center of the curriculum.* 2d ed. New York: Merrill.

Highlights the natural connection between play and learning and demonstrates how to draw from children's spontaneous play both the methods and content of a successful K–3 curriculum. The authors combine clear explanations of theories of development and play with practical approaches to subject matter, including appropriate use of technology such as e-mail and digital cameras.

Ward, C.D. 1996. Adult intervention: Appropriate strategies for enriching the quality of children's play. *Young Children* 51 (3): 20–25.

Provides a concise discussion of methods that teachers in preschool can use to extend children's play in appropriate ways so that children can grow into *master players.*

Wasserman, S. 1990. Serious players in the primary classroom: Empowering children through active learning experiences. New York: Teachers College Press.

Twenty-nine activities in the four curriculum areas of science, social studies, mathematics, and language arts form this book's core. Specific strategies enable teachers to use play to help children learn important concepts and organize "play-debrief-replay" active learning within the primary-school curriculum.

Widerstorm, A.H., & S.R. Sandall. 1995. *Achieving learning goals through play.* Tucson, AZ: Communication Skill Builders.

Encourages naturalistic play that addresses the learning goals of all children, including those with special needs.

Wolf, D.P., S. Grollman, L. McCune, & W.G. Scarlett. 1994. Make-believe-play. *Child Care Information Exchange* (94): 31–50.

Includes articles on the importance of make-believe play, approaching play through fantasy and exploration, make-believe play in the lives of infants, and solving problems in make-believe.

Fostering social and emotional competence

It was especially difficult to develop subcategories in this section because often one kind of social behavior leads to or makes possible another. For example, the discipline system used by the teacher can become the foundation for cooperative learning; helping an individual child develop a relationship contributes to caring classroom communities. Although many of the resources in this area cover more than one component of social or emotional competence, they have been placed in one of five categories according to their primary focus.

Nurturing friendship, self-esteem, and autonomy

This group of resources focuses largely on the teacher's role in fostering individual social competence as the child interacts spontaneously with peers and adults in the course of a day. Teaching attitudes and actions that help a child engage in satisfying interactions, make friends, become autonomous, understand and use his/her feelings constructively, and develop self esteem are some examples of topics that are included.

Bos, B. 1990. *Together we're better—Establishing a co-active learning environment.* Roseville, CA: Turn-the-Page Press.

Focuses on the social and emotional philosophy that doing things together fosters cooperation and the social skills children need to survive in this world. Includes activities that illustrate co-active environments.

Curry, N., & C. Johnson. 1990. *Beyond self-esteem: Developing a genuine sense of human value.* Washington, DC: NAEYC.

Uses research to document how children develop a sense of significance and value and the implications for teachers. In a chronology of the infant and toddler years through kindergarten and primary, the authors illuminate such topics as acceptance, power and control, autonomy, virtue, and moral worth. The second part of the book provides classroom strategies for helping children as they meet the challenges in these areas.

Gonzalez-Mena, J. 1998. *The child in the family and the community.* Upper Saddle River, NJ: Merrill.

An examination of the socialization process of young children, with a focus on the development of attachment, autonomy, initiative, and self-esteem in the family and the child's community. Discusses how society's goals, cultural patterns, and values affect childrearing environments (including group and family child care settings).

Greenberg, P. 1992. Ideas that work with young children. How to institute some simple democratic practices pertaining to respect, rights, roots, and responsibilities in any classroom (without losing your leadership position). *Young Children* 47 (5): 10–7.

Looks at practices in early childhood classrooms that will help build each child's self-esteem, competence, independence, initiative, and sense of significance.

Heidemann, S., & D. Hewitt. 1992. *Pathways to play: Developing play skills in young children*. St. Paul, MN: Redleaf.

Describes ways to promote preschool children's social competency by supporting cooperative play skills. An enclosed checklist is useful in pinpointing where a child is having problems.

Hurst, C.O., & R. Otis. 1999. *Friends and relations: Using literature with social themes, K–2*. Greenfield, MA: Northeast Foundation for Children.

Covers social issues that are central to 5- to 7-year-olds: the give and take of friendship, bullies, pests and teasing, isolation, families, and learning to cooperate and negotiate. Suggestions are offered for using trade books to pique children's interests and start discussions. Books are accompanied by developmental comments, summary of the story, possible questions, and activities to enhance understanding.

Jewett, J. 1992. Aggression and cooperation: Helping young children develop constructive strategies. *ERIC Digest*. ED351147. Urbana-Champaign, IL: ERIC Clearinghouse on Elementary and Early Childhood Education.

Summarizes the emerging knowledge of the complex factors entering into the development of social competence in the young child and how teachers' support and guidance can help children develop constructive strategies for dealing with challenging peer relationships.

Katz, L.G., & D.E. McClellan. 1997. *Fostering children's social competence: The teacher's role*. Washington, DC: NAEYC.

Drawing from research and expert practice, these authors suggest principles and strategies to guide teachers in strengthening children's social skills. They identify very common well-intentioned practices in early childhood classrooms that undermine children's social competence.

Kostelnik, M., L. Stein, A. Whiren, & A. Soderman. 1998. *Guiding children's social development*. 3d ed. New York: Delmar.

Answers the who, what, where, why, and how questions associated with child guidance and discipline. Presents current theory and links that theory to specific guides for skill development as well as pitfalls to avoid. Prepares teachers with a comprehensive framework for interpreting children's social behavior and implementing appropriate strategies to enhance children's social competence.

McCracken, J.B. 1993. *Valuing diversity: The primary years.* Washington, DC: NAEYC.

Discusses how adults can support children's self-esteem and self-discipline, teach children to respect individual differences, resolve conflicts peaceably, and encourage cooperation.

Roe, D. 1998. *Young children with attention difficulties—how can we help?* Watson, ACT: Australian Early Childhood Association.

Ideas about helping children who have difficulties with attention, whether a short-term or ongoing difficulty. Offers practical and positive techniques for helping these children manage their behavior and build self-esteem to overcome learning or social difficulties.

Wittmer, D.S., & A.S. Honig. 1994. Encouraging positive social development in young children. *Young Children* 49 (5): 4–12.

Research-supported ways to encourage prosocial development in young children. Part 1 of a two-part series focuses on interpersonal interactions of caregivers with individual or small groups of young children.

Honig, A., & D.S. Wittmer. 1996. Helping children become more prosocial: Ideas for classroom, families, schools, and communities. *Young Children* 51 (2): 62–71.

Part 2 discusses helping children become less aggressive or shy and more prosocial is a critical goal for early childhood teachers. This pair of articles provides background research and dozens of excellent ideas to promote prosocial behaviors among children.

Achieving positive guidance, discipline, and conflict resolution

This category contains resources that address how rules for behavior are established in a classroom, systems teachers use to help children meet expectations, and how teachers handle situations when children do not meet expectations or conflict arises.

A number of materials underscore the need to go beyond eliminating negative behavior or controlling children and to helping them establish constructive dispositions and effective ways of accomplishing their goals.

Bailey, B. 1994. *There's got to be a better way: Discipline that works!* Orlando, FL: Learning in Action.

Discusses child-centered discipline that is in accordance with developmentally appropriate philosophy. Ideas provided allow teachers to consider their discipline methods and make changes that are appropriate for children, 3 through 6 years old, in group/early childhood settings.

Carlsson-Paige, N., & D.E. Levin. 1998. *Before push comes to shove: Building conflict resolution skills with children.* St. Paul, MN: Redleaf.

Begins with a discussion of the developmental factors, concepts, and skills underlying conflict resolution for the 3- to 8-year-old. This guide to developing curriculum presents themes that have meaning to children, activities and facilitation strategies to promote perspective-taking, and alternatives to put-downs, bias statements, or other actions that escalate conflict. Includes a children's book.

Dinwiddie, S.A. 1994. The saga of Sally, Sammy and the red pen: Facilitating children's social problem solving. *Young Children* 44 (5): 15–19.

Discusses how to facilitate children's social problem solving; gives a hypothetical classroom conflict and illustrates different ways in which a teacher can guide children's own conflict resolution.

Essa, E. 1998. *A practical guide to solving preschool behavior problems.* 4th ed. Albany, NY: Delmar.

Provides a practical approach to working with young children with behavior problems and includes a new focus on working with children with disabilities and special needs. The book presents more than 40 behavior problems with examples and explanations, allowing the reader to review approaches for specific problems.

Fields, M.V., & C. Boesser. 1998. *Constructive guidance and discipline: Preschool and primary* education. Columbus, OH: Merrill.

Examines guidance and discipline concepts based on child development theory, appropriate practice, and the constructivist viewpoint. Focusing on preventing discipline problems, the authors explore how effective teaching can alleviate or prevent many common discipline problems.

Gartrell, D. 1997. Beyond discipline to guidance. *Young Children* 52 (6): 34–42.

Stresses the importance of using positive guidance technique that assist children in learning how to control their own behavior. Explains the difference between punishment, discipline, and guidance and provides six key guidance practices that describe why and how teachers use guidance strategies.

Gartrell, D. 1998. *A guidance approach for the encouraging classroom.* 2d ed. New York: Delmar.

Provides a comprehensive, caring, developmentally appropriate approach to guiding children's personal and social development. Conflict management is highlighted as an integral part of the classroom.

Hitz, R., & A. Driscoll. 1988. Praise or encouragement? New insights into praise: Implications for early childhood teachers. *Young Children* 43 (5): 6–13.

Discusses effective and ineffective ways to praise children and delineates differences between encouragement and praise.

Hymes, J.L., Jr. [1955] 1995. *Behavior and misbehavior: A teacher's guide to discipline.* West Greenwich, RI: Consortium.

This classic book describing the essence of good teaching is useful today. Offers thoughtful, commonsense suggestions for guiding children's behaviors.

Kaiser, B., & J.S. Rasminsky. 1999. *Meeting the challenge: Effective strategies for challenging behaviors in early childhood environments.* Ottawa, Ontario: Canadian Child Care Federation.

Contains proven strategies for succeeding with children whose behaviors present particularly tough challenges. Easily understandable ideas and strategies proven to work with children having the most challenging behaviors and to benefit every child in the setting.

Kohn, A. 1993. *Punished by rewards: The trouble with gold stars, incentive plans, A's, praise, and other bribes.* Boston: Houghton Mifflin.

Presents persuasive arguments against depending upon extrinsic rewards to obtain desired behaviors. The author concludes that the use of incentives lowers performance, reduces interest and risk taking, and doesn't change long-term behavior. A resource for early childhood education students, teachers, administrators, and parents.

Linke, P. 1998. *Let's stop bullying.* Watson, ACT: Australian Early Childhood Association.

A comprehensive handbook on the nature and causes of bullying and how it can be prevented or handled. Designed for early childhood teachers in infant/toddler settings, preschools, or primary grades. Techniques are offered for supporting children (and their parents) who are victims of bullying as well as children who bully.

Marion, M. 1999. *Guidance of young children.* 4th ed. Upper Saddle River, NJ: Merrill/Prentice Hall.

Conveys the research supporting positive discipline and an authoritative caregiving style and practical strategies teachers can use to help children deal with stress, anger, and promote prosocial behaviors. Case study examples from birth through age 8 illustrate a suggested eclectic approach to child guidance.

McCloskey, C.M. 1996. Taking positive steps toward classroom management in preschool: Loosening up without letting it all fall apart. *Young Children* 51 (3): 14–16.

Suggests eight steps for positive classroom management.

Reynolds, E. 1996. *Guiding young children: A child-centered approach.* 2d ed. Mountain View, CA : Mayfield.

Stresses techniques that promote children's ability to solve their own problems. Techniques outlined include natural and logical consequences, active listening, limit setting, and taking responsibility for actions.

Rodd, J. 1996. *Understanding young children's behavior.* New York: Teachers College Press.

Suggests a range of positive strategies for managing inappropriate behavior in ways that enhance children's development and confidence in their own ability to change their behavior. Techniques are offered to help the teacher assess her own internal value system.

Scarlett, W.G. 1998. *Trouble in the classroom: Managing the behavior problems of young children.* San Francisco: Jossey-Bass.

Introduces a classroom management system that centers on supporting the child's long-term development as the cure for problem behavior in preschool settings. In addition to the usual methods of guidance, prevention, and control, the authors present many options that help children build and use inner resources.

Stone, J.G. 1978. *A guide to discipline.* Rev. ed. Washington, DC: NAEYC.

Discusses how to teach children to respect themselves and others and show that respect. Presents ways in which teachers can help children to take control over their behavior—inner control—and establish a classroom that functions in a peaceful and constructive way.

Considering gender and sexual development

This collection of resources discusses the development of gender role in children and offers approaches for teachers to promote nonsexist attitudes and behavior in the classroom. A number also address the meaning of sexuality, how children develop sexually, and common issues about sexuality that are likely to arise in early childhood settings. Authors also suggest responses to these situations and discuss the role of love in early childhood classrooms.

Boutte, G., S. Hendley, & I. Van Scoy. 1996. Multicultural and nonsexist prop boxes. *Young Children* 52 (1): 34–39.

Stresses the importance of a rationale for using prop boxes to facilitate dramatic play and expands on ways to integrate multicultural and nonsexist learning experiences in curricula and activities.

Brown, B. 1998. *Unlearning discrimination in the early years.* Staffordshire, England: Trentham.

Encourages students and adults working with young children to enable the children to talk constructively about issues of discrimination. Author explains relevant research and theory about how racism, sexism, and homophobia develop and how to help engage in antidiscriminatory practice with preschoolers. (Distributed by Stylus Publishing, Herndon, Virginia.)

Cahill, B.J., & R. Theilheimer. 1999. "Can Tommy and Sam get married?" Questions about gender, sexuality, and young children. *Young Children* 54 (1): 27–31.

Address four questions: How can teachers become more comfortable with questions about sexual orientation and social conventions? What does research tell us about children's developing sexuality and how can that information be useful to teachers? How should teachers respond when such issues arise in the classroom? What are appropriate ways to talk to families about sexual orientation and societal mores?

The Children's Foundation. 1994. *Helping children love themselves and others: Resource guide to equity materials for young children.* Washington, DC: Author.

Contains a checklist of books, toys, and materials to assist in determining equity resources; annotated bibliographies of children's literature and resources for adults that include books, curricula, magazines, newsletters and pamphlets; a listing of companies with antibias and/or multicultural books and materials available; and a listing of national support organizations. (Distributed by The Children's Foundation, 725 Fifteenth Street, NW, Suite 505, Washington, DC 20005-2109.)

Corbett, S.M. 1991. Children and sexuality. *Young Children* 46 (2): 71–77.

If we do not wish to perpetuate negative patterns of sexual development and opt to allow our children access to healthy growth in this area, we need to open ourselves to our children's questions and activities even as we open ourselves to our sexual feelings and values.

Crawford, S.H. 1996. *Beyond dolls and guns: One hundred and one ways to help children avoid gender bias.* St. Paul, MN: Redleaf.

Includes information on stereotypes and antibias activities. Offers suggestions for recognizing and overcoming sexism and gender bias and for developing healthy, respectful relationships.

Dyson, A.H., & C. Genishi, eds. 1994. *The need for story: Cultural diversity in classroom and community.* Urbana, IL: National Council of Teachers of English.

Nineteen contributors explore the nature of *story*—the basic functions it serves, its connections to the diverse sociocultural landscape of our society, and its power in the classroom. Emphasizing the complex relationships between story, ethnicity, and gender, the book includes stories both told and written, those authored by children and by teachers, ones professionally produced, and those created in the classroom.

Edwards, C.P. 1986. *Promoting social and moral development in young children: Creative approaches for the classroom.* New York: Teachers College Press.

Examines the social-cognitive growth of children from ages 2 through 6 and discusses six critical areas of development: age identity and roles, gender identity and sex roles, racial and cultural categories, concepts of family and friendship, societal institutions, and moral decisionmaking.

Francis, B. 1998. *Power plays: Primary school children's constructions of gender, power and adult work.* Stoke on Trent, Great Britain: Trentham.

Investigates primary school children's constructions of gender in relation to their own lives and the issue of adult occupations. Concludes that the only way to address the power inequalities is to deconstruct the notions of gender as relational, and suggests how this can be achieved in primary classrooms. (Distributed by Stylus Publishing, Herndon, Virginia.)

Gallas, K. 1998. *Sometimes I can be anything: Power, gender and identity.* New York: Teachers College Press.

From research conducted over a four-year period, this book explores young children's experience and understanding of gender, race, and power as revealed by their interactions in the author's first/second-grade classroom.

Goldstein, L.S. 1997. *Teaching with love: A feminist approach to early childhood education.* New York: Peter Lang.

Addresses the nature, scope, and dimensions of "teacherly love"— the caring, emotion, and intuition traditionally viewed as female ways of thinking. Explores the ways that love contributes to the educational practices of kindergarten and primary teachers, discussing such topics as the discomfort some educators feel in using the term *love,* or in creating a loving atmosphere in which students can learn in a way that relates to their own lives.

Gonzalez-Mena, J. 1998. Modeling and teaching sex roles. In *The child in the family and the community.* Upper Saddle River, NJ: Merrill.

Examines how children learn sex roles and the components of the socialization process that result in differential treatment of boy and girls by parents and teachers. Guidelines are offered for parents and teachers.

Henkin, R. 1998. *Who's invited to share? Using literacy to teach for equity and social justice.* Portsmouth, NH: Heinemann.

Reveals how teachers can use classroom discourse and parts of the literacy program to address inequitable behaviors and attitudes that force some children to become outsiders in the classroom. Begins with examples of gender bias in a first-grade writing workshop and describes the problems of establishing social justice in the classroom and how teachers can address these problems.

Kantrowitz, B., & C. Kalb. 1999. Boys will be boys. In *Annual editions: Early childhood education, 1999/2000, 20th edition,* eds. K. Panciorek & J. Munro. Gilford, CT: Dushkin/McGraw-Hill.

Focuses on the developmental abilities of boys—a close examination of what makes them tick and how educational settings can be responsive to their unique qualities and gender characteristics.

Leipzig, J. 1992. Helping whole children grow: Nonsexist childrearing for infants and toddlers. In *Alike and different: Exploring our humanity with young children,* rev. ed., ed. B. Neugebauer, 32–42. Washington, DC: NAEYC.

Written for infant and toddler caregivers. The author emphasizes the importance of self-observation in interactions with children and becoming aware of gender-related bias. Suggestions for engaging in nonsexist caregiving are discussed.

Linke, P. 1997. *Pants aren't rude: Responding to children's sexual development and behaviour in the early childhood years.* Watson, ACT: Australian Early Childhood Association.

Tells about how children develop sexually and how they express this in behavior. Presents suggested responses to children's sexual behavior and skills that can assist early childhood educators as they respond to and guide children's learning in this fundamental part of their development.

MacNaughton, G. *The power of mum! Gender and power at play.* AECA Resource Book Series, vol. 2, no. 2. Watson, ACT: Australian Early Childhood Association.

Explores the interplay between power and gender in early childhood settings, especially in children's storylines in dramatic play. Insight into children's gender relations is offered, with a range of strategies teachers can use to promote nonsexist attitudes and behavior.

McCormick, T.M. 1994. *Creating the nonsexist classroom: A multicultural approach.* New York: Teachers College Press.

Challenges restrictions on the growth of sex equity and provides educators with theoretical and practical guidelines for implementing nonsexist education in the classroom. Includes appendices of resources.

Paley, V.G. 1984. *Boys and girls: Superheroes in the doll corner.* Chicago, IL: University of Chicago Press.

In vignettes the author re-creates a year of kindergarten teaching in which she explores the differences in the ways children play and fantasize. Paley questions the prejudices of the teacher's curriculum that rewards girls' domestic play while discouraging boys' adventurous fantasies. Discussion of her own discomfort with boys' play and approval of that of girls raises an important educational issue.

Ramsey, P. 1998. *Teaching and learning in a diverse world.* 2d ed. New York: Teachers College Press.

Part 3

Offers a comprehensive discussion of children's identity development in several areas such as race, culture, gender, class, disabilities, and family structure. Also provides principles and strategies for creating quality environments that support children of all backgrounds.

Rothbaum, F., A. Grauer, & D.J. Rubin. 1997. Becoming sexual: Differences between child and adult sexuality. *Young Children* 52 (6): 22–28.

Explores the difference between adult and child sexuality. Presents situations and analysis of the difference between what behavior means for adults and for young children. Provides recommendations for dealing with children's developing sexuality, including problematic behaviors and suggestions for how to talk to children about sexual matters.

Tobin, J., ed. 1997. *Making a place for pleasure in early childhood education.* New Haven: Yale University Press.

Proposes that the "moral panic" following much-publicized incidents of abuse in child care settings has produced environments where the authentic feelings of young children about their bodies and emotions are denied and repressed. The relationship of children's developing sexuality to genuine teaching interactions, disciplinary regime, "no-touch" policies, and classroom activities such as dramatic play in infant/toddler, preschool, and primary school settings is considered.

Wellhousen, K. 1996. Girls can be bull riders, too! Supporting children's understanding of gender roles through children's literature. *Young Children* 51 (5): 79–83.

Sketches children's understanding of gender as they mature cognitively, then lists and describes briefly children's books that have themes of nontraditional pursuits of boys and girls, nontraditional jobs for men and women, and females who take the initiative. Finally, the author presents suggestions for guiding discussions about these books.

Zeitlin, S. 1997. Finding fascinating projects that can promote boy/girl partnerships. *Young Children* 52 (6): 29–30.

A kindergarten teacher describes how she paired boys and girls to work together on a project dissecting owl pellets. She finds that an engaging activity is a good opportunity to pair children who would not usually play together.

Establishing the classroom community

This section offers help to teachers in understanding the concept and steps they can take to establish a sense of community in class or the school. A majority of suggestions involve whole-class activities and routines or are integrated into small-group curriculum activities. Topics such as social responsibility, mutual respect, shared values and ethics, collaboration, and school traditions are highlighted through activities that include class meetings, cooperative learning, give-and-take dialogues, and role playing. Ideas for children's participation in classroom maintenance and curriculum decisions are evident.

Bigelow, B., L. Christensen, S. Karp, B. Miner, & B. Peterson, eds. 1994. *Rethinking our classrooms: Teaching for equity and justice.* Milwaukee, WI: Rethinking Schools Ltd.

This collection for primary-school teachers includes stories and poetry of teachers' and students' struggles to create fair and just classrooms. Includes hands-on examples of ways teachers can promote values of community and equality while enhancing academic skills.

Charney, R.S. 1997. *Habits of goodness: Case studies in the social curriculum.* Greenfield, MA: Northeast Foundation for Children.

Six experienced K–6 teachers study problems from their classrooms concerning the social curriculum, and the author presents their practical approaches for bringing caring into the classroom and integrating ethical practice into daily classroom life.

Dalton, J., & M. Watson. 1997. *Among friends: Classrooms where caring and learning prevail.* Oakland, CA: Developmental Studies Center.

Using their observations of and interviews with 15 teachers, the authors describe concrete suggestions on integrating social, ethical, emotional, and academic learning in the classroom every day toward helping 5- through 11-year-olds get to know and respect one another, practice applying values, understand the academic and ethical goals of their work together, and build habits of planning and reflection.

Developmental Studies Center. 1996. *Ways we want our class to be: Class meetings that build commitment to kindness and learning.* Oakland, CA: Author.

This theoretically sound, practical guide on the what, why, and how of classroom meetings aims at helping teachers build caring communities of learners, all of whom contribute to classroom decisions, including those involving curriculum. A video version of this resource is available.

Developmental Studies Center. 1997. *Blueprints for a collaborative classroom: Twenty-five designs for partner and group work.* Oakland, CA: Author.

Offers collaborative-learning formats, and supports these with specific activities that can be used across the curriculum so that collaboration becomes part of each classroom day. Discusses the why, when, and how of using each format for maximum effectiveness and provides advice on developmental and grouping differences among young children.

Developmental Studies Center. 2000. *Company in your classroom: Building a relationship with your student teacher.* Oakland, CA: Author.

Although designed to help elementary school teachers work effectively with a student teacher, this book shows how all adults in a classroom are a part of establishing classroom community. The anecdotes and voices of the mentor teachers and their student teachers provide insights in bringing all to a common understanding of how to participate in the classroom.

DeVries, R., & B. Zan. 1994. *Moral classrooms, moral children.* New York: Teachers College Press.

Provides a constructivist approach to creating a caring classroom community of 3- through 8-year-olds. Describes how sociomoral development can be promoted through everyday activities and interactions.

Edwards, C.P. 1986. *Promoting social and moral development in young children: Creative approaches for the classroom.* New York: Teachers College Press.

Examines the social-cognitive growth of children from ages 2 through 6 and discusses six critical areas of development: age identity and roles, gender identity and sex roles, racial and cultural categories, concepts of family and friendship, societal institutions, and moral decisionmaking.

Elias, M.J., J.E. Zins, R.P. Weissberg, K.S. Frey, M.T. Greenberg, N. Haynes, R. Kessler, M.E. Schwab-Stone, & T.P. Shriver. 1997. *Promoting social and emotional learning: Guidelines for educators.* Alexandria, VA: Association for Supervision and Curriculum Development.

Provides a straightforward, practical guide to establishing high-quality social and emotional educational programs. Appendices include a curriculum scope for preschool through grade 12 and an extensive list of available contacts for firsthand knowledge about effective programs.

Gallas, K. 1998. *Sometimes I can be anything: Power, gender, and identity in a primary classroom.* New York: Teachers College Press.

Explores how 6 and 7 year-olds come to understand gender, race, and the power structure as they interact in the classroom and collectively construct their social world. Implications for the teacher are portrayed through teacher commentary and the voices and actions of the children.

Hyson, M.C. 1994. *The emotional development of young children: Building an emotion-centered curriculum.* New York: Teachers College Press.

In proposing specific teaching strategies that advance children's understanding and appropriate expression of their emotions, the author focuses on suggestions for practice through the lens of classroom anecdotes drawn from direct observation.

Kohn, A. 1996. *Beyond discipline: From compliance to community.* Alexandria, VA: Association for Supervision and Curriculum Development.

Questions traditional assumptions underlying classroom management, contrasting the idea of discipline in which things are done *to* students to control how they act with an approach in which things are done *with* students to create caring communities in which decisions are made together. Kohn lays out an alternative vision, one that is connected to the curriculum, the nature of children, and the teacher's goals.

Levin, D. 1994. *Teaching young children in violent times: Building a peaceable classroom.* Cambridge, MA: Educators for Social Responsibility.

This violence-prevention and conflict-resolution guide for working with 3- through 8-year-olds details ways to counteract the negative impact of violence on children by creating a classroom environment in which children feel safe. Also includes practical guidelines growing out of developmental theory.

Noddings, N. 1992. *The challenge to care in schools: An alternative approach to education.* New York: Teachers College Press.

Argues that schools have become uncaring places and offers ideas for how to turn elementary schools into caring environments: places where children experience stability of place, personal relationships, and caring communities.

Northeast Foundation for Children. 1997. *Off to a good start: Launching the school year* and *Familiar ground: Traditions that build school community.* Greenfield, MA: Author.

The first two booklets in The Responsive Classroom series offer information about schooling that promotes the intellectual, social, and ethical development of children 4 through 14 years old.

Paley, V. 1997. *The girl with the brown crayon.* Cambridge, MA: Harvard University Press.

The personal story of a teacher and a child in her kindergarten classroom. Interweaves the themes of race, identity, gender, and the essential human needs to create and to belong. A young girl of color discovers herself in the storybook characters created by writer Leo Lionni and inspires her class in the experience of a whole year of discussion.

Schiller, P., & T. Bryant. 1998. *The values book.* Beltsville, MD: Gryphon House.

Written to help introduce the teaching of values in any early childhood setting. Each chapter addresses one of 16 different values, including patience, understanding, and tolerance. The concept of each value is defined and questions are addressed to help clarify the meaning of the values.

Wichert, S. 1989. *Keeping the peace: Practicing cooperation and conflict resolution with preschoolers.* Philadelphia: New Society.

A handbook for parents, day care providers, kindergarten teachers, and playgroup leaders striving to create harmonious groups, bolster children's self-esteem, and foster cooperative and creative interactions between children from age 2 to 6. Includes carefully designed and clearly presented activities, the theories behind these designs, anecdotes from the author's extensive journals, and a bibliography.

Woodfin, L. 1998. *Familiar ground: Traditions that build school community.* Greenfield, MA: Northeast Foundation for Children.

Characterizes the traditions and ceremonies that help children feel they are on familiar ground and unite staff and children through the common language, signals, and experiences that are shared. Using snapshots from her own K–8 school, the author describes how all-school or morning meetings familiar to us all and unique rituals like the magic-penny ceremony can nurture a sense of belonging, openness, and welcome.

Zavitkovsky, D., K. Read Baker, & M. Almy. 1986. *Listen to the children.* Washington, DC: NAEYC.

Uses short stories along with full-page photos of typical child care and family settings to provoke thought and conversation. Also includes an analysis of each story and questions to consider.

Coping with crisis, stress, and violence

Readings in this category deal with the effects of stress and crisis on young children and make recommendations for how teachers can help children and families cope with situations such as serious illness or the death of a family member or pet, violence in the community or home, and other traumas that may occur. The origins of violence and rage receive attention, as do ideas for teachers on how to incorporate early violence prevention education into the curriculum.

Biderman, E., L. Carbajal, V. La Cerva, & L. Whitener, eds. 1998. *Voices of violence/Visions of peace.* Santa Fe, NM: Santa Fe Children's Museum.

This 75-page publication that evolved in response to increasing violence is a collection of captivating photographs and stories—personal accounts of violence, poignant quotes from children and adults, and "Poco á Poco se Anda Lejos," which sets forth stories of transformation. Suggestions for parents and teachers are offered to promote caring and experiencing more peace within our lives and families. (Distributed free by the Santa Fe Children's Museum, 505-989-8359, children@trail.com)

Cherry, C. 1981. Think of something quiet: A guide for achieving serenity in early childhood classrooms. Belmont, CA: Pitman Learning.

Provides strategies for achieving a low-stress classroom environment, techniques for responding to tension and stress, and activities for helping children relax.

Craig, S. 1990. The educational needs of children living with violence. *Phi Delta Kappan* (September): 61–71.

Details the range of ways in which young children's experiences with violence can affect their performances in school and how educators can effectively respond.

Daniel, J. 1995. New beginnings: Transitions for difficult children. *Young Children* 50 (3): 17–23.

This author describes the "new beginnings" received in her center by children who had been expelled or threatened with expulsion from other programs. Includes discussions on the key elements of the new beginning, important staff teaching behaviors, working with the family, and the transition process between programs.

Fox, S.S. 1988. *Good grief: Helping groups of children when a friend dies.* Boston, MA: New England Association for the Education of Young Children.

An excellent resource that discusses a child's understanding of death and suggests ways of helping children cope with grief. Includes an extensive list of books, films, and other resources.

Fraiberg, S. 1987. Ghosts in the nursery. In *Selected writings of Selma Fraiberg.* Columbus: Ohio State University Press.

Gives a glimpse into the clinical genius of Fraiberg's "kitchen therapy" model for family healing and the promotion of infant mental health. Serves as a clinical description of the grave crises some infants face.

Gabarino, J. 1998. *Children in danger: Coping with the consequences of community violence.* San Francisco, CA: Jossey-Bass.

Shows teachers, psychologists, counselors, and social workers how they can work together to help children who live amid chronic community violence. Offers a plan for how we can strengthen children and ward off the development of deep anger and aggression.

Goldman, L. 1996a. *Breaking the silence: A guide to help children with complicated grief—Suicide, homicide, AIDS, violence, and abuse.* Washington, DC: Accelerated Development.

Provides specific ideas and techniques for teachers and caregivers who work with children chronically exposed to violence. Describes ways of helping children understand and deal with grief. Includes a listing of national support resources and an annotated bibliography.

Goldman, L. 1996b. We can help children grieve: A child-oriented model for memorializing. *Young Children* 51 (6): 69–73.

Describes how one family and school responded to the sudden death of a child by holding a child-oriented memorial. Also describes children's view of death and suggests books as resources for children and teachers and parents.

Greenberg, J. 1996. Seeing children through tragedy. *Young Children* 51 (6): 76–77.

Describes how one program dealt with the death of the mother of one of the children. Suggests ways to deal with terminal illness and to plan for helping children deal with tragedy.

Gronlund, G. 1992. Coping with Ninja Turtle play in my kindergarten classroom. *Young Children* 48 (1): 21–25.

Suggests some actions adults can take to help children construct their own understandings of violence and aggression with regard to super-hero play.

Hepburn, M. 1999. TV violence: Myth and reality. In *Annual editions: Human development, 1999/2000, 27th edition,* ed. K. Freiberg. Guilford, CT: Dushkin/McGraw-Hill.

Reports studies of children in the 5- to 12-year-old group and the effects of viewing television violence. The author cites that television programs in the United States are the most violent in the industrialized world and offers childhood activities that can foster critical viewing skills.

Humphrey, J.H. 1998. *Helping children manage stress: A guide for adults.* Washington, DC: Child and Family Press.

Helps teachers understand how stress escalates and how to identify stressful environments. Presents principles adults can apply to their own lifestyle to alleviate stress in young children. Stress reduction techniques and activities such as story games, are offered for the preschool and primary classrooms.

Koplow, L. 1996. *Unsmiling faces: How preschools can heal.* New York: Teachers College Press.

Filled with examples of teachers working with young children in emotionally enhancing ways, this book presents a developmentally framed discussion of how to create a classroom that can help children who have experienced trauma to feel safe.

Levin, D.E. 1997. *Remote control childhood? Combating the hazards of media culture.* Washington, DC: NAEYC.

A handbook for reducing media culture's negative impact on children's lives—the heavy doses of violence, stereotypes, and commercialism, the hours spent watching instead of doing. Provides effective guidance and strategies for teachers and parents to minimize harmful media effects and reshape the media environment in which children grow up.

Levin, D.E., & N. Carlsson-Paige. 1994. Developmentally appropriate television: Putting children first. *Young Children* 49 (5): 38–44.

Discusses the ways in which caregivers can develop a framework for assessing television programs.

Miller, K. 1995. *The crisis manual for early childhood teachers: How to handle the really difficult problems.* Beltsville, MD: Gryphon House.

Addresses the most challenging issues faced by teachers of 3- through 8-year-olds, including death of a family member, domestic violence, substance abuse, sexual abuse, homelessness, natural disasters, and children with HIV/AIDS.

Rimer, P., & B. Prager. 1998. *Reaching out: Working together in identifying and responding to child victims of abuse.* Albany, NY: Delmar.

A resource for people working with children and families to help them identify and respond effectively to children who may have been abused or are at risk for abuse. Takes the reader through steps of a multifactor analysis of child abuse and physical and behavioral indicators, being attentive to disclosure, reporting to appropriate authorities.

Roe, D. 1996. *Young children and stress: How can we help?* AECA Resource Book Series, vol. 3, no. 4. Watson, ACT: Australian Early Childhood Association.

Defines stress and the causes and symptoms in young children. Suggests a range of techniques that adults can teach children to help them recognize and manage stress. The goal of this short informative booklet is to help children learn lifelong ways of coping with difficult or tense situations.

Slaby, R.G., W.C. Roedell, D. Arezzo, & K. Hendrix. 1995. *Early violence prevention: Tools for teachers of young children.* Washington, DC: NAEYC

Provides practical strategies to help reduce and deal with the effects of young children's exposure to violence. Assists early childhood professionals in controlling violent incidents in the classroom and with helping children learn to control aggressive behavior and respond to the aggression of others without becoming a victim or an accomplice or co-perpetrator as a bystander.

Stephens, K., K. Miller, M. Marsh, L. Buffin, & R. Duffy. 1996. When children are difficult. *Child Care Information Exchange* (Sept/Oct): 43–62.

Special section includes articles on responding professionally and compassionately to challenging behavior, developmental issues that affect behavior, teaching student teachers to handle challenging behavior, managing behavior with a creative mind and playful spirit, and understanding how time-out is abused and how it should be used.

Wallach, L. Helping children cope with violence. In *Annual editions: Early childhood education, 1995/1996, 16th edition,* eds. K. Paciorek & J. Munro. Guilford, CT: Dushkin/McGraw Hill.

Reports on the effects of child abuse, other domestic violence, and neighborhood violence on children and what makes some children more resilient than others. Presents many ways teachers can offset the social/emotional and cognitive damage that can occur and start the healing process.

All aspects of teaching and curriculum that pertain to programs for infants and toddlers are given under this single heading. Sample topics address developmental issues such as the current thinking about the process of learning to talk, emerging literacy, and the development of character and temperament. These are discussed along with the critical nature of quality relationships between caregiver, child, and family, and the need to create special spaces to meet the unique needs of this age group.

Barclay, K., & Benelli, C. 1997. Opening the world of literacy with infants and toddlers. *Dimensions of Early Childhood* 25 (4): 9–16.

> Encourages child care providers and parents to observe young children's responses to print-filled environments as a way of becoming better prepared to support children's emergent literacy. Summaries of observation studies of infants and toddlers illustrate the earliest beginnings of literacy.

Brazelton, T.B. 1992. *Touchpoints: The essential reference—Your child's emotional and behavioral development.* Reading, MA: Addison-Wesley.

> This child care resource by a distinguished pediatrician offers a comprehensive explanation of all aspects of child development from physical and emotional to cognitive and behavioral.

Chang, H.N., & D. Pulido. 1994. The critical importance of cultural and linguistic continuity for infants and toddlers. *Zero to Three* 15 (2): 13–17.

> Explores various strategies for ensuring that caregiving is a cultural and linguistic reflection of the family and its community. Strategies include employing caregivers of the children's cultural backgrounds, drawing upon the cultural expertise of staff, developing cultural sensitivity, and rethinking the language of care.

de Villiers, P.A., & J.G. de Villiers. 1979. *Early language, the developing child.* Cambridge, MA: Harvard University Press.

> Documents how the toddler learns language, with a focus on infants, toddlers, and preschoolers. Vivid examples illustrate the course of learning to talk and communicate, with attention to how the adult learns what a child knows about language.

Division for Early Childhood Task Force on Recommended Practices. 1993. *DEC recommended practices: Indicators of quality in programs for infants and young children with special needs and their families.* Reston, VA: Council for Exceptional Children.

Includes validated practices in the areas of assessment, family participation, IFSPs (Individualized Family Services Plans) and IEPs (Individualized Education Programs), intervention strategies, transition, personnel competence, evaluation, and specific skills interventions.

Dombro, A.L., L.J. Colker, & D.T. Dodge. 1998. *A journal for using the creative curriculum for infants and toddlers.* Washington, DC: Teaching Strategies.

Helps caregivers and teachers think about their own experiences, apply what they are learning, and reflect on their work. This guidebook leads caregivers and teachers through each of the 23 chapters of the curriculum (see the entry that follows).

Dombro, A.L., L.J. Colker, & D.T. Dodge. 1999. *Creative curriculum for infants and toddlers.* Rev. ed. Washington, DC: Teaching Strategies.

Provides a practical yet comprehensive framework for planning infant and toddler programs in both family and center settings. Focuses on relationships among children, parents, caregivers/teachers, and the community as the basis for appropriate curriculum.

Dombro, A.L., & L. Wallach. 1988. *The ordinary is extraordinary: How children under three learn.* New York: Simon & Schuster.

Provides readers with a look at the world through the eyes of infants and toddlers. Readers see how children learn physical, cognitive, emotional, and social skills by participating in daily routines with their parents and providers.

Edwards, C.P., & D. LeeKennan. 1992. Using the project approach with toddlers. *Young Children* 47 (4): 31–35.

Explores the possibility and applicability of in-depth study projects for toddlers. The author provides classroom examples and guidelines.

Fenichel, E. 1992. *Learning through supervision and mentorship.* Arlington, VA: Zero to Three/National Center for Clinical Infant Programs.

Assists supervisors and the clinicians they mentor in handling issues related to the crises of families and infants at risk.

Goldschmeid, E., & S. Jackson. 1994. *People under three: Young children in day care.* New York: Routledge.

Describes a child-centered approach developed in Britain for working with infants and toddlers in group care. Topics include values and principles, space organization, managing the day, the treasure basket, heuristic play with objects, mealtimes, out-of-doors, and working with parents.

Golinkoff, R.M., & K. Hirsch-Pasek. 1999. *How babies talk.* New York: Dutton/ Penguin Group.

A chronology of oral language development in easy-to-read language highlights the linguistic accomplishments in the first three years and the most current understanding of what it takes to make language happen. Authors report on new methods of studying language and how caregivers can use the latest knowledge to enhance everyday interactions.

Gonzalez-Mena, J. 1992. Taking a culturally sensitive approach in infant-toddler programs. *Young Children* 47 (2): 4–9.

Helps caregivers become more sensitive to cultural and individual differences and suggests helpful strategies for increasing communication across cultural barriers.

Gonzalez-Mena, J., & D.E. Widmeyer. 1997. *Infants, toddlers, and caregivers.* 4th ed. Mountain View, CA: Mayfield.

Provides an insightful look at life in a child care setting. In addition to learning about the experiences of different age children, providers come to appreciate that there is nothing more important than their relationships with the children they care for.

Greenberg, P. 1991. *Character development: Encouraging self-esteem and self-discipline in infants, toddlers, and two-year-olds.* Washington, DC: NAEYC.

Twelve essays cover all aspects of the curriculum, with practical problem-solving points of view. For reflective teachers, directors, and student teachers who care about developing "good people" while working with young children.

Greenman, J., & A. Stonehouse. 1996. *Prime times: A handbook for excellence in infant and toddler programs.* St. Paul, MN: Redleaf.

Helps the reader understand in what context good child care exists and how to establish and keep vital quality caregiving in infant and toddler programs. Includes illustrations, charts, and forms.

Greenspan, S., with N.B. Lewis 1999. *Building healthy minds: The six experiences that create intelligence and emotional growth in babies and young children.* Reading, MA: Perseus.

Describe the six types of essential experiences between caregivers and children in the early years to help maximize children's potential as learners without undermining their emotional vitality. These core experiences begin in the first few months to help the infant organize his senses and progress to the older toddler at the sixth stage involving the logical bridges between ideas. Charts parallels to growth in key parts of the brain and includes a developmental growth chart.

Harrison, L. 1996. *Planning appropriate learning environments for children under three.* AECA Resource Book Series, no. 1. Rev. ed. Watson, ACT: Australian Early Childhood Association.

A short easy-to-read booklet covering learning experiences, effective organization of equipment and space, and all the components of a secure, consistent yet challenging environment for infants and toddlers in group care. Photos and diagrams of workable places focus on the unique spatial needs of this age group.

Hast, F., & A. Hollyfield. 1999. *Infant and toddler experiences.* St. Paul, MN: Redleaf.

Curricular experiences that focus on the way children relate to the materials, the caregivers, and each other. Experiences are organized around the curiosity of the child, the connections children make with peers and other adults, and the physical coordination necessary for skill integration.

Honig, A.S. 1996. *Behavior guidance for infants and toddlers.* Little Rock, AR: Southern Early Childhood Association.

Dozens of ideas to help young children become more cooperative.

Honig, A. 1997. Infant temperament and personality: What do we need to know? *Montessori Life* 9 (3): 18–21.

Infant temperament is a topic every caregiver needs to be aware of and empathetic with. This concise summary helps infant educators increase their knowledge about tuning into temperament styles for optimal caregiving.

Klein, A. 1992. Storybook humor and early development. *Childhood Education* 68 (4): 213–17.

Demonstrates the role of humor in supporting toddlers' social, emotional, and cognitive growth and providing a context for learning.

Lally, J.R. 1995. The impact of child care policies and practices on infant/toddler identity formation. *Young Children* 51 (1): 58–67.

Suggests five policies for infant and toddler care based on the role the caregiver has in identity formation.

Lally, J.R., A. Griffin, E. Fenichel, M. Segal, & E. Szanton. 1995. *Caring for infants and toddlers in groups: Developmentally appropriate practice.* Washington, DC: ZERO TO THREE.

Provides examples of appropriate and inappropriate caregiver responses to typical young children's behavior and interaction. A chart of milestones for infants and toddlers is included.

Leavitt, R.L. 1994. *Power and emotion in infant-toddler day care.* Albany: State University of New York Press.

Presents a provocative ethnography of the lived experiences of infants and toddlers in day care centers. The application of multiple theoretical perspectives—interpretive, interactionist, critical, feminist, and postmodern—yields powerful insights into the problematic emotional experiences and relations between infants and caregivers.

Lieberman, A.F. 1993. *The emotional life of the toddler.* New York: Free Press.

Uses examples to address commonly asked questions and issues about the explosive, contradictory, and ever-changing emotions of the active toddler. Provides an insightful profile of the toddler's emotional world.

Lowman, L., & L. Ruhmann. 1998. Simply sensational spaces: A multi-"S" approach to toddler environments. *Young Children* 53 (3): 11–17.

Filled with color photographs portraying how to set up toddler environments both indoors and out. Suggested spaces meet the special needs of toddlers for simplicity, seclusion, softness, sensory appeal, stimulation, stability, safety, and sanitation.

Mangione, P. 1995. *A guide to culturally sensitive care.* Sausalito, CA: Far West Laboratory for Child and Family Studies.

Focuses on cultural aspects of care for infants and toddlers in center-based care settings.

McMullen, M.B. 1999. Achieving best practices in infant and toddler care and education. *Young Children* 54 (4): 69–75.

Describes what constitutes best practices with infants and toddlers, based upon recent research. The author discusses how an understanding of best practices and the growing need for caregivers influence teacher education in preservice and inservice professional development programs.

Miller, K. 1999. *Simple steps: Developmental activities for infants, toddlers, and two-year-olds.* Beltsville, MD: Gryphon House.

Helps caregivers develop the necessary skills and knowledge to recognize and capture the emerging interests and intentions of infants and toddlers in their charge to provide an appropriate learning environment. Other topics include becoming partners with parents, dealing with challenging behaviors, and staff development.

O'Brien, M. 1997. *Inclusive care for infants and toddlers: Meeting individual and special needs.* Baltimore, MD: Brookes.

Gives child care providers the practical guidance they need to serve infants and toddlers with and without disabilities in inclusive settings. Topics include handling daily care tasks, teaching responsively, meeting individual needs, developing rapport with parents, understanding toddlers' behavior, working with IFSPs (Individualized Family Services Plans), and maintaining high standards of care. Suggested play activities and intervention approaches help promote healthy development in all children.

Pawl, J.H. 1990. Infants in day care: Reflections on experiences, expectations, relationships. *Zero to Three* 10 (3): 1–6.

Emphasizes the need for providers to understand as much as possible about infants and toddlers and then to apply their understandings to the individual child's experience in the child care setting. Discusses the importance of providing a predictable setting in which infants and toddlers experience their needs being recognized and responded to appropriately.

Provence, S., J. Pawl, & E. Fenichel, eds. 1992. *The Zero to Three child care anthology (1984–1992)*. Arlington, VA: ZERO TO THREE.

An excellent source of information for caregivers, student teachers, parents, and others in early care on all aspects of infant and toddler care. The collection includes 18 classic articles as well as the consensus statement on child care policy developed by researchers at an infant day care summit sponsored by ZERO TO THREE.

Pruett, K.D. 1999. *Me, myself and I: How children build their sense of self, 18 to 36 months*. New York: Goddard.

Conveys key aspects of toddlerhood. Features topics such as brain development and how everyday patterns of sensation, perception, and cognition transform behavior into personality; emerging temperament and style; language explosion and behavior that speaks when words fail; anxieties of toddlerhood; and good ways to help children establish inner controls.

Raikes, H. 1996. A secure base for babies: Applying attachment concepts to the infant care setting. *Young Children* 51 (5): 59–67.

Explains some attachment principles and shows how they can be drawn upon in infant programs to ensure that more programs use practices based on principles.

Reinsberg, J. 1995. Reflections on quality infant care. *Young Children* 50 (6): 23–25.

Moving an infant and toddler program to a new classroom initiated these reflections on the environment and policies needed for a quality infant-toddler program.

Ross, H.W. 1992. Integrating infants with disabilities? Can ordinary caregivers do it? *Young Children* 47 (3): 65–71.

Encourages caregivers to work with special educators and parents to provide part-time developmental care in regular child care settings for babies with special needs.

San Fernando Valley Child Care Consortium, A. Godwin, & L. Schrag. 1996. *Setting up for infant/toddler care: Guidelines for centers and family child care homes*. Washington, DC: NAEYC.

Focuses on the kinds of equipment, personnel practices, room arrangements, uses of time and space, toy selection, and health and safety practices that every family child care provider or child care center director must consider when the decision has been made to include infants and toddlers in a program.

Shimoni, R., J. Baxter, & J. Kugelmass. 1992. *Every child is special: Quality group care for infants and toddlers.* San Francisco: Addison-Wesley.

Well-organized and developmentally sound, this guidebook describes how the caregiver can protect, support, and observe children and enrich their lives in each developmental area. The authors integrate children with special needs.

Szanton, E.S. 1997. *Creating child-centered programs for infants and toddlers: Step by step. A program for children and families..* Washington, DC: Children's Resources International.

Introduces a program that has been successful in twenty-four countries and is designed to be easily implemented by caregivers. Content includes current research on quality care; techniques for observing, assessing and guiding learning; and ideas for setting up healthy, safe, and responsive environments.

Thompson, D.S. 1993. *The promotion of gross and fine motor development for infants and toddlers: Developmentally appropriate activities for parents and teachers.* ED361104. Urbana-Champaign, IL: ERIC Document Reproduction Service.

In recognition of the close relationship between motor skill and cognitive development in the first two years of life, this guide presents 78 developmentally appropriate activities that parents and teachers can use to enhance infant and toddler motor development.

U.S. Army, Child and Youth Services. 1995. *Infant and toddler care. . . . A very special endorsement.* Arlington, VA: Military Child Development Program.

Provides information on how to identify and respond to the individual and developmental needs of infants and toddlers. Suggestions are outlined for appropriate materials, equipment, activities, environment, guidance, and interactions. (Distributed free from the National Clearinghouse for Department of Defense Child Development Programs, 888-237-3040.)

Watson, L.D., M. Watson, & L.C. Wilson. 1999. *Infants and toddlers: Curriculum and teaching.* 4th ed. Albany, NY: Delmar.

Describes the skills necessary to provide high-quality care for infants and toddlers in any child care setting. Emphasizes individual care and includes helpful information on incorporating individualized techniques and activities for each child in care.

Encompassing a broad spectrum of issues that may arise in family child care settings, these resources include recommendations on setting up the home environment and planning a program for children of varying ages. Several resources highlight the unique aspects of family child care.

Baker, A., & L. Manfredi/Petitt. 1998. *Circle of love: Relationships between parents, providers and children in family child care.* St. Paul, MN: Redleaf.

Focuses on high quality family child care and the issues that arise when loving and caring for someone else's children. It is based on interviews with providers and parents who have found unique ways to work together to meet the young child's needs for loving bonds. Authors present ideas for forming the parent-caregiver connection and handling the many complicated and sensitive situations that arise in family child care.

Baker, A.C. 1992. A puzzle, a picnic, and a vision: Family day care at its best. *Young Children* 47 (5): 36–38.

Contains the story of a family day care provider and her commitment to the children in her care.

Bassett, M.M. 1998. *The professional nanny.* Albany, NY: Delmar.

This handbook is written for those who want to apply their early childhood skills by working with young children and their families as nannies in a private home setting. Includes practical information about the business and professional side of nanny employment.

Cherry, C., & B. Harkness. 1991. *Family day care providers management guide.* Torrance, CA: Frank Schaffer.

Provides a complete guide to family child care and includes information on setting up the home for business, getting licensed, recruiting children, child development, health and safety, and activities for children.

The Children's Foundation. 1990. *Helping children love themselves and others: A professional handbook for family day care.* Washington, DC: Author.

Stresses the importance of an antibias, multicultural approach in developing activities for children. It includes a resource guide to equity materials and an annotated bibliography of resources for adults.

de la Brosse, B. 1987. *Children with special needs in family day care homes: A handbook for family day care home providers.* Washington, DC: El Centro Rosemount.

Provides information to help providers include children with special needs in their family day care homes. Topics include questions, concerns, and advantages surrounding this decision; providers' attitudes and feelings about children with special needs; child development and assessment issues; working with specialists; and the importance and components of positive parent-provider relationships with parents of children with special needs.

Debord, K. 1993. A little respect and eight more hours a day: Family child care providers have special needs. *Young Children* 48 (4): 21–26.

Stresses that sufficient attention to professional development needs and cooperative planning of training opportunities must take place for family child care providers.

Dodge, D.T., & L.J. Colker. 1991. *The creative curriculum for family child care.* Washington, DC: Teaching Strategies.

Shows how to implement a developmentally appropriate program for children in a home setting. It offers suggestions on how to organize a home environment for child care, establish a daily schedule, involve children of different ages, guide children's behavior, build partnerships with parents, and help children learn through play.

Galinsky, E., C. Howes, S. Kontos, & M. Shinn. 1994. *The study of children in family child care and relative care: Highlights of findings.* New York: Families and Work Institute.

Presents findings from a multistate observation investigation of mothers and their children who were enrolled in regulated family child care, unregulated family child care, and unregulated relative care, and the providers of this care. Key findings address definitions and child effects of quality experiences, predictors of quality, and causes for concern.

Gonzalez-Mena, J. 1991. *Tips and tidbits. A book for family day care providers.* Washington, DC: NAEYC.

Provides "bits and pieces" of practical strategies and suggestions that can help family child care providers in their daily work with children. Each section includes a bibliography of additional readings.

Gonzalez-Mena, J. 1998. *The child in the family and the community.* Upper Saddle River, NJ: Merrill.

An examination of the socialization process of young children, with a focus on the development of attachment, autonomy, initiative, and self-esteem in the family and the child's community. Discusses how society's goals, cultural patterns, and values affect child care settings and family child care settings.

Harms, T., & R. Clifford. 1989. *Family Day Care Rating Scale (FDCRS).* New York: Teachers College Press.

Designed to aid in evaluating family day care settings, FDCRS consists of 32 items organized under six headings: space and furnishings for care and learning, basic care, language and reasoning, learning activities, social development, and adult needs.

Koralek, D.G., L.J. Colker, & D.T. Dodge. 1993. *Caring for children in family child care.* Washington, DC: Teaching Strategies.

Offers practical ideas for setting up a home child care environment and planning a program for children of varying ages, birth through 12 years. Learning activities allow providers to assess their knowledge and apply new information to enhance what they already do in their family child care home. A trainer's guide also is available.

Lambert, L., & J. Trawick-Smith. 1995. The unique challenges of the family child care provider: Implications for professional development. *Young Children* 50 (3): 25–32.

Highlights unique aspects of family child care in order to inform workshop presenters who often have only center-based experience. This article is a collaboration between a professor and workshop presenter and a family child care provider.

Laurion, J. 1997. *Village of kindness: Providing high quality family child care.* Madison, WI: Madison Education Extension Programs, School of Education, University of Wisconsin.

Comprehensive view of family child care, with lots of everyday examples and a solid grounding in research and practice. The author is a family child care provider with many years of experience and academic credentials. A video series accompanies the book. Available from the Agency for Instructional Technology, 800-457-4500.

Lawrence, M., J. Brown, Y. Lincroft, D. Williams, & D. Bellum. 1994. *Resources/ Recursos: A bibliography of Spanish-language family day care training materials.* San Francisco: California Resource and Referral Network.

One-sentence descriptions, in English, of Spanish-language resources for California providers.

Linke, P. 1998. *Let's stop bullying.* Watson, ACT: Australian Early Childhood Association.

Designed for early childhood family care providers and teachers in infant/toddler settings, preschools, or primary grades. This book is a comprehensive handbook on the nature and causes of bullying and how it can be prevented or handled. Techniques are offered for supporting children (and their parents) who are victims of bullying as well as children who bully.

Litman, M., with C. Anderson, L. Andrican, B. Buria, C. Christy, B. Koski, & P. Renton. 1999. Curriculum comes from the child! A Head Start family child care program.*Young Children* 54 (3): 4–9.

A northern Minnesota community action program demonstrates project success in family child care for preschoolers. Teacher-providers build on family life, nature and the outdoors, culture and foods, and parent/older sibling/community involvement in creating a rich curriculum. Discusses project funding needs and collaboration; makes a recommendations on transitioning projects into successful options.

Mandredi/Petitt, L.A. 1991. Ten steps to organizing the flow of your family day care day. *Young Children* 46 (3): 14–16.

Describes 10 ways to organize the flow of a day in a family child care setting.

Modigliani, K., M. Reiff, & S. Jones. 1987. *Opening your door to children: How to start a family day care program.* Washington, DC: NAEYC.

Discusses a wide variety of issues involved with starting up a family day care program. Includes information about hours, ages, fees, activities, parents, and taxes.

Modigliani, K., & J. Bromer. 1998. *Quality standards for NAFCC accreditation.* Boston: Wheelock College Family Child Care Project.

Defines standards for high-quality child care in the provider's home for accreditation by the National Association for Family Child Care. Includes specific standards for relationships, the environment, activities, developmental learning goals, safety and health, and professional and business practices.

Modigliani, K., J. Bromer, & A. Lutton. 1998. *Training resources for family child care accreditation.* Boston: Wheelock College Family Child Care Project.

Recommended training curricula, books, and videocassettes are described in detail with suggestions for use in family child care training. Resources that support the new NAFCC accreditation quality standards are highlighted.

Nash, M., & C. Tate. 1986. *Better baby care: A book for family day care providers.* Washington, DC: Children's Foundation.

Includes practical suggestions for setting up the home to accommodate babies, information on child development, recommended business practices, and suggestions for developing partnerships with parents.

Osborn, H. 1994. *Room for loving, room for learning. Finding the space you need in your family child care home.* St. Paul, MN: Redleaf.

Filled with diagrams and practical advice on how to set up family child care in any type of home and how to best use available space. Includes ideas for activity areas and better storage.

Roemer, J., & B. Austin. 1989. *Two to four from 9 to 5: The adventures of a daycare provider.* New York: Harper & Row.

Depicts life in a family child care home through a series of vignettes. Providers will identify with many of the situations presented in the book.

Shatoff, D. 1998. *In-home child care: A step-by-step guide to quality, affordable care.* St. Louis, MO: Family CareWare.

Tells how to find a child caregiver to provide in-home care for your child. The interview questions concerning optimal caregiver characteristics, systems for maintaining a positive care partnership, and child care agreement will be of interest and practical use to those providing child care in their own homes.

Squibb, S. 1986. *Family day care: How to provide it in your home.* Boston: Harvard Common Press.

Offers a wealth of practical ideas that would be helpful to both new and experienced providers. The book's scope ranges from tax-related information to recipes for making peanut butter and chicken soup. Extensive resources are cited in the appendices.

Enhancing School-Age Care

For practitioners who work with children in before- and after-school programs, this section covers such topics as arranging the environment, planning activities, encouraging children's growth in all developmental areas, and developing partnerships with families and in the community.

Albrecht, K., & Plantz, M. 1993. *Developmentally appropriate practice in school-age child care programs.* Dubuque, IA: Kendall/Hunt.

Outlines and discusses seven principles of developmentally appropriate school-age child care programs. Illustrates the principles with specific practices, both appropriate and inappropriate, related to various program components. Also provides examples of program planning and assessment tools.

Arns, B. 1994. *The survival guide to school-age child care.* 2d ed. Huntington Beach, CA: School Age Workshop.

Presents a wide variety of ideas, resources, and examples to help caregivers deal with the many demands of school-age care.

Bender, J., B. Elder, C.H. Flatter. 1984. *Half a childhood: Time for school-age child care.* Nashville, TN: School-Age Notes.

Provides practical information based on developmental theory that can be used in a school-age child care program. Tips cover topics such as planning for growth, discovery, and enrichment, while providing a homelike atmosphere.

Blakley, B., R. Blau, E.H. Brady, C. Streibert, A. Zavitkovsky, & D. Zavitkovsky. 1989. *Activities for school-age child care*. Washington, DC: NAEYC.

Discusses approaches to working with parents, staff, and community. Includes planning and resource ideas for working with children ages 5 to 10.

Bumgarner, M.A. 1999. *Working with school-age children*. Mountain View, CA: Mayfield.

Presents developmental information and issues children bring to a broad array of school-age care settings and adult roles in the development of personality, social skills, problem solving, competence, moral reasoning and values. Sections on creating environments in shared space, planning interesting activities, and administration of school-age programs.

Click, P. 1998. *Caring for school-age children*. Albany, NY: Delmar.

Covers such topics as how children grow and develop in early and middle childhood, program administration, creating the indoor and outdoor environment, and behavioral guidance. An entire section addresses all aspects of the curriculum, including games, the arts, and science and math activities for school-age programs. A final section discusses outreach and how to involve community members in the program.

Developmental Studies Center. 2000. *The after-school literature project*. Oakland, CA: Author.

Uses carefully selected children's books in after-school programs to help 5- to 13-year-olds become better, more motivated readers and to improve their understanding of themselves and others. Helps for after-school staff include read-aloud strategies, techniques for shared discussion, and ideas for art, drama, music, word play, and writing journals.

Fink, D.B. 1988. *School-age children with special needs: What do they do when school is out?* Westport, CT: Greenwood.

Describes different approaches to funding, staffing, administration, and training in programs dedicated to meeting the child care needs of school-agers and adolescents with disabilities.

Fink, D.B. 1995. *Discipline in school-age care: Control the climate, not the children*. Nashville, TN: School-Age Notes.

Engages school-age care staff in rethinking their attitudes toward behavior and discipline of children. Six key elements of a school-age care program are included.

Haas-Foletta, K., & M. Cogley. 1990. *School-age ideas and activities for after school programs*. Nashville, TN: School-Age Notes.

Provides strategies for programming for school-age care. Also includes activities and games that are program tested. Discusses factors affecting room arrangement and areas to include in the environment.

Koralek, D.G, R. Newman, & L.J. Colker. 1995. *Caring for children in school-age programs*. Washington, DC: Teaching Strategies.

Provides a comprehensive, self-instructional training program in two volumes for staff in school-age programs. Content and skills addressed reflect quality standards for school-age care as defined by national groups of school-age professionals and experts. Also available is a trainer's guide that explains how to implement and oversee the program and assist staff in assessing their training progress.

Kreidler, W.J. 1984. *Creative conflict resolution*. Glenview, IL: Scott, Foresman.

Contains conflict-resolution techniques, activities, and cooperative games for school-age children. Practical strategies help children improve their communication skills, understand and settle their own disputes, and deal with strong feelings in productive ways.

Kreidler, W.J., & L. Furlong. 1995. *Adventures in peacemaking: A conflict resolution activity guide for school-age programs*. Boston: Educators for Social Responsibility.

Discusses a variety of activities designed to teach school-age children how to use conflict resolution to solve problems and disagreements.

Linke, P. 1998. *Let's stop bullying*. Watson, ACT: Australian Early Childhood Association.

Designed for early childhood teachers in infant/toddler settings, preschools or primary grades. This book is a comprehensive handbook on the nature and causes of bullying and how it can be prevented or handled. Techniques are offered for supporting children who are victims of bullying (and their parents) as well as children who bully.

Middlebrooks, S. 1998. *Getting to know city kids: Understanding their thinking, imagining, and socializing*. New York: Teachers College Press.

Challenges misconceptions about children from low-income urban settings by taking a closer look at six children ages 8 through 12. The author describes alternative approaches to looking at children's capacities to learn, urging teachers to build on and extend the complexity of children's play as it relates to the intellectual work of the classroom.

Miller, B. 1997. *I wish the kids didn't watch so much TV: Out-of-school time in three low-income communities*. Wellesley, MA: School-Age Child Care Project.

Describes the findings of a study of children's out-of-school time. One hundred eighty randomly selected families in three communities were interviewed about current out-of-school activities and aspirations for their children who were enrolled in Head Start, kindergarten, or first-grade. This resource has an accompanying training manual.

Musson, S. 1994. *School-age care: Theory and practice*. New York: Addison Wesley Longman.

Offers a rich overview of the issues related to school-age child care and a developmental perspective. Gives child care providers practical ideas for planning appropriate programs.

O'Connor, S. 1995. *ASQ: Assessing school-age child care quality.* Wellesley, MA: School-Age Child Care Project.

Self-guided resource outlines the elements of quality, provides instruments to assess quality, and offers a process to improve programs. The ASQ self-assessment instruments are parallel to NSACA's (National School-Age Care Alliance) piloted accreditation standards.

Richard, M.M. 1991. *Before and after school programs: A start-up and administration manual.* Nashville, TN: School-Age Notes.

This "policies and procedures" book provides models, applications, forms, and data about starting and operating a school-age program. Information concerning budgets, nonprofit status, job descriptions, and staff and parent handbooks is provided.

Román, J., ed. 1998. *The NSACA pilot standards for quality school-age care.* Rev. ed. Boston: National School-Age Care Alliance.

Details the standards that will be used to assess programs applying for NSACA accreditation. The 149 standards with over 420 specific examples are designed to describe "best practices" in school-age child care.

Seligson, M., & M. Allenson. 1993. *School-age child care: An action manual for the 90s and beyond.* Westport, CT: Auburn House/Greenwood.

Authors of this new edition explore the challenges that child care providers will encounter as the twenty-first century begins.

Simpson, R.L. 1996. *Working with parents and family of exceptional children and youth: Techniques for successful conferencing and collaboration.* 3d ed. Austin, TX: Pro-Ed.

Focuses on school-age children and their families as they deal with special needs. The role of the teacher as collaborator is emphasized.

Sisson, L.G. 1990. *Kids club: A school-age program guide for directors.* Nashville, TN: School-Age Notes.

Details five types of activities and how to program for them. Also includes easy-to-use developmental checklists and checklists for full-day programming and field trips.

Whitaker, D.L. 1996. *Games, games, games: Creating hundreds of group games and sports.* Nashville, TN: School-Age Notes.

Games and sports children play can be child-initiated and directed instead of adult-initiated. Includes 45 games and sports that children can play both indoors and out, with variations of each, leading to hundreds of additional games.

Spanish-language materials

Several early childhood educators were specifically asked to recommend resources that are easily accessible to practitioners who speak languages other than English and who work with children and families whose home language is not English. Not surprisingly, almost all of the resources recommended are in Spanish, which reflects the increased demand for early care and education resources published in Spanish. A few additional recommended resources are in Chinese and French. This limited selection will serve as a beginning or as an expansion of your collection of such resources. Videos in Spanish are listed under the heading "Videorecordings," which follows next in these pages.

Armstrong, G., & M.P. Hansen. 1993. *En el seno del hogar: Experiencias familiares para desarrollar el Alfabetismo.* San Francisco, CA: Addison-Wesley.

Provides instructional, cartoon-style letters that can be sent home to parents or other family members. The authors offer ideas for developing literacy skills during activities at home. In Spanish.

Biderman, E., L. Carbajal, V. La Cerva, & L. Whitener, eds. 1998. *Voices of violence/Visions of peace.* Santa Fe, NM: Santa Fe Children's Museum.

This 75-page publication that evolved in response to increasing violence is a collection of captivating photographs and stories—personal accounts of violence, poignant quotes from children and adults, and "Poco á Poco se Anda Lejos," which sets forth stories of transformation. Suggestions for parents and teachers are offered to promote caring and experiencing more peace within our lives and families. In Spanish. (Distributed free by the Santa Fe Children's Museum, 505-989-8359, children@trail.com)

Cadena de Comunidades de Aprendizaje. 1997. Aprendiendo de nuestras diferencias: Color, cultura, y clase seconda parte. *Narraciones de las Comunidades de Aprendizaje.* Cleveland, OH: Cadena de Comunidade de Aprendizaje.

Containing both personal essays and papers written for professional development, this journal deals with issues of race, color, and class. In Spanish and English within the same binding. (Distributed by Cadena de Comunidade de Aprendizaje, Inc., 1422 Euclid Avenue, Suite 1668, Cleveland, OH 44115-2001.)

Children's Foundation. 1994. *Helping children love themselves and others: Resource guide to equity materials for young children.* Washington, DC: Author.

Contains a checklist of books, toys, and materials to assist in determining equity resources; annotated bibliographies of children's literature and resources for adults that include books, curricula, magazines, newsletters and pamphlets; a listing of companies with antibias and/or multicultural books and materials available; and a listing of national support organizations. In Spanish. (Distributed by The Children's Foundation, 725 Fifteenth Street, NW, Suite 505, Washington, DC 20005-2109.)

Dennis, B.C., S.T. Tyndall, & P. Wesley. 1997. *Quicknotes: Inclusion resources for early childhood professionals.* Chapel Hill: University of North Carolina.

A 10-module set of bilingual, in Spanish and English, information sheets in a portable crate. Modules include these titles: Developmental Disabilities, Setting Up the Early Childhood Environment, Early Childhood Curriculum, What Is Early Childhood Inclusion, Including Children with Special Needs, Health and Safety, Promoting Appropriate Behavior, Families, and Early Intervention Lending Library Catalog.

Developmental Studies Center. 1994-1999. *Reading, thinking, and caring (K–3).* Oakland, CA: Author.

A literature-based program in which students read with partners, hear literature read aloud, and discuss important ideas with classmates and families at home. Each grade level includes read-aloud teacher guides and partner-teacher guides. Some of these teacher guides include student-partner pages and a take-home activity that have been translated into Spanish.

Developmental Studies Center. 1995. *Homeside activities: Conversations and activities that bring parents into children's schoolside learning (Grades K–9).* Oakland, CA: Author.

The volumes (kindergarten and grades one, two, and three) provide a simple way for teachers to initiate parent involvement in their children's learning. The activities, which honor cultural diversity, structure conversations or simple games between child and parent that encourage an exchange of ideas, develop the child's critical thinking and communication skills, and provide an open-ended framework for adult and child to explore significant social and ethical issues. Each activity is printed in Spanish and English.

Developmental Studies Center. 2000. *Homeside math.* Oakland, CA: Author.

Supports parent involvement in mathematics through a series of activities introduced in kindergarten and first-grade classrooms and sent home for children and a home partner to do together. Activities are designed to foster discussion and exploration between children and their families in the areas of number, geometry, and measurement and will culminate in a class discussion or project. In Spanish.

Dodge, D.T., & L.J. Colker, Translation by C.C. Núñez. 1996. *El curriculo creativo para educación preescolar.* Washington, DC: Teaching Strategies.

Explains how to work with children at different developmental levels, how to adapt the environment to make it increasingly challenging, and how to actively involve parents in the program. The book also includes a child development and learning checklist to help teachers learn about each child in their class and individualize the curriculum. In standard Spanish, appropriate for the majority of Spanish speakers.

Dodge, D.T., & J. Phinney. Translation by C.C. Núñez. 1996. *Guía para los padres sobre educación preescolar.* Washington, DC: Teaching Strategies.

Uses concise language and clear illustrations to explain the goals of a developmentally appropriate program. The authors detail what children learn through play, the learning environment, daily schedule, and conversations. The book explains how parents and teachers can work together to help children acquire the skills, attitudes, and habits to excel in school and throughout life. In Spanish; also available in Chinese.

Dodge, D.T., A.L. Dombro, & L.J. Colker. Translation by C.C. Núñez.1998. *Guía para los padres sobre programas de cuidado infantil de 0–3 años.* Washington, DC: Teaching Strategies.

Shows parents how warm and responsive care helps shape the future development of infants and toddlers and their ability to learn. Outlines what children learn and how during these crucial years and suggests ways that caregivers/teachers and parents can work together. In Spanish.

Early Childhood Today. Every issue (eight times a year) of this periodical for teachers has a parent involvement activity that is included in Spanish as well as English. New York: Scholastic.

ERIC Digest. Digests on specific topics selected by the ERIC Clearinghouse on Elementary and Early Childhood Education (also available online; see section on "Internet Websites"). Many in Spanish and Chinese. Urbana-Champaign: University of Illinois.

Escamilla, K., A.M. Andrade, A.G.M. Basurto, O.A. Ruiz, & M. Clay. 1995. *Instrumento de observacion de los logros de la lecto-escritura inicial: Spanish reconstruction of an observational survey, A bilingual text.* Portsmouth, NH: Heinemann.

Draws on the theoretical framework of Marie Clay's *An Observation Survey* not as a literal translation, but a conceptual re-creation. It provides teachers with a tool for considering how children who come into contact with two languages use those languages to make sense of their world and monitor their progress. Based on extensive research in bilingual education, this book expands the knowledge base of K–3 bilingual teachers in a way that enables them to be better observers of children's literacy behaviors and improve their teaching.

Arena: Del cuento "Sand" por Marie Clay. 1995. Portsmouth, NH: Heinemann.

Includes "Concepts About Print" tests (M. Clay) that can be used with new entrants or nonreaders to enable children to point to certain features as the examiner reads the book. The foregoing reference *Instrumento de observacion* presents the theoretical background, administration details, and scoring interpretation of the tests. In Spanish.

Forsten, C., J. Grant, & I. Richardson. 1999. *The multiage evaluation book.* Peterborough, NH: Crystal Springs.

Contains detailed checklists for understanding the concept of multiage and the reason for implementing it. Provides suggestions on how to design, prepare for, implement and assess, and begin a multiage classroom. For those educators already engaged in multiage practice, this book will help in evaluating which components are working well and which need revising. Support pages include sample parent questionnaires in English and Spanish.

Freeman, Y.S., & D.E. Freeman. 1998. *La enseñanza de la lectura y la escritura en espanõl en el aula bilingüe.* Portsmouth, NH: Heinemann.

Provides a readable explanation of second-language teaching methodology supported by numerous primary classroom examples. Includes detailed discussions and examples of EFL (English as a Foreign Language) teaching as well as many scenarios from ESL (English as a Second Language) classes. The emphasis is on teaching language through meaningful content. In Spanish.

George, Y.S., S.M. Malcom, V.L. Worthington, & A.B. Daniel, eds. 1995. *In touch with preschool science.* Washington, DC: American Association for the Advancement of Science.

Includes information on starting a preschool science program and a wide selection of activities for young children and their families. In Spanish and English.

Hendrick, J.B. 1995. *The whole child: Developmental education for the early years.* Upper Saddle River, NJ: Prentice Hall.

Offers teachers of children ages 2 to 5 a complete developmental approach to early childhood education, providing them the specific skills they need to function effectively with the children in their care. Focuses on the whole child and what he or she needs from the learning environment so as to thrive. Recommends methods and materials for enhancing growth in emotional, social, physical, creative, and cognitive areas of child development. In French, Chinese, and English only.

Katz, L.G. 1994. *The project approach.* Champaign, IL: ERIC Clearinghouse on Elementary and Early Childhood Education.

In Spanish as *El metodo llamado proyecto*, this digest explains what a project is, what the goals of a project are, and notes that project work is complementary to the systematic parts of a curriculum. The digest explains how projects differ from themes and units and describes the three phases of a project.

Lawrence, M., J. Brown, Y. Lincroft, D. Williams, & D. Bellum. 1994. *Resources/ Recursos: A bibliography of Spanish-language family day care training materials.* San Francisco: California Resource and Referral Network.

One-sentence descriptions, in English, of Spanish-language resources for California providers.

Olsen, L., & C. Dowell. 1997. *Las escuelas que necesitamos hoy: De como los padres, las familias y las comunidades pueden participar en el cambio escolar.* San Francisco, CA: California Tomorrow.

Written for anyone interested in how schools are changing and how parents and teachers can work together to improve schools. It calls on parents to continue fighting for their children's educational rights and lays out strategies for communities and schools to create equitable education for all students. In Spanish.

Power, B. 1999. *Parent power: Energizing home-school communication.* Portsmouth, NH: Heinemann.

Enhances connections with parents through a collection of 30 letters to parents and a teacher's guide with ideas such as personalizing the communication, designing newsletters, best books for promoting learning at home, and making involvement easier for parents. The letters address curriculum and school concerns and general parenting issues such as coping with sibling conflict. All letters are translated into Spanish as well and one chapter, which addresses strategies for relating to non-English speaking parents.

Rossano, J., & P. Schiller. 1990. *500 actividades para el curriculo de educacion infantil.* Beltsville, MD: Gryphon House.

Allows children to immerse themselves in 500 hands-on activities that encompass music, math, social studies, science, art, language, and dramatic play. These fun and easy activities promote self-esteem, imagination, thinking, problem solving, and fine- and gross-motor skills. In Spanish.

Vopat, J. 1994. *The parent project: A workshop approach to parent involvement.* York, ME: Stenhouse.

Provides a framework for increasing parent involvement. Materials are provided for conducting workshops with parents in areas of writing, reading, self-esteem, and community building. In Spanish.

Videorecordings

We received a limited number of recommendations in response to the request for video resources. The editors offer the following listing as a starting point from which we encourage readers to expand.

The videos are listed in the categories for which we have resources. The categories are given in alphabetical order and include the following: creating quality family child care (Part 3), enhancing school-age care (Part 3), developmental and theoretical bases of practice (Part 2), including children with special needs and abilities (Part 2), partnerships with families (Part 2), promoting health and safety (Part 3), Spanish-language materials (Part 3), teaching and curriculum for infants and toddlers (Part 3), and teaching and curriculum for preschool and primary (Part 3). To increase the accessibility of the video resources, the distributor's address, phone number, or e-mail address is listed.

Creating quality family child care

Caring and learning. 1991. Produced by Diane Trister Dodge for Teaching Strategies. 23 min.

Shows four family child care providers using the activity areas designed to help children learn and grow as described in the Teaching Strategies book *The Creative Curriculum for Family Child Care.* A user's guide provides suggestions for leading discussions and conducting workshops based on the video. (Distributed by Teaching Strategies, Inc., P.O. Box 42243, Washington, DC 20015; 800-637-3652; http://www.teachingstrategies.com)

Head Start at home. 1993. Produced by the Head Start Bureau, U.S. Department of Health and Human Services. 17 min.

Emphasizes the significance of the home as a natural environment for learning and discusses the components of the home-based program option: home visits, parent meetings and workshops, and group socialization activities. (Distributed by Head Start Publications Management Center, P.O. Box 26417, Alexandria, VA 22313-0417; fax 703-683-5769; e-mail hspmc6@idt.net)

Learning through play: Planning for success in family child care. 1990. Produced by Child Care Providers Coalition of Kansas. 20 min.

Offers ideas for planning a balanced family child care program in mixed-age group settings including children through age 6. (Distributed by Redleaf, 450 North Syndicate, Suite 5, St. Paul, MN, 55104-4125; 800-423-8309.)

Let babies be babies: Caring for infants and toddlers with love and respect. 1993. Produced by Family Day Care Association of Manitoba. 123 min.

Set of six videos and accompanying guides describe important relationships and aspects of being a family child care provider. Topics include Rethinking Infants and Toddlers, Keeping Babies Healthy and Safe, Helping Babies Learn, Guiding the Journey to Independence, Understanding the Partnership with Parents, and Caring for the Caregiver. (Distributed by Family Day Care Association of Manitoba, #203-942 St. Mary's Road, Winnipeg, Manitoba, Canada R2M 3R5.)

Yes, you can do it! Caring for infants and toddlers with disabilities in family child care. 1995. Produced by The Children's Foundation. 16 min.

Offers positive images and messages from parents and child care providers on the benefits of serving young children with disabilities. The accompanying manual *Caring for Infants and Toddlers in Family Day Care: Annotated Resources* offers additional resources such as training materials to support inclusion. (Distributed by The Children's Foundation, 725 Fifteenth St., NW, Suite 505, Washington, DC, 20005-2109; 202-347-3300.)

Enhancing school-age care

Before and after school: Creative experiences. 1993. Produced by Indiana Steps Ahead in cooperation with Indiana's Public Broadcasting Stations (current producer Ball State University). 28 min.

Illustrates school-age children experiencing the responsibilities of independence within safe environments and with the support of caring and helpful adults. Available in English and Spanish. (Distributed by NAEYC, 1509 16th St., NW, Washington, DC 20036-1426; 800-424-2460.)

Between school-time and home-time: A look at quality SACC programs. 1988. Produced by National Institute on Out-of-School Time (formerly School-Age Child Care Project) in cooperation with the New York State Council on Children and Families. 18 min.

Illustrates the components of quality school-age child care in various settings. (Distributed by the National Institute on Out-of-School Time, Wellesley College Center for Research on Women, Wellesley, Massachusetts; 781-283-2547; http://www.wellesley.edu/WCW/CRW/SAC)

Between school-time and home-time: Planning quality activities for SACC programs. 1990. Produced by National Institute on Out-of-School Time (formerly School-Age Child Care Project) in cooperation with the New York State Council on Children and Families. 28 min.

Focuses on three separate activities in school-age child care programs and explores what makes them work. Observes how program space, scheduling, and positive staff relationships support each activity. (Distributed by the National Institute on Out-of-School Time, Wellesley College Center for Research on Women, Wellesley, Massachusetts; 781-283-2547; http://www.wellesley.edu/WCW/CRW/SAC)

Keys to quality in school-age care: Video and viewer's guide. Produced by Summerwind Communications Group, Union Bridge, MD. 25 min.

Contains a practical, step-by-step approach to using *Keys to Quality* to unlock the doors to quality programs: Planning with School-Age Children in Mind, Organizing for Diversity and Choice Staffing, Scheduling and Using Space Effectively, Viewing Parents as Partners with Programs, and Collaborating with Others Who Can Help. (Distributed by School-Age NOTES, P.O. Box 40205, Nashville, TN 37204; 615-242-8464; fax 615-242-8260; http://www.schoolagenotes.com)

Developmental and theoretical bases of practice

Child development: The first two years. 1993. Produced by Special Interest Productions. 47 min.

Provides information on child development from birth to 2 years and the role parents play in promoting a child's development. Highlights general information about physical, social, emotional, cognitive, and language development, in addition to specific childrearing tasks. (Distributed by Special Interest Productions, New York, NY; 212-674-5550.)

Cooing, crying, cuddling: Infant brain development. 1998. Produced by Indiana Steps Ahead in cooperation with Indiana's Public Broadcasting Stations (current producer Ball State University). 28 min.

Explores the fascinating process of brain development during the first 15 months of life. Understanding how to stimulate this process can help to "build a better brain." (Distributed by NAEYC, 1509 16th St., NW, Washington, DC 20036-1426; 800-424-2460.)

The first years last forever. 1997. Produced by The Reiner Foundation, with funding from Johnson & Johnson. 27 min.

Shares information on brain research and translates the findings into meaningful advice. Discusses seven aspects of parent involvement: bonding and attachment, communication, health and nutrition, discipline, self-esteem, child care, and self-awareness. (Distributed by The Reiner Foundation, 888-447-3400.)

Flexible fearful and feisty: The different temperaments of infants and toddlers. 1990. The Program for Infant/Toddler Caregiver series developed by Far West Laboratory for Educational Research and Development Center for Child and Family Studies (currently named WestEd) and California State Department of Education. 29 min.

Alicia Lieberman, a developmental psychologist, explains that children behave differently from one another beginning at birth, in part because of temperamental differences. Also discusses the impact of temperamental differences in group care situations. (Distributed by California State Department of Education, P.O. Box 271, Sacramento, CA 95802; 800-995-4099.)

Growing minds: Cognitive development in early childhood. 1996. The Human Development Series. Produced by Davidson Films. 25 min.

David Elkind contrasts the work of Jean Piaget and Lev Vygotsky and uses their research and his own work to look at three aspects of intellectual growth: reasoning, visual perception, and the use of language. Shows young children both in interview situations and busily participating in an accredited center as illustrations of Elkind's points about their ever changing intellectual abilities. (Distributed by Davidson Films, Inc., 668 Marsh St., San Luis Obispo, CA 83401; 888-437-4200; http://www.davidsonfilms.com)

How caring relationships support self-regulation. 1999. Produced by Marie Goulet at George Brown College, Toronto, Canada. 68 min.

Illustrates children's acquisition of self-regulatory skills through interaction with caregivers. Explores child development, including what is known from brain research, in relation to self-regulation, with accompanying 50-page video guide. Filming in care settings illustrates caregiver practices that support self-regulation at different ages. (Distributed by NAEYC, 1509 16th St., NW, Washington, DC 20036-1426; 800-424-2460.)

Infants, children and adolescents in action. 1997. Produced by Laura E. Berk. 90 min.

This observational video accompanies Laura Berk's book by the same name and illustrates milestones of development of birth through 8-year-olds. Places special emphasis upon the early years. (Distributed by Allyn and Bacon; 309-438-5235; Cornkids@aol.com)

Laughing, learning, loving: Toddler brain development. 1998. Produced by Indiana Steps Ahead in cooperation with Indiana's Public Broadcasting Stations (current producer Ball State University). 28 min.

Throughout the toddler period the brain continues to develop at an astonishing rate, and there is much adults can do to promote optimal development. (Distributed by NAEYC, 1509 16th St., NW, Washington, DC 20036-1426; 800-424-2460.)

Mastering the tasks of toddlerhood. 1990. Produced by Davidson Films. 25 min.

Bettye Caldwell examines the intellectual and emotional growth that results from a child mastering her environment, developing a sense of autonomy, and acquiring language during this period. Shows children in the home and in child care settings. (Distributed by Davidson Films, Inc., 668 Marsh St., San Luis Obispo, CA 83401; 888-437-4200; http://www.davidsonfilms.com)

Nourishing language development in early childhood. 1996. Produced by Davidson Films. 31 min.

Using vignettes filmed at a children's center, students are introduced to the vocabulary of language studies. Alice Honig describes the development of spoken language in infancy, toddlerhood, and preschool years. She details strategies caregivers should use to nourish language development during the early stages of language acquisition. (Distributed by NAEYC, 1509 16th St., NW, Washington, DC 20036-1426; 800-424-2460.)

Play: A Vygotskian approach. 1996. Produced by Davidson Films. 26 min.

Reviews traditional ways of viewing play according to emotional content, symbolic representational content, and socialization. Vygotsky's view emphasizes play as a rule-making activity that supports children's mastering of their own behavior. (Distributed by Davidson Films, Inc., 668 Marsh St., San Luis Obispo, CA 83401; 888-437-4200; http://www.davidsonfilms.com)

Sensory play: Constructing realities. 1994. Produced by South Carolina Educational Television. 18 min.

Examines how a child's firsthand sensory experience contributes to overall development. Sensory play is a natural and concrete means of supporting each child's individual learning style. (Distributed by NAEYC, 1509 16th St., NW, Washington, DC 20036-1426; 800-424-2460.)

Ten things every child needs. 1997. Produced by WTTW Chicago and the Chicago Production Center. 60 min.

Child development experts describe 10 things every child needs for optimal brain development: interaction, loving touch, stable relationships, safe/healthy environments, self-esteem, quality child care, play, communication, music, and reading. Illustrates each need through images and vignettes of typical family interaction, showing a diversity of ways that parents and caregivers can provide for these basic needs. (Distributed by Robert R. McCormick Tribune Foundation, 435 N. Michigan Ave., Suite 770, Chicago, IL 60611; 312-222-3512.)

The whole child: A caregiver's guide to the first five years. 1998. Produced by the Detroit Educational Television Foundation in association with Merrill-Palmer Institute of Wayne State University. 30 min.

Thirteen 30-minute programs in English or Spanish are divided into six major content areas: physical well-being, infancy, emotional health, special needs, social development, and cognitive development. Teacher testimonials and comments by Joanne Hendrick highlight scenes videotaped in Head Start, family child care, independent and university child care centers. (Distributed by Annenberg/CPB Collection, P.O. Box 2345, South Burlington, VT 04507; 800-532-7637.)

Including children with special needs and abilities

Can I play too?—Provider version. 1993. Produced by Partnerships for Inclusion, Frank Porter Graham Child Development Center, University of North Carolina–Chapel Hill. 20 min.

This series including three cassettes is about inclusion of young children with special needs, birth through 5 years of age, in community child care programs. Each presents a different look at inclusion, including an overview, a provider's perspective, and a parent's perspective. (Distributed by Frank Porter Graham Child Development Center, UNC at Chapel Hill, Sheryl-Mar Building, 521 S. Greensboro St., Suite 100, Carrboro, NC 27510; 919-962-7364; http://www.fpg.unc.edu)

A circle of inclusion: Facilitating the inclusion of young children with severe disabilities in mainstream early childhood programs. 1989. Produced by Learner Managed Designs. 27 min.

Provides images of children, ages 3 to 6, with severe and multiple disabilities, effectively integrated in Montessori classrooms. Special educators, early educators, and parents of both disabled and typically developing children share initial concerns, experience, and outcomes. (Distributed by Learner Managed Designs, Inc., P.O. Box 747, Lawrence, KS 66044; 913-842-9088.)

Early intervention: Natural environments for children. 1996. Produced by Indiana Steps Ahead in cooperation with Indiana's Public Broadcasting Stations (current producer Ball State University). 22 min.

This program demonstrates how inclusion benefits all children and families. Available in English and Spanish. (Distributed by NAEYC, 1509 16th St., NW, Washington, DC 20036-1426; 800-424-2460.)

Include us. 1996. Produced by TiffHill Productions. 33 min.

Offers a lighthearted and realistic portrayal of children. Combines music and activities to promote understanding and confidence for the inclusion of children with different abilities in inclusive settings. The accompanying educator's guide provides follow-up activities based on the ages and abilities of participants. (Distributed by TiffHill Productions, P.O. Box 1138, Sioux City, IA 51102; 888-462-5833; http://www.IncludeUs.com)

Just friends. 1994. Produced by the Texas Planning Council on Developmental Disabilities. 16 min.

Introduces teachers to individuals with disabilities and the friends they have made through Community Connections projects in Texas. Shares personal stories, thoughts, and experiences while offering examples of the role that friendship can play in breaking the social isolation of individuals with disabilities. (Distributed by Texas Planning Council on Developmental Disabilities; 800-262-0334.)

Welcome to my preschool! Communicating with technology. 1994. Produced by the National Center to Improve Practice, Education Development Center. 14 min.

Visits an integrated preschool classroom where children with disabilities have full access to the curriculum through the use of high- and low-technology tools. Teachers discuss specific challenges, the technologies that have been selected to address these challenges, and the benefits. (Distributed by Education Development Center, Inc., P.O. Box 1020, Sewickley, PA, 15146-1020; 800-793-5076; e-mail edcorders@abdintl.com)

Partnerships with families

Becoming a family of readers. 1995. Produced by Reading Is Fundamental and Literacy Volunteers of America. 10 min.

Features parents and their children modeling book sharing; advocates reading as a family-friendly activity; and encourages viewers to become involved in family literacy programs. (Distributed by Reading Is Fundamental, Inc., 600 Maryland Ave., SW, Suite 600, Washington, DC 20024; 202-287-3220; http://www.si.edu/rif)

Head Start at home. 1993. Produced by the Head Start Bureau, U.S. Department of Health and Human Services. 17 min.

Emphasizes the significance of the home as a natural environment for learning and discusses the components of the home-based program option: home visits, parent meetings and workshops, and group socialization activities. (Distributed by Head Start Publications Management Center, P.O. Box 26417, Alexandria, VA 22313-0417; fax 703-683-5769; email: hspmc6@idt.net)

Homeside activities: Overview. 1995. Produced by Developmental Studies Center. 12 min.

Designed to help teachers and parents build partnerships around kids. Typically the 15- to 20-minute activities are introduced once or twice a month in class, completed at home with a parent or other caregiver, and then incorporated into a follow-up classroom activity or discussion. (Distributed by Developmental Studies Center, 2000 Embarcadero, Suite 305, Oakland, CA 94606-5300; 800-666-7270.)

My kind of place. 1992. Produced by the Greater Minneapolis Day Care Association. 26 min.

Helps parents identify high-quality child care for infants and toddlers. A family day care provider and a day care center teacher talk about how they organize their settings, meet the children's needs, and support the families. Shows them interacting with the children in their care. Other topics covered include staff-parent communication and health and sanitation. (Distributed by Greater Minneapolis Day Care Association; 612-341-1177.)

Our stories keep us connected. 1997. Produced by the Head Start Bureau, U.S. Department of Health and Human Services. 24 min.

Features six Head Start families across the country; describes the creative ways the families support their children's growth and learning. Has an accompanying guide that explains learning as the building of new ideas from the stories we live, see, and hear all around us. (Distributed by Head Start Publications Management Center, P.O. Box 26417, Alexandria, VA 22313-0417; fax 703-683-5769; e-mail hspmc6@idt.net)

Parents, kids and books. The joys of reading together. 1993. Produced by KERA-TV. 30 min.

Profiles parents and children from diverse backgrounds; demonstrates the rationale for reading with children at home and models best practices. (Distributed by KERA-TV, courtesy of J.C. Penney, 3000 Harry Hines Blvd., Dallas, TX 75201; 800-368-KERA.)

Partnership with parents. 1993. Produced by the Head Start Bureau, U.S. Department of Health and Human Services. 23 min.

Outlines the role of the home visitor in the Head Start home-based program and follows two home visitors as they work with four families. Depicts the elements of the home-based program: establishing and maintaining partnerships with families, using the home as a learning environment, planning and conducting individualized home visits, leading group socialization activities with families, and engaging parents in planning and assessing program activities. (Distributed by Head Start Publications Management Center, P.O. Box 26417, Alexandria, VA 22313-0417; fax 703-683-5769; e-mail hspmc6@idt.net)

Protective urges. 1995. Program for Infant/Toddler Caregiver series developed by Far West Laboratory for Educational Research and Development Center for Child and Family Studies (currently named WestEd) and California State Department of Education. 27 min.

Parents speak candidly about their concerns; caregivers discuss ways to provide assistance; and both groups work out conflicting feelings about caregiver/child relationships. Available in English, Spanish, and Chinese. (Distributed by California Department of Education, P.O. Box 271, Sacramento, CA 95812; 800-995-4099.)

Read to me! Sharing books with young children. 1991. Produced by Educational Productions. 25 min.

Demonstrates the value of reading aloud to young children and provides simple guidelines parents can follow to start read-aloud habits. Presents four guidelines for reading aloud: read aloud during infancy; choose books the child enjoys; try to read for 15 minutes every day; and help children get involved in the book by commenting, questioning, and exploring. (Distributed by Educational Productions, Inc.; 503-644-7000.)

Read with me and *Read with me: The teacher-parent relationship.* 1997. Produced by Carol Duffy. 10 min. each.

Two videos packaged together with a guide for viewers. The first features two Head Start families who offer guidance on reading aloud through words and actions. The second, filmed in two Head Start classrooms, focuses on reading aloud and strategies for creating literacy-rich classroom environments. (Distributed by Reading Is Fundamental, 600 Maryland Ave., SW, Suite 600, Washington, DC 20024; 202-287-3220; http://www.si.edu/rif)

Promoting health and safety

Caring for our children. 1995. Produced by the American Academy of Pediatrics and NAEYC, with support by AT&T, the Communications Workers of America, and the International Brotherhood of Electrical Workers. 30 min. each.

Six-part series designed to ensure the health and safety of all young children, including children with disabilities, in out-of-home settings—child care centers, schools, and family child care homes. Titles include *Standards and You, Basic Caregiving, Ready for Anything, Setting Up for Healthy and Safe Care, Keeping It in Shape,* and *Illness in Child Care.* (Distributed by NAEYC, 1509 16th St., NW, Washington, DC 20036-1426; 800-424-2460.)

Food for thought: Nutrition and children. 1996. Produced by Indiana Steps Ahead in cooperation with Indiana's Public Broadcasting Stations (current producer Ball State University). 28 min.

Discusses children's dietary needs, food preparation and sanitation, as well as the social experience of mealtime. (Distributed by NAEYC, 1509 16th St., NW, Washington, DC 20036-1426; 800-424-2460.)

Safe active play: A guide to avoiding play area hazards. 1997. Produced by Video Active Products. 35 min.

Designed to help caregivers identify and avoid the most common causes of serious injuries during active play. The 12 hazards identified are based on a list by the National Playground Safety Institute. Describes each of the hazards and suggests how to avoid them while also maintaining the quality of active play. (Distributed by NAEYC, 1509 16th St., NW, Washington, DC 20036-1426; 800-424-2460.)

Taking good care of you. 1998. Produced by The Mister Rogers' Neighborhood Child Care Partnership. 57 min. total.

Set of four modules offers basic health and safety information for early childhood educators. The training package is comprised of four modules, each with its own video and manual, workshop outlines, background materials, and handouts. Workshop content includes hands-on activities, discussion of issues, and short video elements. Modules cover controlling infectious diseases (15 min.), keeping children well (13 min.), managing the sick child (12 min.), and supporting emotional development (17 min.). (Distributed by Family Communications, Inc., 4802 Fifth Ave., Pittsburgh, PA 15213; 412-687-2990, ext. 237.)

Spanish-language materials

Actividades familiares: Overview. 1997. Produced by Developmental Studies Center. (DSC) 12 min.

Introduces Spanish-speaking families to DSC's parent involvement program. Details 15- to 20-minute activities that can be completed at home with a parent or other caregiver and then incorporated into a follow-up classroom activity or discussion. (Distributed by Developmental Studies Center, 2000 Embarcadero, Suite 305, Oakland, CA 94606-5300; 800-666-7270.)

Como inícoar ima giarderoa en el hogar. 1997. Produced by Doris Raphael with Doug Weisman for Day Care Video Programs. 49 min.

Spanish edition of *How to Start a Family Day Care.* Provides scenes from child care homes and interviews with providers that take the viewer through the steps involved in starting a home child care program. Topics include startup, daily schedules, planning for health and safety, elements of quality, accreditation, and record keeping. (Distributed by Redleaf Press, 800-423-8309; and also Day Care Video Programs, 781-251-0720, fax 781-326-3911, e-mail march1931@aol.com)

Dilemas diarios: Manejando dificultades. 1998. Produced by Indiana Steps Ahead in cooperation with Indiana's Public Broadcasting Stations (current producer Ball State University). 28 min.

Offers specific techniques to help ease the challenges of transition times, arrivals/departures, naptime, and washing/toileting and to deal with issues such as biting. (Distributed by NAEYC, 1509 16th St., NW, Washington, DC 20036-1426; 800-424-2460.)

Discoveries of infancy: Cognitive development and learning. 1992. The Program for Infant/Toddler Caregiver series developed by Far West Laboratory for Educational Research and Development Center for Child and Family Studies (currently named WestEd) and California State Department of Education. 32 min.

Demonstrates how infants and toddlers concentrate, solve problems, and experiment. The video shows six major discoveries infants and toddlers make as they play and interact: learning schemes, use of tools, cause and effect, object permanence, spatial relationships, and imitation. Explains the various ways adults can facilitate this development. Also available in English and Chinese. (Distributed by California Department of Education, Bureau of Publications; 800-995-4099.)

Experiencias creativas para antes y después de la escuela. 1993. Produced by Indiana Steps Ahead in cooperation with Indiana's Public Broadcasting Stations (current producer Ball State University). 28 min.

Illustrates school-age children experiencing the responsibilities of independence within safe environments and with the support of caring and helpful adults. (Distributed by NAEYC, 1509 16th St., NW, Washington, DC 20036-1426; 800-424-2460.)

Intervención temprana: Ambientes naturales para los niños. 1996. Produced by Indiana Steps Ahead in cooperation with Indiana's Public Broadcasting Stations (current producer Ball State University). 22 min.

This program demonstrates how inclusion benefits all children and families. (Distributed by NAEYC, 1509 16th St., NW, Washington, DC 20036-1426; 800-424-2460.)

El jugar dramático. 1998. Produced by Indiana Steps Ahead in cooperation with Indiana's Public Broadcasting Stations (current producer Ball State University). 28 min.

Discusses the benefits of dramatic and sociodramatic play for children's development and across the curriculum. Offers ideas for prop boxes and thematic play and explains the important role of adults in supporting dramatic play. (Distributed by NAEYC, 1509 16th St., NW, Washington, DC 20036-1426; 800-424-2460.)

Nuevos juegos para los sitios donde se culda a los niños. 1998. Produced by Indiana Steps Ahead in cooperation with Indiana's Public Broadcasting Stations (current producer Ball State University). 28 min.

Emphasizes the benefits of active play for young children and suggests simple games that offer enjoyable, noncompetitive physical activity for preschoolers and school-agers. (Distributed by NAEYC, 1509 16th St., NW, Washington, DC 20036-1426; 800-424-2460.)

La nutrición del niño. 1996. Produced by Indiana Steps Ahead in cooperation with Indiana's Public Broadcasting Stations (current producer Ball State University). 28 min.

Discusses children's dietary needs, food preparation and sanitation, as well as the social experience of mealtime. (Distributed by NAEYC, 1509 16th St., NW, Washington, DC 20036-1426; 800-424-2460.)

Pintando un cuadro positivo: El manejo del comportamien. 1994. Produced by Indiana Steps Ahead in cooperation with Indiana's Public Broadcasting Stations (current producer Ball State University). 28 min.

Shows how adults help children manage their behavior in an encouraging, nurturing, and positive manner while supporting each child's self-esteem. (Distributed by NAEYC, 1509 16th St., NW, Washington, DC 20036-1426; 800-424-2460.)

Planeando dias apropriadas para el desarrollo. 1994. Produced by Indiana Steps Ahead in cooperation with Indiana's Public Broadcasting Stations (current producer Ball State University). 28 min.

Demonstrates the fundamentals of developmentally appropriate practice for all children. (Distributed by NAEYC, 1509 16th St., NW, Washington, DC 20036-1426; 800-424-2460.)

The program for infant/toddler caregivers. 1995. Developed by Far West Laboratory for Educational Research and Development Center for Child and Family Studies (currently named WestEd) and California State Department of Education.

A series supplemented by print materials, including curriculum guides and trainers' manuals on infant and toddler caregiving. Based on sound developmental research and theory, the four modules include *Social-Emotional Growth and Socialization; Group Care; Learning and Development; and Culture, Family, and Providers.* Available individually or as a set; also in English and Chinese (Cantonese). (Distributed by California Department of Education, P.O. Box 271, Sacramento, CA 95812-0271; 800-995-4099.)

The whole child: A caregiver's guide to the first five years 1998. Produced by the Detroit Educational Television Foundation in association with the Merrill-Palmer Institute of Wayne State University. 30 min. each.

Thirteen programs are divided into six major content areas: physical well-being, infancy, emotional health, special needs, social development, and cognitive development. Teacher testimonials and comments by Joanne Hendrick highlight scenes videotaped in Head Start, family child care, and independent and university child care centers. (Distributed by The Annenberg/CPB Collection, P.O. Box 2345, South Burlington, VT 04507; 800-532-7637.)

Teaching and curriculum for infants and toddlers

Building quality child care relationships. 1991. Produced by South Carolina Educational Television. 15 min.

Focuses on the essential ingredient of quality child care—the importance of relationships, especially the teacher-child relationship. Also addresses different temperaments and styles in infancy. (Distributed by NAEYC, 1509 16th St., NW, Washington, DC 20036-1426; 800-424-2460.)

Cooing, crying, cuddling: Infant brain development. 1998. Produced by Indiana Steps Ahead in cooperation with Indiana's Public Broadcasting Stations (current producer Ball State University). 28 min.

Explores the fascinating process of brain development during the first 15 months of life. Understanding how to stimulate this process can help to "build a better brain." (Distributed by NAEYC, 1509 16th St. NW, Washington, DC 20036-1426; 800-424-2460.)

Discoveries of infancy: Cognitive development and learning. 1992. Program for Infant/Toddler Caregiver series developed by Far West Laboratory for Educational Research and Development Center for Child and Family Studies (currently named WestEd) and California State Department of Education. 32 min.

Demonstrates how infants and toddlers concentrate, solve problems, and experiment. Shows six major discoveries infants and toddlers make as they play and interact: learning schemes, use of tools, cause and effect, object permanence, spatial relationships, and imitation. Explains the various ways adults can facilitate this development. In English, Spanish, and Chinese (Cantonese). (Distributed by the California Department of Education, P.O. Box 271, Sacramento, CA 95812; 800-995-4099.)

Early messages: Facilitating language development and communications. 1999. Program for Infant/Toddler Caregiver series developed by Far West Laboratory for Educational Research and Development Center for Child and Family Studies (currently named WestEd) and California State Department of Education. 28 min.

Opens by describing infants' biologically built-in potential to learn language and underscores that early communication is rooted in the child's family and culture. Through examples of infant-caregiver communication and infant's early language, the video illustrates 10 strategies caregivers can use to enhance communication and language development, including being responsive to infants initiating communication, using child-directed language, supporting bilingual development, and engaging infants with books and stories. (Distributed by the California Department of Education, P.O. Box 271, Sacramento, CA 95812; 800-995-4099.)

Essential connections: Ten keys to culturally responsive care. 1995. Program for Infant/Toddler Caregiver series developed by Far West Laboratory for Educational Research and Development Center for Child and Family Studies (currently named WestEd) and California State Department of Education. 36 min.

Provides guidelines and strategies for creating culturally responsive, nurturing programs for infants and toddlers. Includes clips of teachers interacting with children and parents, and comments from child development specialists from various backgrounds. (Distributed by the California Department of Education, P.O. Box 271, Sacramento, CA 95812; 800-995-4099.)

Infant curriculum: Great explorations. 1993. Produced by South Carolina Educational Television. 20 min.

Focuses on stages of development from birth through 15 months, individual temperament and style, shaping the environment, and using routines to support infants' explorations. (Distributed by NAEYC, 1509 16th St., NW, Washington, DC 20036-1426; 800-424-2460.)

Laughing, learning, loving: Toddler brain development. 1998. Produced by Indiana Steps Ahead in cooperation with Indiana's Public Broadcasting Stations (current producer Ball State University). 28 min.

Throughout the toddler period the brain continues to develop at an astonishing rate, and there is much adults can do to promote optimal development. From the Child Care Collection. (Distributed by NAEYC, 1509 16th St., NW, Washington, DC 20036-1426; 800-424-2460.)

Let babies be babies: Caring for infants and toddlers with love and respect. 1993. Produced by Family Day Care Association of Manitoba. 123 min.

Set of six videos and accompanying guides take viewers on a journey through the latest thinking on a variety of early care issues. Drawing on the personal experience of caregivers from both family and center-based child care settings, as well as the work of leading experts, this series provides practical advice for caregivers. A facilitator's discussion guide is also included. (Distributed by Family Day Care Association of Manitoba, St. Mary's Road, Winnipeg, Manitoba, Canada R2M 3R5. 204-254-5437.)

The program for infant/toddler caregivers. 1995. Developed by Far West Laboratory for Educational Research and Development Center for Child and Family Studies (currently named WestEd) and California State Department of Education.

A series of videos supplemented by print material, including curriculum guides and trainers' manuals on infant and toddler caregiving. Based on sound developmental research and theory, the four modules are titled *Social-Emotional Growth and Socialization; Group Care; Learning and Development; and Culture, Family, and Providers.* Available individually or as a set; in Spanish and Chinese (Cantonese). (Distributed by the California Department of Education, P.O. Box 271, Sacramento, CA 95812-0271; 800-995-4099.)

See how they move. 1994. Produced by Resources for Infant Educarers. 30 min.

Sitting on the sidelines of a large room containing floor mats, toys, and climbing equipment, Magda Gerber observes the behavior of infants of various ages—some immobile, some crawling, and a few walking—and describes what she sees in terms of readiness and skills level. Gerber explains the natural progression of gross-motor development, stressing that the timing is different for each baby. (Distributed by Resources for Infant Educarers, 1550 Murray Circle, Los Angeles, CA 90026; 323-663-5330.)

Toddler curriculum. 1991. Produced by South Carolina Educational Television. 20 min.

Shows how toddlers develop and learn. Depicts developmentally appropriate curriculum for 2- and 3-year-olds. (Distributed by NAEYC, 1509 16th St., NW, Washington, DC 20036-1426; 800-424-2460.)

Teaching and curriculum for preschool and primary

Active learning. 1991. Produced by High/Scope Educational Research Foundation. 65 min.

Demonstrates how children learn and teachers teach in active learning K–3 classrooms. Viewers see children in a materials-rich environment as they make choices and decisions, use materials and language to solve problems, budget their time, seek and receive support from adults, engage in hands-on, active-learning experiences. Shows how adults focus on the learning process at the child's level of development and expertise. (Distributed by High/Scope Press, 600 North River, Ypsilanti, MI 48198-2898; 800-407-7377.)

Adult-child interactions: Forming partnerships with children. 1996. Produced by High/Scope Educational Research Foundation. 60 min.

Focuses on two teachers' interactions with children throughout their daily routines. Part 1 shows teachers using conversations, questions, and other strategies to encourage children's active learning. Part 2 contains additional classroom scenes to facilitate discussion. (Distributed by High/Scope Press, 600 North River, Ypsilanti, MI 48198-2898; 800-407-7377.)

Block play: Constructing realities. 1993. Produced by South Carolina Educational Television. 20 min.

Examines how children acquire knowledge and skills through block play. Describes skills and the stages of building. (Distributed by NAEYC, 1509 16th St., NW, Washington, DC 20036-1426; 800-424-2460.)

Chelsea has a great day! Produced by Early Childhood Initiatives, Colorado Department of Education. 20 min.

In this program and discussion guide, the viewer follows Chelsea to preschool and the introduction of quality standards for child care facilities and educators. The quality standards introduced are also portrayed in a print publication, *Colorado Quality Standards for Early Childhood Care and Education Services*. (Distributed by Colorado Department of Education, 201 E. Colfax Ave., Denver, CO 80203; 303-866-6629.)

*Children at the center: Reflective teachers at work.*1997. Produced by Margie Carter for Harvest Resources. 24 min.

Emphasizes creating environments for discovery, beauty, and an appreciation of nature. Teachers discuss their changing notions of child-centered play and the importance of helping children feel powerful and competent each day. (Distributed by Harvest Resources, P.O. Box 22106, Seattle, WA 98122-0106; 206-325-0592.)

Creating caring communities: A responsive classroom for urban children. 1996. Produced by Beacon Communications. 35 min.

Portrays a responsive classroom as implemented in a large urban school district. Includes an overview of the six components of this model, including Morning Meeting, Rules and Logical Consequences, Classroom Organization, Guided Discovery, Choice, Assessment, and Reporting to Parents. (Distributed by Northeast Foundation for Children, 71 Montague City Road, Greenfield, MA 01301; 800-360-6332.)

The creative curriculum video. 1988. Produced by Diane Trister Dodge for Teaching Strategies. 37 min.

Demonstrates how teachers set the stage for learning by creating a dynamic, well-organized environment. Shows children involved in seven interest areas discussed in the book *The Creative Curriculum for Early Childhood* and explains how children learn in each area. Also available with Spanish subtitles. (Distributed by Teaching Strategies, Inc., P.O. Box 42243, Washington, DC 20015; 800-637-3652; http://www.TeachingStrategies.com)

Curriculum in Head Start/Individualizing in Head Start. 1986. Produced by the Head Start Bureau, U.S. Department of Health and Human Services. 33 min.

Presents the concept that early childhood curriculum relates to the child's whole interaction with the world and that children learn through active involvement. Also emphasizes the importance of teamwork on the part of parents and staff in the growth and development of each child. (Distributed by Head Start Publications Management Center, P.O. Box 26417, Alexandria, VA 22313-0417; fax 703-683-5769; e-mail hspmc6@idt.net)

Daily dilemmas: Coping with challenges. 1998. Produced by Indiana Steps Ahead in cooperation with Indiana's Public Broadcasting Stations (current producer Ball State University). 28 min.

Offers specific techniques to help ease the challenges of transition times, arrivals/departures, naptime, and washing/toileting and for dealing with issues such as biting. In English and Spanish. (Distributed by NAEYC, 1509 16th St., NW, Washington, DC 20036-1426; 800-424-2460.)

A day in the life of Mrs. Wishy Washy. 1986. Produced by The Wright Group. 20 min.

Demonstrates how to integrate a theme into the classroom and provides ideas for art projects, dramatizing, and emergent reading that can take place in a kindergarten classroom. (Distributed by The Wright Group, 19201 120th Ave, NE, Bothell, WA 98011; 800-523-2371.)

Designing developmentally appropriate days. 1994. Produced by Indiana Steps Ahead in cooperation with Indiana's Public Broadcasting Stations (current producer Ball State University). 28 min.

Demonstrates the fundamentals of developmentally appropriate practice for all children. In English and Spanish. (Distributed by NAEYC, 1509 16th St., NW, Washington, DC 20036-1426; 800-424-2460.)

Detroit Head Start inspired by the Reggio Emilia approach. Produced by Merrill-Palmer Institute. 16 min.

Highlights the ongoing Head Start staff development project, inspired by the Reggio Emilia approach. Viewers meet the teachers and hear their reflections concerning the principles and their experiences in adapting to the Reggio Emilia approach. Features vignettes of the children engaged in a variety of interesting classroom situations and shares impressions of some of the parents. (Distributed by Merrill-Palmer Institute, Wayne State University, 71-A E. Ferry Ave., Detroit, MI 48202.)

Developmentally appropriate first grade. 1993. Produced with the North Central Regional Educational Laboratory. 30 min.

Presents a day in David Burchfield's first grade, a classroom suited to children's development. Viewers see how teachers can provide children with opportunities for problem solving and creativity as they explore academic content. (Distributed by NAEYC, 1509 16th St, NW, Washington, DC, 20036-1426; 800-424-2460.)

Dramatic play: More than playing house. 1998. Produced by Indiana Steps Ahead in cooperation with Indiana's Public Broadcasting Stations (current producer Ball State University). 28 min.

Discusses the benefits of dramatic and sociodramatic play for children's development and across the curriculum. Offers ideas for prop boxes and thematic play and explains the important role of adults in supporting dramatic play. In English and Spanish. (Distributed by NAEYC, 1509 16th St., NW, Washington, DC 20036-1426; 800-424-2460.)

The early childhood program: A place to learn and grow. 1996. Produced by Stark County (Ohio) School District, North Central Regional Educational Laboratory, Iowa Department of Education, Nebraska Department of Education, Ohio Department of Education, Jennings Foundation, and NAEYC. 30 min. each.

Seven programs cover the key issues faced by early childhood programs serving children age 3 through 8. Filmed in public schools and child care centers in rural and urban communities, the videos feature children, parents, teachers, administrators, and other experts. (Distributed by NAEYC, 1509 16th St., NW, Washington, DC 20036-1426; 800-424-2460.)

Emergent literacy: Kindergartners write and read. 1998. Produced through the University of Michigan with support from the North Central Regional Educational Laboratory. 30 min.

Demonstrates an easy technique to get 4-and-5-year-olds writing and reading in school settings. The accompanying teacher's guide defines emergent literacy, shows examples of emergent writing, and suggests a lesson structure. (Distributed by the Agency for Instructional Technology, Box A, Bloomington, IN 47402-0120; 800-457-4509.)

An investigation of liquids: A documentary of project work. 1999. Produced by the Head Start Early Childhood Transition Demonstration Project. 22 min.

Tells the story of a project conducted by Kathryn Lee's second-grade class at Beall Elementary School in Rockville, Maryland, and documents children's several-months-long investigation of liquids. Children reflect about their experience with project work and compare it with more traditional instruction. (Distributed by Montgomery County Public Schools, Division of Early Childhood Services, 4910 Macon Road, Rockville, MD 20852.)

Linking literacy and play. 1995. Produced by International Reading Association (IRA). 12 min.

Provides ideas about how to use the natural environment of play to foster literacy development in 3- and 4-year olds. An accompanying facilitator's guide includes a book of articles about children's literacy development in play situations. (Distributed by IRA, 800 Barksdale Road, PO Box 8139, Newark, DE 19714; 302-731-1600.)

Math time: The learning environment for K–2 mathematics. 1997. Produced and narrated by Kathy Richardson. 24 min.

Shows examples of dynamic and supportive learning environments in real classrooms. Includes a facilitator's guide with the videotape. (Distributed by Educational Enrichment, Inc., P.O. Box 1524, Norman, OK 73070; 405-321-3275.)

Mathematics: What are you teaching my child? 1996. Produced by Scholastic in cooperation with Cuisenaire and Marilyn Burns Education Associates. 20 min.

Addresses how to integrate manipulatives into the classroom to help implement the National Council of Teachers of Mathematics Standards; collaborative learning; the role of problem-solving and reasoning skills; and how to build parental understanding and support for a mathematics curriculum. (Distributed by Cuisenaire Company of America, Inc., P.O. Box 5026, White Plains, NY 10602-5026; 800-237-0338.)

New games for child care settings. 1998. Produced by Indiana Steps Ahead in cooperation with Indiana's Public Broadcasting Stations (current producer Ball State University). 28 min.

Emphasizes the benefits of active play for young children and suggests simple games that offer enjoyable, noncompetitive physical activity for preschoolers and school-agers. In English and Spanish. (Distributed by NAEYC, 1509 16th St., NW, Washington, DC 20036-1426; 800-424-2460.)

Observing young children: Learning to look, looking to learn. 1995. Produced by Teaching Strategies. 30 min.

Helps new and experienced early childhood educators to learn about individual children, evaluate their programs, and measure children's progress and acquisition of skills. Appropriate for both self-instruction or group training sessions. The narrator describes objective observation techniques and how to apply them and then walks viewers through several practice observations. (Distributed by Teaching Strategies, Inc., P.O. Box 42243, Washington, DC 20015; 800-637-3652; http://www.TeachingStrategies.com)

Painting a positive picture: Proactive behavior management. 1994. Produced by Indiana Steps Ahead in cooperation with Indiana's Public Broadcasting Stations (current producer Ball State University). 28 min.

Shows how adults help children manage their behavior in an encouraging, nurturing, and positive manner while supporting each child's self-esteem. Available in English and Spanish. (Distributed by NAEYC, 1509 16th St., NW, Washington, DC 20036-1426; 800-424-2460.)

Performance assessment: A teacher's way of knowing. 1993. Produced by Davidson Films. 21 min.

Samuel J. Meisels presents the rationale behind the move to performance assessment in primary grades and early childhood settings. The video proposes that a wider range of information is possible when assessment is a part of daily classroom life and not a once-a-year event. (Distributed by Davidson Films, Inc., 668 Marsh St., San Luis Obispo, CA 83401; 888-437-4200; http://www.davidsonfilms.com)

Reading and young children: A practical guide for childcare providers. 1992. Produced by the International Reading Association. 15 min.

Intended as an introductory training tape for child care professionals and others who work with young children. Demonstrates techniques for reading aloud, choral reading, using Big Books, and storytelling and suggests inexpensive resources that can help child care facilities become reader friendly. (Distributed by International Reading Association, 800 Barksdale Road, PO Box 8139, Newark, DE 19714; 302-731-1600.)

Scaffolding self-directed learning in the primary grades. 1996. Produced by Davidson Films. 35 min.

Provides examples of structuring learning so that children are active learners while teachers use their knowledge base to meaningfully guide their learning. Explains and demonstrates three essential elements of scaffolding as children in urban classrooms become literate and ever more responsible for their weekly learning plans. (Distributed by Davidson Films, Inc., 668 Marsh St., San Luis Obispo, CA 83401; 888-437-4200; http://www. davidsonfilms.com)

Setting sail: An emergent curriculum project. 1997. Produced by Harvest Resources. 19 min.

Outlines the elements of developing long-term curriculum projects with preschoolers. Shows teachers and children designing an environment that provokes interest and engagement, observing and documenting the unfolding curriculum, and communicating the curriculum to others. (Distributed by Harvest Resources, P.O. Box 22106, Seattle, WA 98122-0106; 206-325-0592.)

Starting small: Teaching tolerance in preschool and the early grades. 1997. Produced by Southern Poverty Law Center. 58 min.

Through lively classroom footage, teacher interviews, commentary from early childhood specialists, and the voices of children, the video explores five equity education programs from Seattle to New Haven. Designed to promote staff discussion and personal reflection on effective ways of fostering respect for differences. (Distributed by Southern Poverty Law Center, 400 Washington Ave., Montgomery, AL 36104; 334-264-0286.)

Structured play: Gross motor activities for every day. 1995. Produced by Indiana Steps Ahead in cooperation with Indiana's Public Broadcasting Stations (current producer Ball State University). 28 min.

Illustrates how gross-motor play is an important contributor to each child's development and can be incorporated throughout the day. (Distributed by NAEYC, 1509 16th St., NW, Washington, DC 20036-1426; 800-424-2460.)

Talking mathematics. 1995. Produced by R. Corwin, J. Storeygard, S.L. Price, & D. Smith for Heinemann.

Program of seven tapes filmed in elementary classrooms. Includes an introductory video; four 20-minute videos on important aspects of children's mathematical talk; a tape of six unedited classroom episodes; and a 20-minute summary tape featuring a Talking Mathematics teacher seminar. (Distributed by Heinemann, 88 Post Road West, P.O. Box 5007, Westport, CT 06881; 800-793-2154; http://www.heinemann.com)

That's my buddy: Friendship and learning across the grades. 1996. Produced by Developmental Studies Center. 14 min.

Overview video offers step-by-step advice on creating partnerships and getting started, how and when to schedule Buddies, and specific activities to engage both younger and older children. (Distributed by Developmental Studies Center, 2000 Embarcadero, Suite 305, Oakland, CA 94606-5300; 800-666-7270.)

Thinking science: Work in progress. Produced by Wendy Saul, University of Maryland–Baltimore County, in collaboration with the Elementary Science Integration Project. 30 min.

Offers a rare opportunity to look inside the classrooms of four teachers as they work with children. After classroom sessions, teachers share their perceptions of what they and their students were doing and discuss how they apply the principles and methods of whole language literacy learning to their science teaching. (Distributed by Heinemann, 88 Post Road West, P.O. Box 5007, Westport, CT 06881; 800-793-2154; http://www. heine mann.com)

Tools for teaching developmentally appropriate practice: The leading edge in early childhood education. 1998. Produced for NAEYC by Resources and Instruction for Staff Excellence. 4 tapes, 3 hours total.

Short stand-alone programs, 3 to 35 minutes in length, teach the key points from NAEYC's best-selling, recently revised book *Developmentally Appropriate Practice in Early Childhood Programs.* Highlights high-quality teaching in urban and rural child care centers, preschools, family child care homes, kindergartens, and primary grade schools. (Distributed by NAEYC, 1509 16th St., NW, Washington, DC 20036-1426; 800-424-2460.)

Using what we know: Applying Piaget's developmental theory in primary classrooms. 1991. Produced by Davidson Films. 35 min.

David Elkind proposes educational practices for today's primary classrooms that reflect thoughtful application of Piagetian theories. Filmed in three public school classrooms, the content deals with setting up a physical and organizational environment, making curriculum decisions, and assessing child growth. (Distributed by NAEYC, 1509 16th St., NW, Washington, DC 20036-1426; 800-424-2460.)

Windows on learning: A framework for making decisions. 1996. Produced by Macomb Projects, Western Illinois University. 20 min.

Shows children working in classroom settings and illustrates how teachers can document children's learning in a variety of ways. Emphasizes the value of careful observation in providing teachers with insight into what children know, what they are beginning to learn, and where their interests lie. (Distributed by NAEYC, 1509 16th St., NW, Washington, DC 20036-1426; 800-424-2460.)

Internet Websites

Selecting Internet resources useful to teachers in the classroom presents many challenges. A primary concern is that the Internet changes rapidly, and there is no guarantee that the sites listed will continue to be accessible from the addresses provided or that they will continue to contain high-quality information.

The following listing of Websites is intended to contribute to teachers' understanding and implementation of developmentally appropriate practice in the classroom. These sites are called hubs because they also provide links to other Websites. The criteria used in selecting the sites include relevance of content, continued availability, frequent updating, and ease of use. The sites have been developed by organizations, as government-funded projects, or at universities. This listing highlights only a few of the available Internet Websites that support developmentally appropriate practices.

Culturally and Linguistically Appropriate Services (CLAS) Early Childhood
  Research Institute
http://www.clas.uiuc.edu/

The CLAS Early Childhood Research Institute is a federally funded collaborative effort of universities and national organizations. CLAS identifies, evaluates, and promotes early intervention practices for children with special needs or who are at risk of educational failure. CLAS specifically identifies materials and resources that are responsive to the influence of culture and language in the lives of families, children, and their service providers. The Website includes descriptions of books, articles, manuals, brochures, videos, and audiotapes; materials that have been reviewed by two or more experts who have listed recommendations for use and adaptation; and several special collections, including literature reviews, program descriptions of Child Find Project brochures, and language assessments. Sections of the Website are available in Spanish.

Division for Early Childhood (DEC) of the Council for Exceptional Children
http://www.dec-sped.org/

DEC advocates for individuals who work with or on behalf of children with special needs, birth through age 8, and their families. Promoting practices that support families and enhance the optimal development of children is a priority. The Website is a hub to early intervention-related sites, including the IDEA (Individuals with Disabilities Education Act) Practices Website. A titles index of articles having appeared in DEC's journals, *Young Exceptional Children* and *Journal of Early Intervention;* a searchable index of publications; and governmental-related information and action alerts are posted.

ERIC Clearinghouse on Elementary and Early Childhood Education (ERIC/EECE)
http://www.ericeece.org

This Website is one of the most reliable and widely used hub sites for early childhood educators and individuals interested in child care, child development, and early learning. Included are the full texts of some of ERIC/EECE's publications, all of ERIC/EECE's Digests (selected ones are available in Spanish and Chinese), sections on Reggio Emilia and the project approach, information on ERIC/EECE's listservs, and the AskERIC question-answering service and the National Parent Information Network. ERIC/EECE links to sites that over time have maintained collections of high-quality information continue to offer full-text information and are reasonably well organized.

National Association for the Education of Young Children (NAEYC)
http://www.naeyc.org

NAEYC offers early childhood educators professional development opportunities designed to improve the quality of services for children from birth through age 8.

The Website includes a wide range of resources, including a searchable index of resources in the NAEYC Catalog; a searchable index and abstracts of articles appearing in the *Young Children* journal over the past 15 years; and *Early Years Are Learning Years* information releases—one page fact sheets on topics of high interest, formatted for easy use by parents, teachers, and caregivers. As a service to NAEYC members this site provides links to other national early childhood related organizations.

National Center for Early Development and Learning (NCEDL)
http://www.fpg.unc.edu/~NCEDL/

NCEDL's mission is to identify and study issues of national significance to young children and their families and to disseminate that information to researchers, practicing professionals, and families. This site contains full-text publications, research, press releases, newsletters, and other resources pertaining to the goals and mission of the organization. The site provides a link to the Frank Porter Graham Child Development Center, University of North Carolina at Chapel Hill, which is one of the nation's oldest multidisciplinary centers for the study of young children and their families. Research and education activities focus on child development and health, especially factors that may put children at risk for developmental problems.

National Institute on Early Childhood Development and Education, Office of Educational Research and Improvement (OERI), U.S. Department of Education
http://www.ed.gov/offices/OERI/ECI

The National Institute on Early Childhood Development and Education sponsors comprehensive and challenging research to help ensure that young children are successful in school and beyond and to enhance their quality of life and that of their families. This Website contains information about the OERI-sponsored National Educational Research and Development Centers, the Early Childhood Research Working Group that links the Institute with other federal agencies and online recent issues of its quarterly newsletter *Early Childhood Update,* and links specifically for teachers and child care providers.

ZERO TO THREE
http://www.zerotothree.org

ZERO TO THREE fosters a multidisciplinary network of people around the country who are concerned about the needs of infants, toddlers, and families. It also functions as an Early Head Start National Resource Center. The Website includes timely, authoritative information for parents of infants and toddlers and for professionals who work with infants, toddlers, and their families. The site provides an online bookstore, professional development opportunities, advocacy links, developmental milestones, guidance on choosing quality child care, new research, and ideas for parents.

List of Publishers

Ablex	203-661-7602
Addison Wesley Longman	800-552-2499
Allyn and Bacon	800-278-3525
American Association for the Advancement of Science	202-216-0743
American Guidance Service	800-328-2560
Association for Childhood Education International	301-570-2111
Association for Supervision and Curriculum Development	800-933-2723
Australian Early Childhood Association	011-61-26-241-6900
Bank Street College	212-875-4467
Basic Books	800-331-3761
Brookes, Paul H.	800-638-3775
Brooks/Cole	800-730-2214
Cambridge University Press	800-872-7423
Centre for Urban and Community Studies	416-978-6895
Children's Defense Fund	202-628-8787
Children's Resources International	202-363-9002
Council for Exceptional Children	703-620-3660
Crystal Springs Books	800-321-0401
Delmar	800-347-7707
Developmental Studies Center	800-666-7270
Dushkin/McGraw-Hill	877-888-1507
ERIC Clearinghouse on Elementary and Early Childhood Education	800-583-4135
Free Spirit Publishing	800-735-7323
Garland	800-968-0042
Greenwood Publishing	203-226-3571
Gryphon House	800-638-0928

Harcourt Brace	800-211-8378
Harvard University Press	800-726-3244
HarperCollins (and Basic Books)	800-331-3761
Heinemann	800-793-2154
High/Scope	734-485-2000
Houghton Mifflin	800-334-3284
International Reading Association	302-731-1600
JAI Press	203-323-9606
Johns Hopkins University Press	800-537-5487
Jossey-Bass	800-956-7739
Merrill/Prentice Hall	800-526-0485
McGraw-Hill/SRA	800-338-3987
National Academy Press	202-334-2812
National Association for the Education of Young Children	800-424-2460
National Association of Elementary School Principals	701-684-3345
National Association of State Boards of Education	701-684-4000
National Council for the Social Studies	202-966-7840
National Council of Teachers of English	800-369-6283
National Education Association	202-833-4000
Northeast Foundation for Children	800-360-6332
Open University Press	800-874-0388
Perseus Books	781-944-3700
Redleaf Press	800-423-8309
Richard Owen Publishers	800-336-5588
Routledge	800-634-7064
Scholastic	800-724-6527
Stenhouse Publishers	800-988-9812
State University of New York Press	800-666-2211
Teachers and Writers Collaborative	212-691-6590
Teachers College Press	800-575-6566
Teaching Strategies	800-637-3652
Trentham Books distributed by Stylus Publishing	800-232-0223
Williamson Publishing	800-234-9791

Information about NAEYC

NAEYC is . . .

an organization of nearly 102,000 members, founded in 1926, and committed to fostering the growth and development of children from birth through age 8. Membership is open to all who share a desire to serve young children and act on behalf of the needs and rights of all children.

NAEYC provides . . .

educational services and resources to adults and programs working with and for children, including

• *Young Children, the* peer-reviewed journal for early childhood educators

• **Books, posters, brochures, and videos** to expand your knowledge and commitment to and support your work with young children and families, including topics on infants, curriculum, research, discipline, teacher education, and parent involvement

• **An Annual Conference** that brings people together from across the United States and other countries to share their expertise and advocate on behalf of children and families

• **Week of the Young Child** celebrations sponsored by more than 400 NAEYC Affiliate Groups to call public attention to the critical significance of the child's early years

• **Insurance plans** for members and programs

• **Public affairs information** and access to information through NAEYC resources and communication systems for conducting knowledgeable advocacy efforts at all levels of government and through the media

• **A voluntary accreditation system** for high-quality programs for children through the National Academy of Early Childhood Programs

• **Resources and services** through the National Institute for Early Childhood Professional Development, working to improve the quality and consistency of early childhood preparation and professional development opportunities

• **Young Children International** to promote international communication and information exchanges

For information about membership, publications, or other NAEYC services, visit the NAEYC Website at **www.naeyc.org**

National Association for the Education of Young Children
1509 16th Street, NW, Washington, DC 20036-1426
202-232-8777 or 800-424-2460